Rohan Daft was b[...] he lives in Lond[...] Consultant, as well as contributing to a number of publications. He is an authority on Irish culture, though his pastimes, for the most part, are best left unmentioned.

Malcolm Bennett was born and raised in a Public House in Wallasey. He now lives in a posh house in London where he is a Commercial Director.

... born in Cheltenham in 1963. Curr...
... lives in ... London and works as a Public Relations
...

DAFT ABOUT LAGER

Rohan Daft
with
Malcolm Bennett

Illustrations by
Aidan Hughes

SPHERE BOOKS LIMITED

SPHERE BOOKS LTD

Published by the Penguin Group
27 Wrights Lane, London W8 5TZ, England
Viking Penguin Inc., 40 West 23rd Street, New York, New York 10010, USA
Penguin Books Australia Ltd, Ringwood, Victoria, Australia
Penguin Books Canada Ltd, 2801 John Street, Markham, Ontario, Canada L3R 1B4
Penguin Books (NZ) Ltd, 182–190 Wairau Road, Auckland 10, New Zealand

Penguin Books Ltd, Registered Offices: Harmondsworth, Middlesex, England

First published in Great Britain by Sphere Books Ltd 1989

Printed and bound and Great Britain by
Richard Clay Ltd, Bungay, Suffolk

For Uncle Arthur

ACKNOWLEDGEMENTS

I would like to thank the following, without whom this book would not have been possible: Dick Bradsell; Mark Paterson; Diane Wheeler-Nicholson; Desmond and Charlotte Skene-Catling; Gill Freer; Benegale Richards; Martin Fletcher and everyone at Sphere Books; my family; Arthur Guiness; all at Lithuanian House; John Humphries at Maison Caurette; David Johnson — a fine, upstanding (before lunchtime) brewer; Robin Evans; Michael Cooke at Continental Lager Distributors; Mary Bull at Off-Licence News; Robert Card and his sister Georgina at The Liquor Store, London SE1 (tel: 01 928 4623); Paul O'Connor at the Uxbridge Arms; Toby Cookson; Janet Hogg; Duncan Ward; Paul Hely; Emma Harrison for feeding me; Russell Cronin; and especially Malcolm Bennett and Aidan Hughes. Cheers!

INTRODUCTION

I first started to appreciate lager on my travels abroad.
Until then I had not been a great fan of beer. Living at
that time in Cheltenham, I found neither the bitters
nor the majority of the available domestic lagers to my
taste. I only really found solace in a pint of Guinness,
or the odd continental brew I happened to discover.

This sorry tale ended for good, however, after a trip
to the United States. I can still remember vividly my
first visit to one liquor store just outside Washington
D.C. It was called 'Rips', and consisted of a small room
full of wines and spirits (including a fine selection of
Scotch whiskies), and a huge 'walk in' refrigerator,
containing over 200 different beers, mostly lagers, from
all over the world. After a little under half-an-hour I
managed to persuade my father to emerge with (and
pay for!) thirty-four different lagers from all corners of
the globe.

That was the first time I had the pleasure to find
Sapporo from Japan, Jamaican brewed Red Stripe, Port
Royal from Honduras, and the American Samuel
Adams Boston Lager, all of which are now available in
the UK.

Holland is another country that I've been lucky
enough to visit which brews a fine range of lagers. I
can clearly remember the enormous disappointment I
felt after returning from Holland and opening a can of
Heineken. I honestly thought that I'd been given a duff
can as I swallowed my first mouthful. But no, a second
can, a week later, confirmed my worst suspicions that
the Heineken produced in the UK is a pale imitation of
the brew of the same name produced in the Netherlands.

It was probably this experience that led me to search
high and low for genuinely good lagers. Two real finds

were the off-licences, The Groggs Bottom, in West Hampstead, London, and, The Liquor Store, in the London Road, London SE1. I also discovered to my great pleasure, that the British can also (in some cases!) brew a decent lager, and are most certainly becoming more 'lager literate'. They are more discriminating in what they drink, and it is regrettable that lager has become associated with what many story-starved sections of the media have labelled our latest species of Saturday night hooligan, namely the 'lager lout'. Lager drinkers are, without doubt, some of the most civilized people in the world.

Lager is now big business in the UK. It is currently the biggest selling type of beer, and its sales are still rising. Approximately 45 per cent of all beer sold in the UK in 1988 was lager. In a little over ten years lager has doubled its share of the UK beer market and it is estimated that by the mid 1990s, it will hold a huge 60 per cent share.

One of the reasons lager has become so popular is advertising. Some of the most memorable television advertisements have been for lagers. Indeed, two of the most successful copy lines in advertising have been: 'Heineken refreshes the parts other beers cannot reach', and 'I bet he drinks Carling Black Label'. In 1987, around £65 million was spent advertising lager. Most of this was consumed by the big selling domestic brands, and, as there is little difference in taste between them, there is certainly more than a modicum of truth in the saying that many people drink the advertising.

However, this book is for the discriminating drinker who enjoys lager for its distinctive, keen and remarkably wide-ranging character and who is prepared to search out new and satisfying tastes. For the true lager drinker the advertising is, at best, an amusing diversion.

Let me point out at this stage of the book, that I am giving a personal view, as a lager drinker, on each lager discussed. As, no doubt, your taste is different from mine, do not dismiss from your sampling list those brews that I do not personally care for! Make up your own mind.

Happy reading . . . and drinking!

Rohan Daft, November 1988

WHAT IS LAGER?

Lager is a bottom-fermented beer, the basic ingredients of which are hops, barley-malt, and water, though adjuncts – such as rice – are added in some brews. The brewing process is very simple, as you can see on page 2.

AAS BOK   Norway

*

Bottles

Clean, crisp and very lightly hoppy, AAS BOK (be careful how you pronounce it!) from Norway is by no means widely available. Indeed, I've only once had the good fortune to stumble across it in Fulham, London, in an off-licence that sadly no longer exists. If you are lucky enough to find it, tell your friends ... and me! It's delicious.

ACE LAGER   UK

OG 1030–34°   *Federation Brewery*
Draught
Cans
PET Bottles

The Federation Brewery was established in 1919 shortly after the end of the First World War as a co-operative on Tyneside. At that time supplies of reason-

* Details of Original Gravity or Alcohol by Volume and packaging details supplied where known.

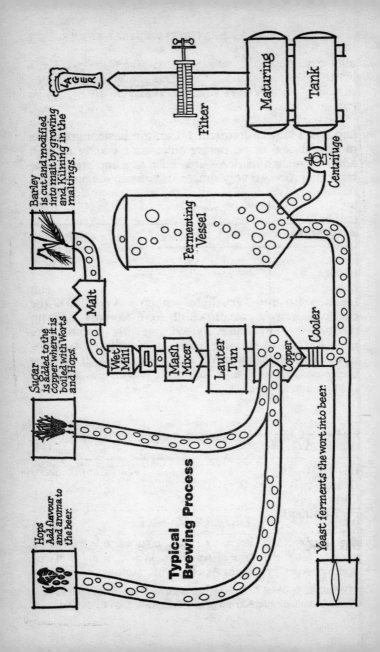

ably priced beer to the working-men's clubs of the North were restricted. They needed a drink at a price they could afford, and thus a brewery was born, to be run by working-men's clubs for working-men's clubs.

Seventy years later the Federation Brewery has grown and is flourishing, no doubt through the loyalty of the northern drinker. However, like all other breweries, Federation has experienced the increasing demand for lager over the past 20 years and now brews a range itself, A CE being one of them. They tell me that it's a 'natural for the new generation of lager drinkers'. Well, that's a matter of opinion. 'Light and refreshing' can be translated as thin and bubbly, and 'mature lager taste' means that it's different from lemonade. Just! Pale, with a very slight hint of a bitter aroma, it's unpleasantly over-carbonated. In all senses of the word it is a throwing lager, and I recommend you do just that. In fact, A CE goes against all the traditions that the brewery was born to protect, and it seems like treason to sell such a weak, tasteless lager. Still, they say that the working man has never had so much money in his pocket so I suppose he can afford to throw it away on twelve pints of this session juice a night, though just why he should want to I really do not know.

SAMUEL ADAMS BOSTON LAGER – *see under* **'S'**.

ADELSHOFFEN BIERS BRUNE France

OG 1060° *Continental Lager Distributors*
Bottles

Produced by the Grande Brasserie Alsacienne d'Adelshoffen, in the Alsace region of France, BIER BRUNE is a very dark, thick and sweet brew much in the style of the French *biers de garde* (beer to be kept).

The one that I sampled went down extremely well with a nice Toulouse sausage from my favourite French butcher in Soho's Brewer Street.

As an occasional tipple BIER BRUNE is *très bon!* You'll be hopping like mad if you miss out on this one!

ALTENMUNSTER STRONG LAGER
West Germany

OG 1048°
50cl swing-top bottles

This lager, brewed by Sailerbrau of Marktoberdorf, West Germany, is imported by Courage as one of their 'Chosen Few' range of classic beers still brewed and bottled in the country of origin. Although not a particularly famous drink, it is a fine brew and bears all the hallmarks of a German beer in as much as it is strong yet very drinkable, with a certain delicately bitter taste. Distinctly German, it comes to our shores a fully qualified ambassador accompanied by all the great traditions of brewing that still survive in Germany. It was once a relatively easy beer to get hold of in Courage land, and if you can still find it I highly recommend that you give it a try. I have, and I will again!

AMARIT
Thai

4.8% ABV   *Continental Lager Distributors*
Bottles (33cl)

Coming in at a little under 4.8 per cent alcohol by volume, AMARIT is said to be one of Thailand's principal brands. Brewed and bottled by the brewery of the same name in Bangkok (which, incidentally, also brews Guinness), it is bound to go down well in the increasing numbers of Thai restaurants now springing up throughout the country at an astounding rate. With its label adorned by a Goddess driving a three-horse chariot, it was first brought to Britain in January 1988 and will do well to hold its own against other Thai beers already established here, notably the excellent SINGHA (q.v.). Having said that I hope it does survive.

I've drunk it several times myself and have found that, with its slightly dry but refreshing taste, it goes down a treat with the spicy cuisine of Thailand.

ANCHOR STEAM BEER USA

OG 1058°   *Majestic Wine Warehouse*
Bottles

The Anchor Brewing Company of San Francisco have been using the term 'steam beer' for more than 60 years, and it is indeed a trade mark of theirs.

In the 19th century 'steam beer' was a local nickname for draught beer produced under pioneering conditions. Steam was an important factor in the production of beer in those days: it was used to heat brewing vessels; it powered engines to drive brewing equipment; and it was also used in the process of pasteurization. Thus it was probably from these uses that the term 'steam beer' originated, although legend has it that during the Californian gold-rush a man by the name of Pete Steam brewed beer!

Now available in the UK through Majestic Wine Warehouses, ANCHOR STEAM is indeed a great brew. With a very creamy head, a full body, a delightful hoppy nose and a slightly malty taste, this one should be sought out! You'll thank me for it!

ASDA LAGER   UK

Cans (440ml)

Surprised? I was! ASDA Lager? Yes, they sell the not 70p, not 50p but the heroic-horse-and-knight-in-armour-decorated 30p can of lager! It's at times like this when my heart goes out to anyone thirsty enough to drink this bland beverage. Visions of Christmas parties spin through my mind like a sea of gaudily coloured polaroids, and there, in the deathly hush of the once-crowded kitchen stands a mountain of untouched ASDA Lager! Probably the only difference between this and the water it is brewed with is that the water has less bubbles. Still, no matter what I say, no matter how many sleepless nights I must endure, sweating, tossing and turning in my bed, I know that this little item will be bought in the thousands of gallons – which is probably how much you need to feel the slightest alcoholic effect. Yup! Little chance of alcohol poisoning with this one.

ASDA LOW-ALCOHOL LAGER   UK

Cans

The supermarket group Asda might have made great financial strides since their divorce from the furniture people MFI a couple of years ago, but unfortunately this success is not reflected in the quality of their low-alcohol lager.

This stuff really is unpleasant. Initially sharp, even tart, in taste, its only redeeming feature is that it's got a head! Indeed, it kept its head a lot longer than I did after being handed a can! All in all it's awful.

ASTICA   Bulgaria

There are many strange stories about lager, none quite so bizarre as the tale of the ASTICA invasion. Until very recently not a drop of the stuff had been drunk by the British. Although it is Bulgaria's leading brand, it has only ever made it through British customs in the diplomatic bags of visiting Bulgarian officials, to be supped quietly in huge state rooms. But, in the next five years, an incredible 5 million litres of the stuff will land in off-licences throughout the length and breadth of Britain. Yes, 600,000 24-can cases will retail at 59p a can. Why? Are the umbrella-toting Bulgarians suddenly ready to compete with the Fosters and Budweiser marketing campaigns? No. Nothing quite so bold, I'm afraid. The truth is much simpler. Rank Xerox have sold Bulgaria's PDS manufacturing business the right to produce its copiers and laser printers. In return, PDS, who are painfully short of foreign exchange to fund imports, are paying for the Xerox franchise with Maritsa typewriters and ASTICA lager! However, before the hearts of the hardened lager drinkers begin to race with excitement at the prospect of exporting coal, ships, cupboards, socks and oil around the world in exchange for their beloved liquid, I'm assured that this is a one-off deal. Still, one can't help but wonder how many 24-can cases we could get for the Crown Jewels . . .

ASTON MANOR EXPORT LAGER   UK

OG 1030–34°   *Aston Manor Brewery Co. Ltd*
Cans
PET Bottles

Rather an intriguingly named lager since I very much doubt this one is exported anywhere!

Yet another low-gravity British-brewed session product that's available in cans and big plastic bottles. The brewers say that they're aiming to give a 'quality drink at as low a price as possible'. Well the price is right, but as for the product . . . !

ASTON MANOR PILS LAGER   UK

OG 1045–50°   *Aston Manor Brewery Co. Ltd*
PET Bottles

From the same brewers as the unexportable ASTON MANOR EXPORT (*q.v.*), ASTON MANOR PILS comes to us in horrible plastic PET bottles.

Introduced in 1986, and with an original gravity of 1045–50° it is certainly a little more qualified than its sister brew.

Another one to either look out for – or avoid – at your local supermarket. I know what I'll be doing!

AYINGERBRAU   UK

OG 1037–41°   *Samuel Smith*
Draught
Bottles (275ml)
Cans (440ml)

Despite a fiercely competitive market AYINGER-BRAU has survived for a full 16 years since being introduced to the palates of Britain's drinkers by Samuel Smith in 1972, who is the beer's sole on-trade outlet, as is the case with all Smith's brews. A first-generation lager, it is surprisingly stronger than a lot of its rivals, while at the same time remaining comfortably within the bounds of being a session lager.

This possibly accounts for its success in Smith's houses for, rather than discontinuing the line as competition increased during the 1970s and 80s, they added to it. Only time will tell, however, whether or not its sister brews meet with the same success. A smooth refreshing lager that comes highly recommended.

AYINGERBRAU SVS (SPECIAL VERY STRONG)

UK

OG 1078–84°
Bottles (275ml)

Samuel Smith

Due to the success of its stable mate, AYINGERBRAU LAGER (*q.v.*), this mind-bending little beverage was introduced to the market in 1984. With more and more lager flooding onto the market all the time, and especially with the new wave of super strength lagers, Samuel Smith found it necessary to update their original portfolio. They had to come up with something with a lot more appeal to the new young lager drinker. More and more of today's youth don't enjoy drinking several pints of their favourite a night when they know that one or two bottles has the same effect. I believe that SVS LAGER suffers the same fate as all other lagers in this original gravity category – they are too strong for their own good. The strength becomes more important than taste, and I find nothing refreshing about super-strength lager even when a person needs something for that very special thirst. Yes, it is thick, and heavy, but having said that it has a surprisingly crisp taste for such a strong brew.

As I've made obvious, I'm not a great fan of super-strength lagers. However, if you are, and there are a lot of you out there, I wholeheartedly recommend that you find a Samuel Smith's pub or off-licence and give this one a go.

AYINGERBRAU 'D' PILS   UK

OG 1042–48°   *Samuel Smith*
Draught
Bottles (275ml)

Of course, how could any self-respecting brewer hope to cover all areas of an expanding lager market without having a pils under their belt? I first noticed pils back in 1976 when a diabetic friend of mine drank it on the grounds that it was sugar-free! Yet as I grew older and traversed the pubs and clubs of the land I began to notice pils everywhere, though usually in the hands of the younger drinker. Indeed, its diet qualities soon caught on with the young trendsetter concerned about an expanding beer-gut.

AYINGERBRAU 'D' is available in draught as well as bottled form, which is unusual for a pils and, in my view, a clever marketing wheeze. As with all Ayingerbrau brews 'D' Pils is brewed by Samuel Smith under licence from the Ayinger Brauerei in Bavaria, using specially imported yeast and hops. Light, crisp, full-bodied and refreshing, this one is again recommended. My local Samuel Smith's pub, The Earl of Lonsdale in London's Portobello Road, stocks the whole range of Ayingerbraus, and whether you are a standard, premium or super-strength drinker, Samuel Smith's pubs have an excellent British brewed lager lying in wait for you!

AYINGERBRAU PRINZ   UK

OG 1044–50°   *Samuel Smith*
Draught

When I tell you that this lager was launched in 1987 you'll be able to see for yourself how Samuel Smith has very competently followed the changing trends in the lager market. In 1972 they released their first generation brew, AYINGERBRAU LAGER (*q.v.*), in draught, bottles and cans, as the demand for lager began to increase. However, by the early 80s drinkers were fed up with just plain old cold, see-through stuff; they wanted something with a higher amount of alcohol in it, a little bit more of a bite. Thus AYINGERBRAU SVS (*q.v.*) appeared in 1984, aimed at a super-strength market. Yet in 1987, with Britain's bars jam-packed with lagers from throughout the globe and the premium market growing by leaps and bounds, the Samuel Smith brewery realized that it would have to update its original draught lager, Ayingerbrau – hence AYINGERBRAU PRINZ, an altogether stronger, more qualified draught lager than its kid sister brew Ayingerbrau.

Again, this is a fine, well-balanced brew and is recommended.

BARBICAN   UK

0.04% Alcohol	*Britvic Corona*
Draught	
Bottles	
Cans	

This latest money-spinning bonanza for the major brewers of producing low- or no-alcohol lager is considered by a number of people to be a 'good move', at least according to the market-research people Gould Mattison and Associates. Their results were announced in March 1988. Quotes gleaned from this research are all pretty much in the same vein: '. . . It means you can go into a pub with your mates and have a drink without them taking the piss' [that is, of course, if you buy the round and don't let them know what you're drinking!]; 'I drink [low-alcoholic drinks] all the time and never have a hangover, and don't look a namby-pamby with my mates'; 'It means that men can have a few jars with their mates without looking daft drinking fruit juice or Coke.' 'Working-class' men, it seems, drink to quench their thirst: 'There's nothing like a cold lager when you're thirsty.' 'Working-class' women, on the other hand, drink to get in the mood, and for the 'middle-class' of both sexes taste is an academic pursuit. Thus, in this amazingly inaccurate analysis of the drinking habits of the British drinker one can see these nasty little brews taking root, and with the advent of licence-loss and stiffening of sentences for drink-drivers, the subsequent demand in the £50-million per annum market-place for them.

The truth of it, of course, is that in the end it's all down to *personal* taste. Attitudes to what we eat and drink have certainly changed over the last decade, if we believe what we read in the papers. This makes it very convenient to believe the claim of the advertising/marketing men that the only difference between these brews and 'real' beers is the lack of alcohol.

BARBICAN was the first real contender in this market in 1980, and today it still claims to be the brand leader in the field with around 38 per cent of the market in the off-trade and 35 per cent in the on-trade. This, as I said, of a £50-million market which I should point out is a measly 0.5 per cent of the total 36- million-barrel beer market. But it does seem destined to grow and grow and the low/no-alcohol sector, referred to by the brewers as the 'lifestyle phenomenon', is seen by them as being 'virtually unlimited'. These same brewers are also at pains to point out that the product has not only changed but is a far cry from the muck they started with nine years ago. Indeed, they are now selling the stuff on draught as the market enters its *second phase*, the logic being that the sight of a barperson pulling a pint of low- or no-alcohol beer (anything between 0.05 per cent and 1.2 per cent is defined as low/no-alcohol – interestingly enough orange juice also carries a measure of 0.05 per cent alcohol by volume!) will act as a further *psychological* push to potential customers. And of course they're right – it will!

But what can we say about BARBICAN itself? Let's try watery to start, then unpleasant and, overall, boring. So why not start with carbonated water in the first place? Well, as I pointed out above, it is all down to the male attitude to beer. It appears, according to the market research companies, that men are so insecure with their friends that they feel like an idiot drinking a soft drink in front of them. They hide this insecurity behind a drink that *looks* like alcohol. Maybe they should simply knock back water in a shot glass and tell their mates it's a vodka!

BAVARIA DUTCH LAGER Netherlands

OG 1030° – 3.2% ABV *Bavaria UK Ltd*
Cans 44cl

Nestled peacefully in southern Holland's Brabant province, lies the sleepy little hamlet of Lieshout where, it goes without saying, the land is flat, but it is also spacious and green and the soil is basically sand – which acts as a natural filter for water. Water is one of *the* most important ingredients for lager and it is fair to say that this region's supply is clean and pure, a magnet for a brewery.

And so it proved to be, for one fine summer's day back in 1719 this small rural community excitedly turned out *en masse* to applaud the arrival of the locality's first brewer. Awarded this warm and somewhat thirsty reception, the man was soon down to work. The brewery grew and grew, and some 50 years later in 1764, one Ambrosius Swinkel was appointed head of the company. Since then they have never looked back. Indeed, six generations of Swinkels have

made the brewery what it is today, even constructing a new plant in 1924 now known as 'the old brewery'. However, it wasn't until Piet, Frans and Jan junior succeeded Jan senior that very same year that they decided to name the company, and therefore also its beer, BAVARIA. But why should a Dutch firm choose such an obviously German name for its product?

During the 20s there was a massive growth in demand for the 'pilsner' lager type, and due to the clear foresight of Jan Swinkel senior, his company was already producing a variant of this beer. Therefore, when he handed over the reins of power the three young executives simply chose a name that matched the beer, and there you have it, BAVARIA, a full-bodied malty little number. Six generations later, the local farmers are still as happy with the region's major brewer as BAVARIA buys thousands of tons of their barley every year. Once the barley has sprouted naturally, a period of eight days is usually enough to allow it to be transformed into 'green malt', then kilning effectively stops the sprouting process. The malt is then ground and the grains pulverized. In the brewing copper the insoluble starch is converted into soluble sugar, which is pumped into a lauter tun where the mixture of wort and spent grains is filtered. This results in clear wort. Hops, the female flowers of the hop plant, are now added, followed by BAVARIA's special yeast strain. Then fermentation – the conversion of sugar into alcohol and carbon dioxide – begins. During a maturation period of several months at a temperature of 0°C more carbon dioxide is formed, ensuring the draught version's perfect frothy head. Thus we have a natural lager and, nature being a capricious thing, it is checked regularly to ensure a fine brew.

Exported around the globe, BAVARIA was introduced to the UK market in January 1985. This fine Dutch lager has rather bravely taken on a market that many would see as already being locked up tight by the major brands. They not only have a 20-year head-start but are also heavily consolidating brand loyalty in their latest promotional packages, in a bid to keep out the newcomers. Therefore, it would appear that the only way to break into the session-lager market now would be on the quality of the product, and as a totally natural product BAVARIA does have a lot going for it. Golden, with a light malty nose, it has a lively hoppy flavour that is very pleasant. With an ABV (alcohol by volume) content of 3.2 per cent, it is certainly a far finer brew than the majority of UK lagers you'll find on draught at your local. If you are a session-lager person, or indeed a person that enjoys a good lager that's brewed with loving care we recommend that you try it.

BAVARIA DUTCH PILS LAGER Netherlands

OG 1048° – 5% ABV *Bavaria UK Ltd*
Cans 44cl

Seventeen months after its sister brew BAVARIA
DUTCH (*q.v.*) was introduced to the UK, BAVARIA
DUTCH PILS appeared. This brew has done extremely
well to survive in the pils market, especially considering
the marketing muscle of some of its competitors. It is
always good to see a product survive by its quality
alone, and this lager certainly has a bit of that. A lager
with all the characteristics of its sister brew, this one is
a little crisper and has a little more bite to it. It is by no
means a widely available lager, so if you do have the
good fortune to find it I recommend that you try it out.

BAVARIA 8.6 SUPER STRENGTH LAGER Netherlands

8.6% ABV *Bavaria UK Ltd*
Cans 44cl

At the time of writing this 'super-heavyweight' lager
had not been introduced although by the time this
book is published it should be available through off-
licences nationwide. Still, in my view, it seems a shame
that the brewery, Bavaria of southern Holland, producers of the excellent BAVARIA DUTCH LAGER and
BAVARIA DUTCH PILS (*qq.v.*) should go to such lengths
to obtain the quality they are after as well as the
specific alcohol by volume content, which they also
incorporate in the brand name, only to export it in
cans and not bottles as well. After all, and I know this
argument will rage on for it is ultimately down to
personal taste, beer experts themselves are pretty much

unanimous in the opinion that a finer brew should be bottled. Indeed some Eastern European brewers would even go so far as to describe the canning of beer as heathen and something one would only do to an extremely inferior brew. This is something that you can decide for yourselves upon sampling, as I intend to do, given the first opportunity.

BECKS   West Germany

O G 1044°	*GB Vintagers/Marblehead*
Bottles 27.5cl	*Maison Caurette*
Cans 33cl	

Exported to 140 countries, this is not only Germany's favourite premium beer but also their biggest export brand, boast brewers Brauerei Beck and Co. Ltd, the largest private brewery group in Germany. BECKS bier is their only product. There is a dark version as well as the lighter, more common one, and though pasteurized for export it remains close to the original in that it is dry, full bodied and has a deep honey colour. Seemingly thick and well-hopped to the palate, it is actually quite light and extremely refreshing, which is no doubt the reason why it's so popular worldwide, though BECKS bier is brewed only in Germany and under licence in Africa.

From Bremen in North Germany Becks have a great brewing tradition to uphold, and one can honestly say that it is a fine brew well worth making space in the fridge for. Since 1985 Becks have become famous for their sponsorship of the arts, including theatre, dance, art exhibitions and film festivals. Their famous green bottle even carried a label designed by the artists Gilbert and George during their 1988 exhibition at London's Hayward Gallery. BECKS can often be found at many arty parties and private views, and has become popular with today's trendy drinkers. Not the best German brew but not far off.

It should also be noted that there are canned versions of both the light and dark BECKS. Although I have yet to taste the contents of one, I recommend you give both varieties a try.

BELHAVEN LAGER   UK

OG 1030–34°   *Belhaven*

Although the Scottish brewers Belhaven state on the bottle that their brewing history extends back into the last century, this does not apply to their lager which they have only been brewing for the past couple of years. This is surprising, considering the enthusiasm with which the Scots have always downed the amber nectar. I found this one in my local Oddbins and was rather looking forward to it.

With a light, malty nose, BELHAVEN is pale and very highly carbonated. It is dry, with a slightly bitter aftertaste that is extremely unpleasant for such a mild lager. It tastes of something unusual, something I can't quite put my finger on. Whatever it is, though, it isn't nice. In fact, it's a great disappointment.

BERGMAN'S LAGER   UK

OG 1032–34°   *Allied*

What can I tell you about BERGMAN'S? Not much, I'm afraid! It is brewed by the mighty brewers Allied, and is currently only available in the north-west, the Midlands and parts of Wales.

However, don't jump on a train in search of it – not without a preliminary phone call at least. I believe BERGMAN'S might be discontinued in 1989. Does this mean that it's a pitiful brew that has failed? Well, who knows? But Allied don't seem to be very proud of it.

BERLINER EXPORT   East Germany

OG 1038–40°
Bottles 33cl
Cans 33cl

Launched nationally through the off-trade in 1986 BERLINER EXPORT was, its importers claim, handsomely received by UK lager drinkers. It is not a bad little lager, in my view, though somewhat lacking in the character of some of its relatives on the other side of the Berlin Wall. Light and smooth, it's again one you should try given the opportunity. At the time of publication the importers expressed themselves as 'over ze moon' with its progress in the already crowded market place. No doubt some of those involved in the brewing process would like to be 'over ze wall'.

BERLINER PILS   East Germany

OG 1044–48°
Bottles 33cl
Cans 33cl

Introduced simultaneously with its sister brew BERLINER EXPORT (q.v.), it shares the same outlets as well as, interestingly enough, the same national success, or so we are told by the flamboyantly happy importers. A slightly more bitter and drier tipple than Berliner Export, with, I thought, an unpleasant metallic tinge to it. This could be put down to the fact that I sampled the canned version. However, don't let this put you off sampling it yourself.

BIG BARREL   Australia

OG 1035°   *Continental Lager Distributors*
Cans

Contrary to traditional belief convicts weren't the only ones who filled those first ships to Australia, but also a proud drinking class, and with them several proud and enthusiastic brewers. One such brewer was the Yorkshireman, Thomas Cooper, who founded his brewery in 1862 and it is still run by his descendants 125 years later, the last family-run brewery on the continent.

As you will gather throughout this book, Australian's are fiercely patriotic about their drink and each state has its own major brewers. Cooper's brewery is South Australia's, and each year, together with the German Club of South Australia, they hold a shooting festival called, naturally, the Schützenfest. Traditionally Coopers brew a new beer for every festival and in 1974 this beer was BIG BARREL LAGER, a pasteurized, bottom-fermented, sweet and dark lager, relatively low in alcohol, which incidentally makes it a fine session lager. It no doubt went down well with the lager-drinking population of South Australia as it has been kept in production ever since, a rare event for Schützenfest beers which are usually one-offs. A sweet tasting but extremely pleasant lager that comes to these shores in a beautifully designed 'Big Barrel' of a can. Heartily recommended.

BIRELL   UK

Watneys

BIRELL is another nasty low-alcohol product that ever since my first mouthful I've managed to avoid. I

suggest that you do the same. Either leave the car at home and have a real beer, drive to the pub and drink fruit juice or water, or stay where you are and put the kettle on.

BITBURGER   West Germany

OG 1045°   *J. A. Cooper & Son*
Draught
Bottles 33cl

BITBURGER PILS has brought great renown and
respectability to the Theodor Simon Brewery and the
town of Bitburg itself in the Eifel region of the Federal
Republic of Germany. Fortunately for the discerning
British tippler, it arrived in the south-east of England in
1980. Today it is available throughout many parts of
England and Wales, although notably still in the
south-east as well as the Midlands and north-west.

In 1987 it was 170 years old. With the sixth generation of the family taking the helm in 1975, Bitburger
has grown steadily over the years from a small family
concern to a major German brewing company, producing some 2,380,000 hectolitres of BITBURGER PILS
per annum. The brewery itself views this success as
residing in the restaurant trade in Germany where
Bitburg firmly holds a huge 40 per cent share of the
draught lager market which amounts to a mighty
900,000 hectolitres a year, making it the greatest
draught beer in West Germany. This success, however,
is not solely due to the home market as BITBURGER
is exported to 21 countries worldwide, although it
should be added that these are the countries most
often favoured by German tourists who dash wholeheartedly to some of the world's finest hotels and clubs
where, they believe, their beloved BITBURGER will
be served as it ought to be – exclusively and in style.
And it's no wonder that the Germans put in an amaz-
ing 300 odd pints each a year when we consider
Germany's excellent brewing standards, and BITBUR-
GER is no different: quality *is* its trademark passed on
from father, Johann Peter Wallenborn, to son, since
1817, and Wallenborn the elder was no fool.

Now, as we all know, apart from malt and hops, just about the most important ingredient for any beer is its water and since 1911, when the brewery sank its first artesian wells into the reservoir under the ancient hamlet cum modern-day town of Bitberg, some 9,000 cubic yards of water have gushed hourly into the brewery's vats. This, together with barley processed by first-rate maltsters, hops from Germany's most famous regions and a strain of yeast cultivated in their own laboratories, as well as the art of master-brewers, go into the making of a truly fine German beer.

BITBURGER has a delicate taste and the rich, full-bodied flavour is instantly recognizable and rewarding. Although it seems slightly dry and bitter at first, one's palate soon warms to its flavour and the pity of it is that it isn't more widely available as it is most certainly recommended. I grant you, German restaurants are hardly ten a penny, and we're not all members of trendy London clubs, but this one is well worth badgering the manager of your local off-licence for.

Get your quid out and plug in one of the very best!

BLEU DE BRASSERIE   UK

OG 1043°   *Allied*
Bottles 27.5cl

Women consume 37 per cent of the canned and bottled lager market, and Allied Breweries, in April 1988, launched the first lager in Britain to be targeted specifically at women. To do this Allied has chosen what it freely admits is a completely meaningless name for its lager, BLEU DE BRASSERIE (blue bars or bar recruit, depending on whether you passed your 'O'-level French). Allied were quick to capitalize on a Mintel survey which pointed out that women working outside the home were the only social group ignoring the trend to reduce alcohol consumption and, further to this, believed that there are therefore a 'large proportion of females who would like their own product'.

Unfortunately at the time of writing there were no figures available to gauge the success of BLEU which was test marketed in London at the beginning of April 1988, backed by a £250,000 press and poster campaign. The area within the M25 was chosen, purely on the grounds that if it couldn't be sold in London then they couldn't sell it anywhere. The label on my bottle was a miserable looking bloke with a prominent dickybow in front of a very dull and serious moon, and if this wasn't bad enough then we should thank our lucky stars that it wasn't a duplicate of the poster on the London Underground – a scruffy, lifeless illustration that made one's eyes wander to the next advertisement almost instantly. BLEU was launched with six different 'art nouveau' labels which Allied believe add sophistication, class and desirability to the brand.

BLEU DE BRASSERIE is a *fashion* drink and will probably survive on the market only as long as other fashions. Still, although targeted at women, men certainly shouldn't scoff at it. After all with a gravity of 1043 the feminine BLEU makes Allied's macho Castlemaine XXXX look like a bucket of Barbican! And rubbish it is not. With a dark, amber colour and a strong hoppy bouquet, it is actually quite pleasant. Dry with a refreshingly mature flavour, it is particularly light for a lager of this strength, and goes down considerably easily without leaving any residue of a sticky aftertaste. Not a bad lager at all.

PS Shortly before the launch of BLEU, traditionally thirsty journalists drank the entire stock of six bottles, held by advertising agency Ayer Barker, only to discover that these were demonstration bottles advertising only the label, the contents of which were not not fit for human consumption.

BOAGS PREMIUM   Australia

OG 1044–46°   *Anglo Australian Wine Co.*
Cans 37.5cl

Mainland Australia might be home to some famous brews, but it should not be forgotten that just over 60 per cent of their hops come from the island state of Tasmania, which is the Australian brewing industry's major producer of malting-barley. Tasmania is also the home of the Cascade Brewery which takes its name from the streams that cascade down the side of Mount Wellington. It was this stream water that was originally used not only in the brewing process but also to supply power to the plant.

Shortly after the turn of the century Cascade bought the Boags Brewery, the producers of BOAGS lager at the other end of the island. A relatively pale brew, BOAGS lager is best served even as cold as 4°C, as any warmer it becomes quite frothy and taste comes a poor second to the struggle to get it down! Served *well* chilled, then, BOAGS is quite rightly a highly-rated premium Australian lager and should be sought out. I first found it on sale in London a couple of years ago and have become quite a fan. A true Aussie product that is often found sitting amongst a shelf full of pretenders!

BOFFERDING   Luxembourg

Bottles   *Luxembourg Wine Co. Ltd*

BOFFERDING is an extremely smooth lager from Luxembourg that I used to buy regularly from my local off-licence when a resident of Fulham. I must say, however, that this was partly due to its very competitive price.

Unfortunately, I haven't seen it for a while, though it is apparently available from the seemingly deaf and dumb Luxembourg Wine Company of Bath. Go on, you try and get a bottle out of them! I can assure you, it's well worth a try!

BOHEMIA   Mexico

Bottles 12fl. oz   *Mexican Beer Co.*

To put it bluntly, the average Britain associates the sombrero with Mexico and that's about all, except, perhaps, for the odd peasant revolution starring Lee Van Cleef and a fistful or two of dynamite. However, if we really stretch ourselves we'll remember the Aztecs and the great and wonderful treasures and architecture they left behind after the Spaniards had put paid to them. But interestingly enough the Aztecs were no strangers to beer, as any Spanish chronicler of history worth their salt will point out. Braver historians have even compared these beers with those of ancient Germany. Although very different from a German brew, this particular lager from the Cuauhtemoc brewery in Monterrey does at least take its name from the country that is the father of all beers.

BOHEMIA comes in a nice squat brown bottle that is fat in the body with a slim neck. Decorated with a gold label adorned with the head of a bronze Aztec Indian, the package itself is very up-market, which is both a reflection of and a tribute to the brew inside. Initial investigation tells us that it is very light, pale and virtually aromaless – in a nutshell, traditionally Mexican. However, unlike most beers from this part of the world, it has a distinctive and far fuller flavour than its Mexican sister brews. Now available in many Mexican restaurants as well as the off-trade, it comes recommended with your tacos, nachos, fritos . . . etc.

BRAHMA
Brazil

OG 1048 – 5% ABV
Bottles 27.5–35.5cl
General Atlantic Ltd

Ninety per cent of the beer market in Brazil is held by two groups, Antarctica Paulista and Brahma. The latter, based in Rio and founded at the turn of the century by 19th-century German settlers, is without question the larger of the two. Indeed, Brahma is not only the largest brewery in Brazil but also in the whole of South America, so it's no surprise to discover that it is the seventh largest brewery in the world, producing 28 million hectolitres of beer every year.

Although described as a pilsner on the label, it is different in that it is brewed with a rice compound as well as malt, yeast and natural hops, yet it no doubt derives this description from its proud German heritage. BRAHMA is one of the worldwide brand leaders for rice-based lagers and has a surprisingly clean, full-flavoured premium lager taste. In fact it's an excellent beer, though somewhat sweeter than the average tippler may be accustomed to, yet its light body is designed to be consumed easily and rapidly, a prerequisite in the Brazilian climate. Despite all the other positive images of Brazil (Copacabana Beach, Sugar Loaf Mountain, *the* festival, Ayrton Senna, and singularly beautiful women), the importers seem so desperate to market the lager that they even describe the bottle as being 'sexy' which, no doubt, might be the case after fourteen glasses.

Though obviously not designed for the British climate, BRAHMA offers a refreshing change from the norm and should most certainly be hunted out. If you buy a bottle the brewers donate a penny to the preservation of the Brazilian rainforests which supply 25 per cent of the world's oxygen, without which we would suffocate. Take it lightly if you wish, but personally I don't like the idea of holding my breath when drinking my lager. Try it. It's a great lager from a great country.

BREAKER   UK

5.4% ABV   *Bass*
Cans

A very similar brew to COLT .45 (*q.v.*). Initially fluffy, thick and sticky with a fine head (at least mine was the next morning!). Served extremely cold, it can be quite refreshing, and the heavy malt taste, when acquired, is stimulating.

In fact, it's precisely this strong malt taste that puts it a cut above many of the major brands on the off-licence shelves, in as much as it does have a taste! Worth trying as a malt brew – one you'll either love or hate.

BREDA	Netherlands

OG 1044°
Draught
Bottles 25cl
Cans 33cl

R. W. Randall

You might think this indulgent of me but I have to tell you a true story. Many years ago when I was young, I set off to hitch-hike to Amsterdam where, I had been assured, they catered for every vice. By the next day I was in Ostend, Belgium, and up to then everything had been rosy, yet once on the Continent my troubles began. I was arrested and fined twice for hitch-hiking on the hard shoulder of the Belgian motorways and this sudden drain on my resources shook me badly. I took a bus to Breda where I thought I might start my adventure afresh. Once there it was equally impossible to get a ride to my original destination. The hours passed and as it got dark I felt more and more morose. I wandered back the short distance towards the town, so depressed that I could have died ... and that's when I saw an old man watching me from his illuminated window. Instantly I stopped and did my best to look as hungry and thirsty as I could.

I let my pack drop to the ground and, following it, clutched at my stomach. Moments later the little old man appeared and helped me back to his home where, upon opening the fridge, I saw my first ever case of BREDA PILSENER. 'It's lucky,' the man said, indicating the three horseshoes on the label. I smiled, peeling off the top of the first of many during my stay in the Netherlands.

That weekend was carnival weekend in Breda and I stayed with the old man all that time. Together we drank BREDA whilst the music blared and laughter splashed to the streets from every bar. The beer itself was great and such a refreshing change from the lagers of England I was used to. It's hoppy, light and strong. A local brew manufactured in the town of the same name, it is now available in the UK. A fine beer with a distinct taste, it should be sampled when found, and held aloft to the old man of Breda. *Prost!* and thank you!

BRITISH HOME STORES LAGER

I haven't been into British Home Stores for years, and I've certainly never bought any lager in one. Therefore, I've never tried this lager, though I understand that it is, or indeed was, brewed by Allied. I'm afraid I suspect the worst with this one – as I do with most supermarket lagers. Your reports please and unless they're favourable I doubt if I'll be buying it!

BROKEN HILL   Australia

OG 1041–45°   *Victon Ross*
Cans 37.5cl

Imagine the sun as a huge orange ball set against a perfectly clear sky. Imagine the sound of flies as they hover around you, flirting, zooming and zipping into your face. Imagine mile upon mile of unbroken desert blurred and dancing in the heat haze. Imagine lips caked with salt, a dry tongue noisily scraping over them, sweat pouring from every pore in your body and a temperature well over the hundreds for the 85th year running. Imagine a town where the only toilet is a shack 300 yards away from the main street, on the edge of the outback, where the 'sh*t truck' stops once a fortnight to pick up the contents – a battered, rattly dust-covered old van, chased by dogs and kids alike as it bounces in and out of town. Imagine a weather-beaten old pine hut with a marble bar full to burst with dusty mineworkers at 6 o'clock every day and reverberating with every *shout* for a fistful of ice-cold beer.

This is Broken Hill.

BROKEN HILL lager, on the other hand, is brewed by the South Australian Brewing Company in Adelaide, a far cry from those work-hardened men baking gently to death in the middle of the continent. Broken Hill is a mining town famous to all Australians simply for what it is and what it requires to survive there: *machismo.* Therefore the SABC have chosen to decorate the can with a rather sluggishly drawn miner with too much on his mind and not a grain of sweat on him – a tough Oz, and a typical Oz to many British lager drinkers. He certainly looks as though he could do with several Broken Hills.

The crack and *phfsssht* of the can releases a rich hoppy smell that is supported by a lively brew set at the lower end of the premium range. BROKEN HILL makes for a refreshing lager that, though difficult to come by, is worth passing the time of day with whenever you can.

BUDWEISER UK

OG 1042–48° Draught		*GB Vintagers*
OG 1045°	Bottles 27.5cl	
	Cans 33cl	

Anheuser-Busch's BUDWEISER is the world's best-

selling beer. However, four years after they brought it to the UK it has flopped badly. It has barely captured 1 per cent of the lager market in the UK, while the likes of FOSTER'S (*q.v.*) have gained a 6 per cent share after a seven-year period. One London-based firm pointed out that BUDWEISER's failure might be due to the initial advertising at the time of its launch. The company was basically selling us America wholesale without addressing the brew itself to British pub culture. You've got to admit that if this is the case, which I think it is, Anheuser-Busch has literally thrown millions of pounds down the drain. As the advertising journal *Campaign* pointed out, in this country 'Pub Culture reigns victoriously'.

One can easily see how Anheuser-Busch made such

a mistake with the UK launch. Beer consumption *per capita* is 20 per cent higher in Britain than the States, but the advertising agency overlooked the fact that nearly 75 per cent of these sales come from drinkers enjoyably quaffing their beer in the sanctum of the local public house. For an advertising agency to apparently overlook this is *absolutely disgraceful*. If I were the brewer I'd not only sack the firm but I'd ask for my money back. What a disaster! I mean, after all, one could barely contemplate a beer like BUDWEISER failing in this country, for not only does it have the millions of pounds worth of clout that could make its name an everyday word in the English language, but it also arrived at a time when the lager market was (and still is) booming. In just a few short years the British beer drinker has rapidly acquired a taste for cold, carbonated, light-coloured lager and its sales in 1987 fell just short of taking 50 per cent of the entire market, over what was for centuries Britain's favourite tipple, ale. Poor old BUDWEISER must be kicking itself to death because its got nothing else to do with its foot now it can't, as yet, get it in the door.

Even before its launch in the autumn of 1984 Anheuser had to spend two years in court where it successfully fought the Czechoslovakian beer BUDWEISER BUDVAR (*q.v.*) over the use of its name; a name which, the Czechs claim, Adophus Busch (the original Busch in Anheuser-Busch) simply took for his own brew in 1876 after experiencing the original in his homeland. This victory, however, only applies to Britain and in other parts of Europe the dispute continues. In Spain it was introduced under the simple name of Bud, and the same name was used in test markets in West Berlin six years ago where, not surprisingly, it failed to impress the discerning German lager drinker. This name was also used in Switzerland with the same depressing results. Tens of millions of pounds have been spent in lengthy litigation as, on a country-by-country basis, the Yanks battle fiercely to register their own trademark. It has been reported that Anheuser offered the Czechs more than $2 million (£1.09 million), a share of Third World markets, and the temptation of several joint ventures. In Ceske Budéjovice, home of the original Budvar, those who drink the local version are adamant that they would 'rather die' than come to an agreement with a firm whose beer is, in their opinion, 'only a pale imitation of our quality product'. Local mythology even goes as far as saying that Adolphus Busch, the venerated 19th-century father of modern American brewing, was sacked from the Bohemian brewery at Budweis (now Ceské Budéjovice) for incompetence before he emigrated to America and sacrilegiously marketed his own beer using the same name. Indeed, a young shopkeeper in Budé-jovice sneered at the American version and pointed out, 'You will never find our beer in a tin. We only keep *sauerkraut* in such things!' So the Czechs don't look like budging – and why should they? They have been brewing for centuries what are generally acknowledged to be some of the world's finest beers, and they consume more beer per capita than most other nations in the world. Indeed, in 1986, the Czechs ranked a heroic third.

Back in Britain, despite its judicial victory, the catalogue of disasters continued: the draught launch was hit with divine intervention when, promoted as an ice-cold drink, because at 3–5°C Bud is served colder than any other beer, it arrived after an unusually cold summer. Thus Anheuser-Busch's boasts of disproving Britain's belief that US beer is tasteless, gassy and weak failed as hardly anyone was bothering to taste the stuff. This position was not helped by the fact that British drinkers believe all American beers are weak, which in BUDWEISER's case with a 5 per cent alcohol by volume content is wrong.

Still, four years later BUDWEISER is still trying. In March 1988 their sponsorship of a four-week radio series, relating to the story of Motown music, on independent radio marked the start of 'a record-breaking marketing spend' for BUDWEISER support activities. In May 1988 they sacked several top executives in their international marketing team in a bid to crack the world market. At the same time they splurged out another £4.5 million on an advertising and promotional package set to coincide with what they consider to be the peak of the lager-drinking season – July. However, the two TV ads, 'Moonshot' and 'Baseball', backed by 66 per cent of the aforementioned £4.5 million are, in the words of one adman, 'slow, boring and lifeless'. We're still being sold America wholesale but 'this time in the pub' – well at least they got one thing right!

Plagued by problems, there was even talk in the middle of 1988 of BUDWEISER leaving the market place altogether! This, though, is a little drastic, and one feels that the beer which is certainly not completely without character, could stand proud compared to the majority of other British lagers, and no doubt could have been a roaring success had the marketing been better. Perhaps Anheuser's biggest mistake was that they never bought a brewery. Without its own pubs BUDWEISER only has 5,800 outlets compared to, for example, Foster's with 20,000. This sort of availability has an awful lot to do with a product's success, especially if the advertising works.

Watneys predicted that BUDWEISER would be the single biggest-selling beer of the decade in the UK, however we feel that it won't come into its own until the 1990s. Despite its initial poor showing, trading figures for the year ending March 1988 showed a 37 per cent increase in take-home sales, and a 38 per cent increase for draught. Promising, after four changes in advertising strategy in as many years, and after Anheuser gave up control, snatched it back again, and then gave it back to Grand Metropolitan Brewing!

As for the beer itself, it certainly isn't unpleasant. With an original gravity of 1045, and a 5 per cent alcohol by volume content it's up there in the strength stakes with a number of fine lagers. It is a very light brew, which is possibly why people wrongly think it is weak. Anheuser is proud to announce that it uses rice as an ingredient and we all know of the roasting over beechwood chips. Although Anheuser has insisted in the UK that BUDWEISER is brewed to the same US recipe, it is unclear just how this rule is adhered to when the water is completely different. However, BUD-WEISER does have a distinctive flavour. The US-brewed variety also has a 32-day lagering period, a fact most certainly not to be snorted at, for the average brew is only given around 14 days.

Although the beer has been a commercial failure up to now, we believe that BUDWEISER will surprise its critics and grow into a household brew within four or five years . . . but we can't say how much we're willing to bet on it.

BUDWEISER BUDVAR   Czechoslovakia

OG 1048–54°   *BB Supply Centre Ltd*
Bottles (33 and 50 cl)

No, not the American variety of BUDWEISER (*q.v.*), but the original from Czechoslovakia, the real home of lager. The reason why there are two lagers called Budweiser, so the Czechs claim, is that in 1876 the American brewer Adolphus Busch simply took the name for his own beverage. A spokesman for Anheuser-Busch, the brewers of the American Budweiser, says that Busch was an American citizen, but they are not sure of his origins. The Czechs of Southern Bohemia, however, are. As local mythology has it Busch was dismissed from the brewery for incompetence shortly before he emigrated to America.

BUDWEISER BUDVAR is named after the town

of Budweis – now called Ceské Budjévice. The legend 'Beer of Kings' has lived with BUDWEISER BUDVAR since it was delivered to the Czech court of King Ferdinand in 1531. Appealing to the discerning drinker who appreciates a good-quality strong lager, it has long been one of my favourites as it has a very mild, sweet-bitter taste with a distinct hoppy flavour and not too much aftertaste. Yet don't let that deceive you: after a few of these you'll wake up with a crowd round you! Made with the finest aromatic hops, grown in nearby Saaz, best malt and natural spring water, it is still faithful to its centuries-old brewing tradition, and is allowed 90 days to mature. Not surprisingly it has doubled its sales in two years and continues to grow as one of the leaders in the imported lager market. It won four gold medals in 1986 alone, being rewarded in Poland as the best beer in Eastern Europe, and in Madrid for outstanding quality. Although BUDVAR has been available in the UK for 20 years, we can thank Courage for bringing it to our attention by importing it in the on-trade since 1984, as one of its strongs, classic, imported lagers, each brewed and bottled in the country of origin. The London-based BB Supply Centre now handles BUDWEISER BUDVAR over here so get your 'offy' to give them a call.

Probably the best lager in the world. Cheers!

CARLING BLACK LABEL | UK

OG 1035–39° Draught *Bass*
OG 1034–38° Bottles and Cans

The biggest-selling lager in the UK! I'm sure a lot of you actually see this beer as a totally British invention, but in fact you are wrong. CARLING BLACK LABEL was originally a Canadian beer. Its founder was

Thomas Carling who established the Carling Brewing and Malting Company in Ontario way back in 1840.

It was first brewed in the UK in 1952 by Hope and Anchor Breweries of Sheffield. It was a reciprocal deal, whereby the Canadians got to brew Hope and Anchor's Jubilee Stout. I wonder who got the best half of the deal?

CARLING BLACK LABEL has been advertised on TV since 1955. Some of their award-winning commercials, made by the advertising agency Wight Rutherford Collins Scott and Mathews Marcantonioni, are among the best adverts ever made for any product, let alone beer. Though the marketing man of Bass might well disagree with me on this point, there has to be some truth in the saying that 'lager drinkers drink the advertising, not the product'.

Brewed by Bass at Burton-on-Trent – which is arguably the capital of the British brewing industry, and indeed, famous the world over for its underground wells of natural spring water – CARLING BLACK LABEL is one of the most successful products ever launched in the UK.

The draught version's original gravity makes it slightly stronger and tastier than its main rivals. While it is by no means one of my favourite lagers, it is nevertheless preferable to many others. I recently sampled a pint at a pub in Mayfair and was happily surprised. With a slightly sweet aroma, and a smooth, not too gassy, character, it was – what shall I say – not unpleasant! To stick my neck out I'd say that it's the best selling lager in the UK because people do drink advertising, and because it's a better drink than your home-produced CARLSBERGs and HEINEKENs (*qq.v.*).

CARLSBERG ELEPHANT BEER   Denmark

OG 1072°   *Global Beer Co. Ltd*
Bottles

Ah! Now this is it – a real CARLSBERG!

ELEPHANT BEER was named after the elephant gates at the Carlsberg Brewery in Denmark (yes, this lager is brewed in Denmark!), and a good friend tells me that it's the same brew that used to be sold over here as CARLSBERG 68.

ELEPHANT is a great lager! Smooth, surprisingly dry and unsticky and, considering its original gravity, it should certainly be sought out.

Forget the Carlsberg that's sold in your local! This is the way the Danes intended CARLSBERG to be, and this is indeed the form in which you should drink it. One of the very best!

CARLSBERG EXPORT

UK

Carlsberg

OG 1040–44°
Draught
Bottles
Cans

This is yet another highly-carbonated mixture that has little in common with the great Danish-brewed CARLSBERG ELEPHANT (*q.v.*). Having said that, however, we should also point out that it is stronger and far more drinkable than the original CARLSBERG PILSNER (*q.v.*), and if you ever have a choice between the two, and find it impossible to abstain, we highly recommend that you drink this one. It really is a great shame that a lager with such a great name and tradition is brewed to such a low standard in this country. A minute's silence please, for Mr Christian Jacobsen, the original Mr Carlsberg, who would surely be turning in his grave if he knew what his successors were up to over here.

CARLSBERG PILSNER

UK

Carlsberg

OG 1030–34°
Draught
Bottles 27.5cl
Cans 27.5cl/44cl

The very first pint of CARLSBERG was brewed on November 10th 1847 and it marked the beginning of an epoch. The brewer, Christian Jacobsen, zealously pursued the finer science of brewing and was friends with all the Gods of Beer, Sedlmayr, Dreher, Pasteur and Velten. With these men the art of brewing became a science: thermometers were used as opposed to elbows, refrigeration explored, yeast cells isolated.

Quickly popular in Copenhagen, after a few teething problems had been resolved, the first CARLSBERG arrived in Britain in 1868 and all was well. Yet over 100 years later in 1973 the Danish brewers made their biggest mistake and built a brewery alongside the River Nene in Northampton, coincidentally within the perimeter of a 9th century Danish settlement. Sadly, though, this seems to be the only thing in common with the original Danish brew and before long the British version flooded the market.

In just seven years, from 1969 to 1976, Carlsberg had negotiated the site of their brewery, built it, brewed and pulled the first pint on August 28th 1973, and expanded the production from one million barrels to over two million. Since then CARLSBERG has become a giant in both the on- and off-trades and even has the 'bottle' to advertise itself as 'Probably the best lager in the world'. With Danish-brewed CARLSBERG ELEPHANT (q.v.) they might well have a claim to that title, but with the Northampton brew ...

Although I'm not a great ale drinker, I must confess that I share the opinion of the CAMpaign for Real Ale who describe CARLSBERG PILSNER as 'Probably the worst lager in the world', and a 'sort of draught Perrier' – probably a slight on the mineral water industry!

CAMRA have pursued their case against Carlsberg and as a result a Carlsberg TV commercial was announced as being 'misleading' by the Independent Broadcasting Authority, who later banned the advert. CAMRA had protested that the commercial shown on ITV, called 'Check-Point', depicted a convoy of lorries crossing Denmark's border with Germany, carrying pure lager, in accordance with the German Pure Beer Law of 1516. However, CAMRA pointed out that the German border 'does not extend as far as Northampton'. They went on angrily, 'The lager is said to be pure because under the German Pure Beer Law of 1516 it must be pure to be allowed into Germany. But the advertisements on ITV are promoting Carlsberg lager in Britain and the lager in the convoy crossing the German border has precious little to do with that! The Carlsberg lager on sale in the UK is brewed in Northampton to a completely different recipe than its Danish namesake!'

The truth of it is that the Carlsberg lager available here has very little in common with the fine brew made in Denmark. It's thin, weak and ghastly.

CARLSBERG SPECIAL BREW   UK

OG 1078–82°   *Carlsberg*
Bottles
Cans

Another 'Carlsberg' that's brewed in the UK and not its native Denmark.

SPECIAL BREW is probably the biggest selling super-strength lager on the market, and it has certainly been around for a lot longer than most others. For me, though, it suffers in the same way that all these lagers do: it is extremely thick. Remember, I'm not a fan of super-strength brews, but if you are there must be something in this one, judging by its popularity alone.

Maybe these lagers are an acquired taste but to be honest I don't have the patience. All I could manage was a few mouthfuls before returning to a can of RED STRIPE (*q.v.*) to wash away the aftertaste. SPECIAL BREW's main appeal to many is its strength, and if that's what you want, then go ahead.

CARLTON SPECIAL LIGHT   Australia

0.9% ABV   *Courage*
Draught
Cans 37.5cl

Imported by Courage in a pleasant cream-coloured can
decorated by dray horses, the brewers, Carlton United
Breweries of Melbourne, claim that it is a full-strength
lager, with the reduction in alcoholic strength being
achieved by 'a unique vacuum process'.

Yawn. Another bland, low-alcohol lager.

CARTA BLANCA   Mexico

Bottles 12oz   *Mexican Beer Co.*

A product of the famous Cuauhtemoc brewery in Monterrey, which, incidentally, is where England played
their first games in the 1986 World Cup finals. The
brewery takes its name from an Indian hero murdered
during the Spanish invasion under Cortes.

From its humble beginnings in the late 19th century,
Cuauhtemoc is now Mexico's second largest brewer.
CARTA BLANCA is a very light pilsner-style brew,
and is definitely atune to the Mexican market in as
much that as a thirst quencher it probably does the
trick very well. Unfortunately in the overcast muggy
atmosphere of England it tastes of nothing.

At the time of writing Mexican beer seems to be
becoming extremely popular. Some of them are very
pleasant, but CARTA BLANCA in my view just isn't
one of them.

CASCADE

Australia

Bottles 34.5cl   *Anglo-Australian Wine Co.*

Peter Degraves was an unsettled man. For years he'd harboured dreams for change, for some sort of adventure as all around him he heard talk of the new world down under. Then, at last, he could hold himself back no longer, and he took the long journey to Australia. Lady Luck was kind to him there, and in 1824 Governor Sorell granted the newly arrived 46-year-old migrant from England 2,500 acres of land on the side of Mount Wellington, Tasmania.

At the Cascades, where two of the mountain's rivers converged, Degraves worked long and hard to build a watermill wheel to power his newly-built sawmill. Naturally, in a fresh colony, timber was in great demand and Degraves prospered with the growth of the young Hobart Town. Yet still he felt frustrated and, despite his wealth, he was unhappy. And so it was that within less than a decade the ever-dreaming Degraves built himself a freestone Georgian-style building – a brewery was born!

A better choice of location could hardly have been made, with an unending supply of pure, clean mountain water at his disposal; not only this for Tasmanian hops are famous throughout the world and 60 per cent of all the hops used in the Australian brewing industry come from there. Thus, as he used only malted barley, brewer's yeast, hops and water, Degraves was able to advertise his brew in 1832: 'At this establishment, publicans and private families can be supplied at all times with genuine beer from malt and hops, either in cask or bottle, and of a very superior quality.'

Launched in the UK in January 1987 in a distinctive green bottle with two Tasmanian Tigers on the label, CASCADE is a refreshing, though slightly bitter lager beer from Australia's oldest continuing brewing operation. Relatively light, it's very pleasant and should

certainly be sampled alongside Australia's other exports. An extremely pleasant find.

CASTLE
South Africa

OG 1044–46° – 4.8% ABV
Bottles 34cl
Cans 34cl

*Continental Lager
Distributors Ltd*

First brewed in Pietermaritzburg in 1896, CASTLE was the first real breakthrough for the pioneers in the production of a genuine imitation of a central European lager beer, and today it is still the South African's favourite swill.

CASTLE is quite bitter with no sweetness. It is light

in colour, as well as texture, and it has a very slightly hoppy aroma. Pretty average.

CASTLEMAINE XXXX DRAUGHT   UK

Draught
Cans

Commercials for CASTLEMAINE XXXX are well-loved by the British beer drinker for their humour. It is true to say that the average Brit has fallen hook, line and sinker for the traditional image of the Aussie lager strangler who, living in a desert surrounded by kangaroos, seems to drink all day and night without ever going to the toilet or sliding under the table. Indeed, the Aussies themselves would have us believe this and at an average of around 148 litres per head per annum, they insist that they are the world's number one national beer drinkers. However, although this isn't exactly true, beer sales are increasing Down Under and they most certainly rank in the world's top five, along with such great lager drinking nations as Czechoslovakia and the mouse that roared, Luxembourg. Brewed under licence by Allied, XXXX has grown to be the sixth best-selling draught lager in Britain, at one time out-selling its Aussie rival, FOSTER'S (*q.v.*), according to independent sources. Still, no matter how briefly XXXX did outgun Elliott's empire, one could hear Alan Bond's champagne corks popping around the planet, for the rivalry between Bond and Foster's John Elliott is legendary Down Under and makes the J.R. *v* Cliff Barnes affair look like two snotty-nosed three-year-olds arguing over a marble in a sandlot. Two things are certain: one is that XXXX has achieved better growth more swiftly than FOSTER'S; and two, that Australian lager has been one of *the* major success stories in the UK drinks market. So what about the lager itself?

When poured from the can this Brit-brewed version of XXXX is most certainly not blond in colour but has a slight copper tint to it. The head that is established by the ferocious number of bubbles soon disappears, although the highly-carbonated bite doesn't. It would be difficult to detect any bouquet in this one, unless, of course, you have a snout on you like a prize hog. The hog used in our test swore to being able to detect a very mild hoppy aroma although to me, a layman, I assure you it smells of nothing. It is slightly bitter and so overcarbonated that it makes it very unpleasant as it is frothy on impact and somewhat furry on the way down. If this isn't bad enough it also seems to produce a strange gluey quality to the interior of the mouth which, for a session lager, is most unusual. So, flavourless and aromaless, it would be difficult to get stuck on this one, and quite frankly it is not recommended. At best it's a refreshing drink when on draught and served well chilled. Don't worry about the whole Aussie reputation thing, as it most certainly isn't brewed Down Under and I doubt whether any Oz in Blighty would give a XXXX if he never saw it again. Keep shopping around.

CASTLEMAINE XXXX EXPORT   Australia

OG 1041–45°
Cans 37.5cl

Originally prepared by the Brisbane firm of Castlemaine Perkins in 1889, legend is uncertain as to whether the XXXX logo was taken from a Mr Fourex or from the brand burnt onto wooden barrels at the time to identify a premium lager content. Still, whichever is true it is certainly Queensland's most popular lager with a full body and a lively hoppy flavour. Like most Australian lagers, it is sweet, reasonably highly carbonated, and goes down a treat! In a nutshell: *Ripper!*

CHALLENGE   UK

OG 1030–34°   *Winerite Ltd*
Cans 44cl
PET Bottles 2 & 3 litres

Launched in a can in 1977, CHALLENGE apparently sold enough to give the brewers confidence to launch it in the infamous plastic PET bottle in 1984. By 1987 they were claiming to sell 32,000 cases of cans and 996,000 litres in PETs. One wonders how.

Marketed in one of the most tasteless and corny cans of the decade, CHALLENGE is basically a real cheapo supermarket lager and I'd feel embarrassed to know someone who drank it. Well worth avoiding.

CHARGER   UK

OG 1030–34°   *Tennent*
Cans

Brewed by Tennents in Glasgow, and with an original gravity of 1030–34°, the canned CHARGER is their lager competing at the cheaper end of the market.

Compared with its competitors, then, it's not that bad, not over-carbonated, and with a very slight hint of malt in the taste. If you're counting your pennies and can't go without, you could do worse than this one.

CHASER UK

OG 1030–34°
PET Bottles 2 litre

It smells and tastes of nothing. Don't bother.

CLAUSEN Luxembourg

OG 1047° – 4.8% ABV
Bottles 25cl

Euroimpex Ltd

Brewed by the Brasseries Réunies de Luxembourg Mousel company at the Mousel Clausen et Funck brewery, Luxembourg's second largest brewery, CLAUSEN was launched nationally through the off-trade in 1980, though it's not by any means an easy brew to find. Light, hoppy and usually competitively priced, CLAUSEN is an excellent little lager that is well worth sampling.

CLAUSTHALER SPECIAL LOW ALCOHOL LAGER West Germany

0.6% ABV
Bottles 33cl

Marblehead

One wonders who is to blame for selecting the extremely lame, unfunny and off-putting cabaret act Bobby Davro to promote this low-alcohol lager in Britain. As if it's not hard enough to establish a foothold in an already overcrowded market place! Still, Scottish and Newcastle Breweries (Sales), who handle off-trade sales and distribution for the importer Surfax, saw fit to invest £1 million plus in 1988 with Davro as the front man. However, one should not be put off by this as CLAUSTHALER is quite rightly the world's number one low-alcohol lager and in its home market of West Germany it accounts for a massive 60 per cent share of low-alcohol product sales, outselling its nearest rival by 2:1.

CLAUSTHALER was launched nationally in the UK in 1983 after successful test marketing in London, Northampton and Essex in the autumn of 1982. As I have said before, I am not a fan of low and no-alcohol lagers, yet taken in context, CLAUSTHALER is the best of a bad bunch.

Most of these 'lagers' claim to be brewed by traditional methods, and then treated to remove the alcohol content. What they won't admit, however, is that the majority of lagers produced in this way lose not only their taste but also their character.

CLAUSTHALER is different in that the exacting German 'Purity Laws' of 1516 require that beer is only made from barley-malt, hops, brewer's yeast and water, and the only nationally available low-alcohol lager in the UK containing only these ingredients is CLAUSTHALER SPECIAL LOW ALCOHOL LAGER.

This lager's low-alcohol content is produced by keeping the fermentable sugar content very low during brewing. This process creates a lager with only trace amounts of alcohol. The character and strength of taste is created by not only brewing it under the traditional 'Purity Laws' but also by lagering it for up to six weeks in conditions akin to any other premium German beer. Now doesn't that sound nice? If you must drink low-alcohol lager than we firmly recommend that CLAUSTHALER is your best buy.

You're welcome to it.

COLT .45 STRONG MALT LAGER UK

OG 1042–48° *Courage*
Cans 44cl

Originally brewed by the Colt Breweries of America, COLT .45 is brewed under licence in the UK by Courage.

As the title suggests, COLT is a very malty-flavoured lager with a strong nose and a somewhat syrupy, though not unpleasant, texture. Dark and full-bodied, COLT .45 can easily fulfil the taste of someone looking for something slightly different in the premium lager sector. It is an interesting brew that has a lot more going for it than many brands to be found packing the off-licence shelves. An acquired taste.

CORONA Mexico

Bottles

A friend of mine who likes to think he knows his lagers, recently tried to get hold of this one to sell in his bar. He swore by it, as in his words it was 'miles ahead of any other Mexican lager'.

Well, to cut a long story short, he couldn't get hold of it. He told me the reason was because British Corona, the lemonade people, held the trade mark 'Corona' in the UK. So there you have it. You can drink the pop but not the lager!

Bottled in clear glass (*Tsk! Tsk!*), it's a relatively dry, smooth-drinking brew that's a pleasure to consume at any time of the day if you can find it!

CRUZCAMPO   Spain

5.4% ABV
Bottle 25cl

There are so many brands backed by a major marketing exercise these days that it's almost impossible to open your eyes without seeing one mega lager or another. That's why it's special to bump into something new – such as CRUZCAMPO. I was thrilled when, in Garcia's, the excellent Spanish grocer's in London's Portobello Road, I happened to notice the light catch something behind a bag of rice. Quickly, my nose aroused, I ran over and removed the rice to reveal four crates of this little-known Spanish lager.

Just then the owner of the shop appeared and threw himself at our feet, begging us not to take the last of his personal hoard. It was his favourite, he explained, and difficult to get. He had been drinking them slowly to make them last and even offered us his eldest daughter, if only we would leave him his beer. No chance. We took the lot and sprinted home to put them in the fridge. This excellent lager is brewed throughout Spain. A typically dry, bitter, Spanish pilsner type that isn't readily available in the UK. Well worth sampling if you can get hold of it.

DAB West Germany

Bottles

From the wonderfully named Dortmunder Actien Brauerei comes DAB. Smooth and malty with a dry character, it is another quality German lager that goes down well at any time of the day.

The shame is that it is not more widely available to all you drinkers out there in lager land.

DANISH LIGHT Denmark

0.9% ABV *Federation Brewery*
Draught
Bottles 27.5cl & 33cl
Cans 44cl

A gaudy, dull bronze can, decorated with a child's drawing of another child holding two pints of lager.

Or is it lager? For the can not only has the gruesome little graphic but for some obscure reason it also proudly boasts that it contains 'carbon dioxide, antioxidant E224, additives E150 and E405' which, I suppose it can be argued, are definitely 'value for money' as these nasty little Es will remain in your body long after the 'lager' has gone down the toilet. It's enough to bring you to tears, knowing that this stuff is brewed and matured in Denmark, a country with a fine brewing tradition.

As if to convince you that it is a beer before your lips can touch it, it has a very deceiving strong malty bouquet. Malt is also evident in the taste though it is very dry with no depth, quality or character. It is watery, with an aggressive aftertaste.

Contrary to zoological opinion a 'yak' is not only an animal with shaggy fur, it is also a word to be yelled after you pour your first and hopefully only glass of DANISH LIGHT.

YAK!

DANSK LA   Denmark

0.9% ABV
Draught
Bottles
Cans 33cl

The International Carlsberg AS Group are responsible for this particular stuff. It is brewed at the Wiibroes Brewery, Elsinore, Denmark, and most of the alcohol is removed by a 'unique' process! Hmm, vacuum cleaner? Unpleasantly sweet, and strong smelling, it is another low/no alcohol lager to avoid.

First introduced to the UK in 1985, Dansk predict that they'll be selling 841,000 barrels of it by 1992 as the low/no-alcohol market explodes by 80 per cent per annum. The market should be worth some £170,000,000 by 1992. No small potatoes.

DIEKIRCH   Luxembourg

Longmans Distribution Ltd

Living in one of the most prosperous of all the communities in the EEC, the people of Luxembourg proudly spend a great deal of their money on drink – though usually not their own – and with a consumption rate of some 130 litres per head per annum, Luxembourg is comfortably within the top six drinking nations in the world (it also rates within the top five spirit-drinking nations and the top ten wine drinkers). The largest brewer of five in the Grand Duchy is Diekirch who produce this full-bodied, malty pilsner-style lager with a delicious hoppy bouquet. Well worth sampling, as are most lagers, DIEKIRCH is, however, nothing extra special.

DIXIE AMBER LIGHT   USA

Bottles

Even small breweries are aware of the cash-flow syndrome. Even small breweries need to make money, and why not? They give us a service we wouldn't like to live without and, naturally, they couldn't live without us. That's why the Dixie Brewery has risen to the task of meeting the current demand for lighter, less alcoholic beers and introduced DIXIE AMBER LIGHT to the market place. They see AMBER LIGHT as the answer to a challenge to produce a superior tasting and quality, super premium beer. They claim that the brew was formulated by the world-renowned consultant to the brewery industry, Dr Joseph Owades who, in their words, is 'the father of light beer'. They claim that their traditional Louisiana cypress vats and their selected roasted malt give this light beer a crisper, smoother flavour, as though the legendary Dr Owades and Dixie have taken light beer to a new dimension. Well, nothing so bold as that, I'm afraid, but still, not a bad lighter version of the original brew. I recommend you give the brew a go, but make sure you drink it before the plain old DIXIE BEER (q.v.) otherwise you'll never taste the stuff. Naturally, Dixie II isn't a patch on Dixie I. Stick with the original.

DIXIE BEER   USA

OG 1049°   *Continental Lager Distributors Ltd*
Bottles

Founded on October 31st 1907, DIXIE is a survivor of New Orleans' once flourishing brewery industry, and continues to ignore the fancy methods of the modern assembly line. It is still brewed with much care by the traditional slow-brew, hands-on method.

Huge cypress seasoning vats from Louisiana's swamps add a certain unique flavour to this delicate lager. Brewed with pride and pure water, yeast, barley-malts, hops and Louisiana rice, it does have a specific flavour that explodes in your mouth without leaving the slightest bitter aftertaste. Sounds all right, huh? But then again, I must ask myself, can the Americans brew anything that resembles a good lager? Yes, of course they can, and especially when it's a small brewery such as this, where pride, as well as profit, comes into it. As far as American lagers go this is one you should taste – then compare it with the rest. But beware, don't make your evaluation on the sheer romanticism of New Orleans alone, famous world over through films and music for its food and lifestyle. Simply sit back and enjoy the brew. Once you've cast those images from your head and simply supped the stuff, then I'm sure you'll agree with me – not bad, huh?

DONKLE   Luxembourg

OG 1070° – 7% ABC   *Euroimpex Ltd*
Draught
Bottles 25cl

It is extremely rare to have such a strong lager as this available on draught in the UK and although I must confess that I've never seen it available, I'd be willing to wager that it would be a popular pint if it were. My reporters tell me that as the strength suggests, it is a very dark lager that's relatively heavy and sweet, with a taste that needs to be acquired. It's brewed in the tiny Grand Duchy by Brasseries Réunies de Luxembourg Mousel, Clausen et Funck, whose history dates back to 1511. It was first introduced to the market in 1987 and, at the time of writing, no figures were available as to sales and it is still far too early to predict whether it will sink or rise. For those who appreciate a super-strength lager DONKLE's cleaner taste will be appealing, and one should remember that Luxembourg, like Germany, has a 'Purity Law' all of its own ... although subordinate brews are allowed.

DORTMUNDER KRONEN ALT   West Germany

OG 1047°
Draught
Bottles

German Lager Importers Ltd

The Dortmunder Kronen brewery is one of the biggest and most modern private breweries in Germany with an annual production of an impressive 1.2 million hectolitres per annum. Its history dates back some 450 years when, as the 'Krone am Markt', it was first mentioned in the town chronicles as early as 1430. After some 300 years of being a brewery and an inn combined, it became the property of the Wenker family in 1729. Under the legendary Heinrich Wenker it soon flourished into a major brewing force and has remained a family business ever since. A visit to the brewery is a must for all the family and not just the connoisseurs as it is an ideal day out where one can view a wonderful mural ceramic that recounts the history of the Kronen brewery from its origins through to the present day. The mural itself is something that the brewers are keenly proud of – that, as well as their lager. There is simply no substitute for 458 years of experience.

Whatever one's tastes or opinions, there is simply no way of avoiding the fact that German beer is unique and usually manufactured from natural ingredients. It is one of the healthiest drinks known to man. Kronen's lager is brewed from the finest hops from a region blessed by nature, Hallertau, specially selected barley and crystal clear brewing water from the subterranean depths of Westphalia's Turonian rock system, which was formed literally millions of years ago, and is regarded as being among the finest in the world. Sticklers for hygiene, not only do they cultivate their yeast in conditions totally protected against the influence of foreign bodies but the slightest sign of dust in their vast, totally automated bottling plant is liable to bring on a condition of cardiac arrest in certain members of the proud Wenker family.

The draught Kronen available here is exactly the same as that consumed in Dortmund. It is only exported in the keg as the brewers feel that this is the only way of guaranteeing the quality of their product. Quality is the all-important word in Germany, where, with a brewery to virtually every square inch of land, quality is the only way to compete. The results of this fierce competition are lagers one can drink with total confidence and DORTMUNDER KRONEN ALT is no different. Cultivated, wholesome and delicious, this full-bodied relatively dark lager was first introduced to the UK in 1981 and I, for one, have been enjoying it ever since. I recommend you do the same.

Prost!

DORTMUNDER KRONEN
CLASSIC
West Germany

OG 1051°
Bottles 25 & 33cl
Cans 33cl

German Lager Importers Ltd

Kegged at the brewery itself, CLASSIC can be drunk safely for it is exactly the same lager that the Germans themselves are enjoying. Another product of Dortmund's oldest brewery, CLASSIC is unpasteurized and should therefore appeal to a daring real-ale buff who, having been weaned on ale, might fancy a tipple of lager should the sun ever come out.

One of the strongest draught lagers available in the UK, it was introduced alongside its sister brews, KRONEN ALT and KRONEN PILS (*qq.v.*), in 1981 and at its very first International Lager Festival, held in Bristol in 1984, it walked off with first prize in the premium lager, 1044–56, category. Proudly full-bodied with a good, strong malty taste, it is a clean, crisp brew that is naturally carbonated and with only a mildly sweet texture. In short, it is a fine pint to be enjoyed by all.

DORTMUNDER KRONEN PILS
West Germany

OG 1048°
Cans 44cl
German Lager Importers Ltd

KRONEN PILS is just another superb brew from this formidable brewing concern. Although it is only available in cans, we genuinely recommend that the pils drinker should give it a whirl as it is most certainly a robust lager with a good clean flavour, still sweet enough to appeal to a Pils person.

I'd just like to take this opportunity to have a word with pils drinkers. All too often I see them drink whatever is put in front of them in the on-trade, yet in the off-trade, their brand loyalty is famous. Let me urge them now not to be so complacent and actually to shop around!

DORTMUNDER RITTER
West Germany

Bottles
Scottish German Beer Imports Ltd

The third largest brewery in the famous city of Dortmund, owned partly by the Dortmunder Union Brauerei, produces DORTMUNDER RITTER, a lively, dry, full-bodied lager that is exceptionally thirst-quenching and refreshing. Its robust qualities are ideal for a person who has genuinely worked up a physical thirst throughout a hard, back-breaking day. Although often difficult to find amongst the variety of Dortmunders now available in the UK, this almost fruity little beverage should definitely be sought out. There is simply no time of day that a lager of this quality cannot be enjoyed!

DORTMUNDER UNION EXPORT
West Germany

OG 1052°
Bottles 33cl
GB Vintagers

Possibly the finest of the three DORTMUNDER UNION lagers available in the UK at the moment. Despite its strength, its light honey colour and delicious malty taste make it an extremely refreshing drink. Capitalizing on their own spring of soft, pure water, from the depths of Westphalia, the Kronen brewery painstakingly combines this with its specially selected barley, yeast and hops to produce an authentic and classic German lager that is sought after throughout the globe. Full-bodied with a unique taste, this is just the sort of lager one should make an effort to seek out.

DORTMUNDER UNION SIEGEL PILS
West Germany

OG 1044°
Draught
Bottles 25cl
GB Vintagers

Dortmund is Germany's biggest brewing city and

DORTMUNDER is produced from the city's oldest brewery, Kronen, which dates back to 1430 and has been in the same family's hands since 1729. However, it was only when the brewery moved to its present site in 1873 that it began to brew the now famous DORTMUNDER to the strict German 'Purity Laws' of 1516.

Tradition, skill and brewing experience have all played their part in producing beers that are full flavoured and immensely refreshing. Other factors that have helped in the manufacture of such an excellent line of lagers are the choicest hops, malt and the brewer's own pure cultured brewing yeast. Still, one can harp on about this legendary 'Purity Law' until one is blue in the face, yet we all know that in this day and age it is not only the wooden keg that has disappeared but also the ancient brewing methods. However, the standard of modern technology employed at certain breweries is such that a description of it would leave us none the wiser, and this is the case with the Kronen brewery and their famous DORTMUNDER lagers, where storage under extremely low temperatures and a maturation period of up to three months create one of the finest beers in Germany. And that's saying something!

We are lucky to have such a brew available in this country so I not only recommend it, not only suggest you hunt it out, but also demand that you do it justice and buy it by the pack. You certainly won't regret it.

DORTMUNDER UNION SPECIAL

West Germany

OG 1052°
Draught
Bottles 33cl

GB Vintagers

Often spotted at airports, DORTMUNDER UNION is

lightly carbonated with a strong, sharp taste that is distinctly German. Pale and strong with a full-bodied bite, it goes down exceptionally easily with no unpleasant aftertaste. Exported throughout the globe it is a lager very much in demand by discerning drinkers and in draught form it comes unpasteurized, which might even tempt one or two hard-core real-ale buffs to give it a crack. DORTMUNDER UNION comes highly recommended as a session lager for the adventurous!

DOS EQUIS – AMBER   Mexico

OG 1049°   *Maison Caurette Ltd*
Bottles 35.5cl

Unusually strongly flavoured with both malt and hops, DOS EQUIS – AMBER is, as the title suggests, a marvellous amber colour with a very rich bouquet. As one might expect from such a dark lager, it has a harsh bitter taste which might seem unpleasant to some at first – although this is certainly not the case once the taste is acquired. Its UK suppliers, Maison Caurette, told us that it is brewed like an old Vienna-style beer, which is not surprising when one discovers that the brewery was founded by a German.

One should also remember that Mexico is one of the top half-dozen brewing nations by volume on the globe and has an extensive brewing history that goes back some 450 years. The Mexicans take their lager very seriously and there are many outrageous stories of mass drunkenness that litter their history, from the Aztecs, through the Spanish conquests to the present, which might stand at odds with what one would expect from such an orthodox Catholic country. Therefore we suggest you acquaint yourselves with AMBER next time you slip into a Tex-Mex restaurant because not only does it go down extremely well on its own, but it is a perfect accompaniment to Mexico's spicy food. A distinctive brew that is well worth sampling.

DOS EQUIS XX   Mexico

OG 1048° – 4.8% ABV   *Maison Caurette Ltd*
Bottles 35.5cl

First brewed in 1899 to celebrate the coming of the new century XX (i.e. 20th), this is the number one imported lager brand from Mexico, selling in excess of 50,000 cases per annum. It was first made available in the UK on November 8th 1982 and now enjoys national distribution through Oddbins, Augustus Barnett and Peter Dominic, to name but a few.

The Moctezuma brewing company was established in 1894 by the emigrant German brewmaster Wilhelm Hasse on the slopes of the formidable Mount Orizaba, the highest peak in Mexico. From here the naturally pure water is supplied for XX as well as the company's other brews, among which are the famous SOL, SUPERIOR, NOCHE BUENA and TRES EQUIS XXX. The water which cascades down the mountain is naturally filtered through 7,000 feet of porous bedrock and therefore makes the ideal ingredient for any great lager and is no doubt the envy of many breweries throughout the world.

In America, where there are over 400 imported brands of beer available, XX is one of the seven top-selling brands. It is brewed from specially grown hops imported from the Yakima Valley in Washington State, along with selected barley-malt from its own malting plant, as well as that famous mountain water. Yet perhaps Hasse's most important legacy was the German

'Krausening' process, the technique of adding unfermented malt, or wort, to the conditioning tank to produce natural carbonation. By so doing, XX is produced as a fine dark, full-bodied malty lager that is both refreshing and strong. Ideal in Mexican restaurants, it can also be enjoyed at home with the television, book or friends. We certainly recommend that you dabble in the wide variety of Mexican lagers now available in the UK, even though you will probably end up on XX. And why not? It's a fine lager that is there to be enjoyed. Go forth and do so.

DOUBLE HAPPINESS China

Double happiness is two pints of lager ... in each hand! Seriously though, this is one we haven't managed to taste. Your reports are most welcome!

DRIKOENIGSBIER Switzerland

OG 1064°   *Shepherd Neame*
Bottles 33cl

Specifically a festival lager, Hurlimann's DRIKOENIGSBIER is actually available all year round in both pale and dark styles and is one of Switzerland's strongest beers, which must contain no more than 5.5 per cent alcohol by volume. You should feel lucky to find it and you should most definitely plug one in and see how you get on. After all, Switzerland, famous for it's cuckoo clocks and bank accounts, can hardly boast of being one of the world's great brewing nations, and therefore when something rare like this turns up you'd be a fool to miss out.

DUVEL LAGER PILS   Belgium

OG 1046°   *GB Vintagers/City Vintagers Ltd*
Bottles 25cl

Most of us look to the Germans as the gods of lager, but let me tell you that the Belgians are up there with them. One only has to wander into a Belgian café to see for oneself the vast range of beers they have to offer. Belgium's brewing talents are a match for anybody on the planet and we should be grateful that they see fit now to export one or two of their beers to the UK, famed thoughout the world as being the Philistines of lager-consuming nations.

One such beverage now available here is the blonde DUVEL lager which, completely natural, is brewed from Czechoslovakian hops and Danish barley-malts. In this sense its most important attribute is its authenticity, and the result is a lager of exceptional quality with a delicious aromatic character. Thankfully there is absolutely no difference between the DUVEL we receive here and that enjoyed on the Continent.

In a country where for centuries brewing has been a practised art, DUVEL has been brewed with great pride by one of the last family-run breweries in Europe, the Brouwerij Moortgat of Breendonk and remains as it has been for generations: smooth, light and very very refreshing. Get them in!

EDELBRAU   UK

OG 1052°   *J. W. Lees & Co.*
Draught
Bottles 10fl. oz

First introduced in 1969 for a beer keller (remember

them?) in Manchester called the William Tell, EDEL-BRAU long suffered the ignominy of being a lager in a land of ale drinkers. But with the sudden boom in lager's popularity, J. W. Lees saw fit to relaunch it in a new, more exciting package in 1977 to celebrate the silver jubilee of H.M. Queen Elizabeth II (remember that?). However, despite this, EDELBRAU still remains basically a regional drink and is only to be found in Lees' tied estate and their free trade customers through-out Manchester and the north-west as well as North Wales. Lees also export it to their one pub on the Continent, the White Grouse at Flaine in the French Alps.

Bearing in mind the McEwan's 'is it alcohol or isn't it?' scandal in 1988 (*see* MCEWAN'S), EDELBRAU's pleasant green bottle also carries no information as to its alcohol content, preferring only to describe itself as an 'extra strong lager'. It certainly has all the visible hallmarks of an extremely potent brew. Exceptionally cloudy and very yellow, it has an overpowering, slightly sweet malty bouquet. It is quite a spritzy little lager, although after the initial taste explosion it leaves an unpleasantly bitter aftertaste. Mighty in alcohol by volume stakes, EDELBRAU is certainly powerful, and it definitely sits in the acquired taste category.

Personally I found this to be a most disagreeable drink. It's odd that a British company, and a regional one at that, should bother to manufacture such an unpalatable lager when there are so many cheery imported lagers to chose from. Still, what do we know? After all, it was judged the best British strong lager at the 1980 Brewex Exhibition, and won the gold medal and a Diploma of Excellence! As I am entitled to my opinion, I must suggest that this is a bad reflection on 'British' strong lagers.

Sorry, Mr Lees.

EDELBRAU DIAT PILS   UK

OG 1048°/6.5% ABV   *J. W. Lees & Co.*
Bottles 10fl. oz, returnable
Cans 16oz

Currently selling some 2,000 barrels per annum, EDEL-
BRAU DIAT PILS was introduced in 1979 to complete Lees' portfolio of lagers available and so pleased
were they by the result that it was relaunched on a
national scale in 1988. Surprisingly there is actually a
distinct difference between the same drink in its different packages. The bottled variety was very dark and
extremely cloudy, almost like one of the ales the
brewers are famous for. Strong in both flavour and
alcohol, it goes down surprisingly easily while at the
same time its bitter-sweet flavour is distinctive enough
to savour, leaving you with a not altogether too unpleasant burnt aftertaste. It actually reminded me of
cold tea and had a certain tannic quality to it. Unusual
in all respects, it should be sampled at least once.

EDELBRAU PILS in the can is seemingly more
carbonated than the bottled drink and it didn't remind
me of tea – cold, hot, Indian, Chinese, or otherwise – in
the slightest. With a full, malty bouquet and flavour,
this one poured from the can with not a cloud to be
seen anywhere and instead settled into an admirably
clear lager with a golden colour. Not unpleasant in the
slightest, it went down just as easily as the bottled
version, if not more so, with a delightful strong flavour.
We actually found it to be most enjoyable and, indeed,
it could be drunk quite easily in twos. Despite its
strength, it's so smooth it tastes, disarmingly, as if it is
a lot lower in alcohol than it actually is, yet the quality
is certainly that of a fine lager in the premium range.
When it is allowed to sit for a minute or two (i.e. when
not drunk instantly on removal from the fridge), the
whole drink appears to change and then its firm, full

body actually tastes a lot stronger and leaves a definite aftertaste – the sort that demands another EDEL-BRAU DIAT PILS. Aye, it's a fine pint that I thoroughly enjoyed, and I for one shall certainly be buying some more. I recommended that you do the same.

EICHBAUM EXPORT ALTGOLD
West Germany

5.1% ABV
Bottles
Eichbaum UK

A brew from the Eichbaum Brewery at Manneheim in West Germany. This one is more golden in colour than the EICHBAUM UREICH PILS (*q.v.*), and a little fuller bodied. With an ABV content of 5.1 per cent, it should find many supporters over here. A great lager that comes recommended.

EICHBAUM LITE OAK
West Germany

2% ABV
Bottles
Eichbaum UK

LITE OAK's contents of 2 per cent ABV is interesting as it makes it slightly stronger than low-alcohol lager (they can have an ABV of up to 1.2 per cent), but slightly weaker than the average session lager.

Therefore, I can't really see which market it is competing in. Slightly fuller in taste than your low-alcohols, but certainly not in my view a tasty drink. I shall be interested to see how this one sells.

EICHBAUM UREICH PILS   West Germany

5.1% ABV   *Eichbaum UK*
Bottles

This one immediately interested me as its importers, Eichbaum UK, are based in Seaton, a small town in Devon. Seaton is only a couple of miles away from a small village where, as a youngster, I spent many enjoyable summers. The name of the village...? BEER!

EICHBAUM UREICH PILS is brewed by the Eichbaum Brewery at Manneheim, West Germany, and is a palatable brew. Dry and lightly hopped, it should be a hit with the many British pils drinkers in the UK. It is becoming more widely available all the time, and it's well worth keeping your eye open for.

EINHORN   UK

OG 1035.5°   *Frederic Robinson & Co.*
Draught
Bottles

EINHORN was first introduced in the UK in 1969 and has no doubt proved popular in the provinces as it is still available alongside the major brands despite their multi-million-pound promotions. Ostensibly a regional lager which you'll have great difficulty finding outside of the Stockport/Manchester area. So, for all the plucky lager veterans steadily drinking your way through the book, it's on yer bike time again!

And don't forget to let us know your experiences on the road in the great lager quest.

EKU PILS   West Germany

Bottles 33cl   *West Country Products*

As you'd expect from the brewers of the world's most potent lager EKU 28 (*q.v.*) their PILS is full-bodied with a powerful malty bouquet. Obviously not as famous as 28, it is certainly no slouch and should quite possibly be purchased at the same time so that you can draw the comparisons of the brewery's two gifts to humankind for yourself. Not what I consider to be one of the greatest lagers of the world, but it is not unpleasant and served well chilled can make an extremely refreshing beverage to be enjoyed at any time of the day.

EKU 28   West Germany

OG 1129° – 12% ABV   *West Country Products*
Bottles 33cl

The strongest lager in the world is produced by the Erste Kulmbacher Actionbrauerei (*Action Brewery* – now that's what I call a good name!) of Kulmbach, Bavaria, and is as famous as it is strong. There is no doubt that EKU 28 is an unrivalled and unforgettable drinking experience, even more so if one isn't careful. It should be lightly sipped and savoured to appreciate to the full its smooth balanced weight and unique flavour. It is brewed with meticulous care and attention, especially during the fermentation process. The brewery claim to give EKU 28 nine months to mature, with a short period of freezing so that water can be extracted, therefore increasing the density and raising the alcohol content.

Although I am not a fan of super-strength lager, I find that EKU is actually quite enjoyable despite its heavy texture and unusual aftertaste. For such a strong lager it is unusually pale and somewhat amber with a rich malty bouquet. The super-strength drinker should most definitely sample it; as for the standard and premium drinkers then a bottle or two should also be supped if for nothing other than the novelty value. It is not an everyday drink by any stretch, but for those big occasions this is one BIG drink in a little bottle. Handle with care.

EVERTON PREMIUM LAGER   UK

OG 1038°   *Team Advance*
Cans

Launched originally in time for Christmas 1987 alongside similar brews for Liverpool and Manchester United football clubs, these beers took a hammering from the press and horrified MPs at a time when all believed that alcohol alone was responsible for a sudden increase in soccer hooliganism.

The company responsible for their birth, Team Advance of Hackney, London, which was established specifically to market the lines, forecast sales worth around £6.5 million a year, with the clubs expecting royalties of an excess of £100,000. Although *canned* by just about all concerned, Everton Chairman Phillip Carter, who was recently dismissed as President of the Football League for being too concerned 'in the promotion of his own club', made the point that there is 'no difference between somebody going to the off-licence or supermarket and buying any of the many brands on offer and people choosing to buy one associated with a football club'.

Despite their bold predictions and the acres of newsprint these lagers attracted, the actual launch was a total disaster and by May 1988 wholesale prices had to be slashed by 25 per cent in an attempt to boost flagging sales. They were originally priced to retail at between 55p and 65p a can with 'free offers' on the ring pulls –

for instance, a United fan could get the cheapest ticket available at Old Trafford for the return of a mere 640 such ring pulls! – and Team Advance director David Gillion wouldn't be drawn on how the wholesale price cut would affect shelf prices. However, he did eventually admit that 'Pricing is very important – and we didn't get it right. By the time we had brewed the lager and added a margin for the club, ourselves and the whole-saler, the price just wasn't competitive. But we've worked out a better deal with Devenish (the Brewer) and now we're talking about a trade price of £6.49 for a case of 24 33cl cans. When we launched it was £8.69.'

Team Advance, however, might already be too late. Distribution was handled by the Midlands cash-and-carry giant M6, as well as Parfett's in Stockport, although now both have declared that they will not handle the lines in future. Stephen Parfett, a director, said, 'Not to put too fine a point on it, the idea has been an unmitigated disaster from our point of view.' Team Advance have thus been forced to deliver direct to the retailers themselves and are also negotiating with two London clubs for a licensing deal. The lager for these two clubs, should it materialize, would be brewed overseas, although not, I feel, by a master brewer, but probably by someone cheap.

EVERTON PREMIUM LAGER, of standard strength, is exactly what one would imagine. Vaguely malty, pale and highly carbonated, it couldn't be distinguished from hundreds of others if the taster were blindfolded. If you don't believe me then find out for yourself.

EXECUTIVE LAGER UK

3.9% ABV
Draught
Federation Brewery

Yet another lager from the Federation Brewery's

ever-expanding portfolio. This one was introduced to the market in 1988, though quite why I do not know. It is my opinion that the FED, founded after the First World War with extremely sound principles, should stick to the brewing of their fine ales and bitters, as lager quite simply is not their forte.

To put it bluntly EXECUTIVE LAGER is bland, bubbly and best left in the tap. If it is intended as an out-and-out session lager, I can understand why it's thin, but what I can't understand is why it has no character, and indeed nothing really going for it at all except the price. I should imagine in a Tyneside working-men's club it would retail at under a quid. Recommendation? Nah!

FAUST DIAT PILS   UK

OG 1033–37° – 4.5% ABV   *Eldridge, Pope*
Bottles 27.5cl, returnable
Cans 16oz

Eldridge, Pope and Company Limited are featured in the Guinness Book of Records as the brewers of the strongest beer in Britain, Thomas Hardy's Ale. They began life in 1833 when Charles Eldridge and his wife Sarah took over the Antelope Hotel in Dorchester where they established the unlikely-sounding Green Dragon Brewery. In 1870 Edwin Pope bought a share of the company and four years later Edwin and his brother Alfred acquired complete control. The business expanded rapidly and in 1880 they built the present brewery. Over a hundred years later the business is still in family hands, being run by Alfred's grandson and three great-grandsons. Although primarily an ale-brewing firm, when the brewery was expanded they installed a modern plant for lager brewing and packaging alongside the traditional ale brewhouse. From the brewery's humble beginnings with one man, his dream and a small south coast hotel, Eldridge, Pope now employ close to 1000 people who, they insist, proudly believe in their products.

First brewed in Dorchester in 1980, FAUST is manufactured, under licence from the Faust family brewery in Miltenberg, Bavaria, to an all-malt recipe which they claim conforms to the famous German 'Purity Laws'. This recipe includes whole-cone Continental hops and the yeast is flown over specially from Bavaria. In 1985 the famous Welsh brewers S. A. Brain and Company also began production of the Faust range. In April 1988 FAUST DIAT PILS was given a 'more elegantly shaped' brown bottle as well as a new yellow label bearing Faust's 'iron-fist' coat of arms, *faust* being the German word for fist.

There is a curious little yarn behind the coat of arms that goes something like this. During the Bavarian War of Succession, one Herr Gotz von Berlichingen (1480–1562), an infamous robber baron, accidentally lost his hand and he quickly had an articulated iron one made to replace it. Well, von Berlichingen led the peasants' revolt in 1525 which was joined by the people of Miltenberg, home of the Faust brewery. For this the brewery rewarded him by bestowing the supreme accolade upon him – they put his articulated iron hand on their coat of arms which, no doubt, his ancestors are proud of to this very day. However, robbing, pillaging and plundering weren't the only things Gotz died famous for as he is also said to be the originator of a well-known phrase in the international vocabulary. When he was hauled up to appear before the Sheriff of Mainz on a bum rap he suggested that the Sheriff could kiss a posterior part of his anatomy! Interesting, huh? Well, you can't say I haven't told you something you didn't know. But enough of this nonsense! On with the lager!

The FAUST range of EXPORT, PILSNER (*qq.v.*)

and DIAT PILS is distributed via Eldridge, Pope's own pubs and free trade, as well as the pubs of Palmers of Bridport along the south coast. National distribution is offered through the Waitrose and Safeway supermarket chains. Sales figures, however, proved unobtainable and one wonders how the new-look label was helping sales, in as much as many pils labels are yellow and therefore make it indistinct. The only real difference is on the green foil collar around the top of the bottle which displays two of FAUST DIAT PILS's awards. Its bottle and can won a gold medal at the Brewing Industry International Awards at Burton on Trent in 1985 and in the same year its can and bottle picked up a first prize at the International Lager Festival held at Bristol, which I proudly attended as well as the 1984 festival. However, DIAT PILS would not have picked up my vote had I been invited to judge, an oversight I hope will be rectified shortly. Although more fully fermented to give it more strength and less carbohydrate than standard lagers, DIAT PILS is actually quite weak in comparison with some of the other splendid pils on the market. With a light bouquet, its golden-coloured body is actually quite thin and tastes like it. Still, pils drinkers should always be on the lookout for it, although I feel that once they have sampled, the majority of drinkers will return to their old brand.

FAUST EXPORT LAGER

UK

OG 1040–44/4.8% ABV
Draught

Eldridge, Pope

Brewed with the same ingredients as their FAUST DIAT PILS (*q.v.*), EXPORT LAGER is also an award winner, picking up third prize at the 1983 Brewex

Festival in Birmingham, a silver at the Brewing Industry International Awards in 1985 and another silver at the same awards in 1987 at Burton on Trent. The genuine FAUST from Miltenberg is a gold medal winner.

EXPORT was introduced at the same time as the DIAT PILS and is obviously distributed in the same manner. Stronger than the Pils, EXPORT is an altogether more qualified lager and although carbonated far more than I personally like, its smooth, crisp flavour makes it a fine session lager. Certainly I found it not disagreeable with no unpleasant aftertaste, but I was left to wonder whether what I was drinking was really that 'traditional full Bavarian flavour' the promotional material would have us believe. Personally I think not and hopefully it won't be too long before I can sample the genuine article on its own ground. Whether or not you yourself think it is genuinely Bavarian is something that you'll have to discover by treating the tongue to a pint or two. As I say, there is nothing wrong with that, because it's not an unpleasant lager, but neither is it exciting or imaginative. As an occasional lager it will do.

FAUST PILSNER LAGER   UK

OG 1033–1037°   *S. A. Brain & Co.*
Draught
Bottles (half-pint)
Cans (16oz)

Faust, you'll remember, was that bloke who sold his soul to the devil for personal profit, the result of which was a harrowing and boring metaphysical death for the man in the final pages of the book. Originally brewed in Miltenberg, Bavaria, by the Faust Family

Brewery it was introduced to Britain in July 1985 when S. A. Brain & Co., a deservedly famous, and even legendary, Welsh brewer of fine, strong ales, began to brew the stuff under licence from the Germans (other beers from the Faust range are brewed by Eldridge, Pope & Co.). As one would imagine from a brewery with its headquarters in Cardiff, FAUST PILSNER LAGER is available through Wales as well as spilling over into Avon and the Midlands. However, neither Brains or Eldridge, Pope seemed happy with this arrangement and, in the great tradition of humankind they dreamt of expansion. To this end the summer of 1988 saw a small advertising campaign break out along the cheery, happy-go-lucky length of England's south coast where, on a hot day – which for England is a rare occurrence – the demand for lager can reach phenomenal proportions. The campaign itself included radio and press ads as well as posters, and was based around the redesigned half-pint bottle described by the brewers as 'elegantly shaped' which, in lay terms, means a pale-ale bottle full of lager. Interestingly, this new design also does away with the usual coloured tin foil wrapped around the top which enables the punter to differentiate between the pils and the porter. Therefore, assuming that the average first-timer buyer is going to run an eye along the available stock before making a purchase, the new bottle could turn out to be a marketing nightmare. For although we're told you can't judge a book by its cover we know that people can and, more importantly, *do*! True, sat up there on the shelf surrounded by dozens of other pilsner lager bottles, FAUST holds its own with its good Germanic-sounding name emblazoned on the label in a nice bit of olde Germanic typesetting but, without the foil on the lid it's going to look very plain, even boring, and the look and image of lager is one of *the* key factors for sales in a market-place swamped with enough beer to flood the globe. The first thing you have to do is to get people to drink *your* lager as opposed to the opposition's, then, if it's any good they'll stay with it.

And Brains have the know-how to brew a mighty pint. For FAUST they use whole-cone Continental hops as well as Continental malted-barley and, to give it a 'genuinely' Bavarian flavour, they import the yeast from Germany. It sounds like a winner. To sum it all up, it's not bad, and praise is indeed due to the brewers for producing a fine, well-balanced lager, using natural ingredients. Not too highly carbonated, it makes for a decent pint that is definitely preferable to many other draught lagers. Not available everywhere by any means, but if you do see it on your travels I certainly recommend that you have a pint, or two, or three ...

FISCHER   France

OG 1045–51°
Bottle

Brewed in the Alsace region of France, the home of many fine beers, one could argue for a long time over the nationality of this lager. Is it German? Is it French? Some would have it that 'French' and 'lager' is a double negative. Isn't it true that the French drink nothing but wine? Not quite ... They certainly know a thing or two about lager as well – give this one a try and you'll soon find out. Though its German origins are clear, it has a certain '*Je ne sais quoi*' about it.

A full-tasting, smooth brew that is certainly worth checking out. Packaged in a swing-top bottle, à la GROLSCH, I've enjoyed FISCHER myself on a number of occasions and, God willing, will continue to do so.

A votre santé!

FOSTER'S   UK

OG 1034–38° – Draught   *Watney Mann Truman/*
OG 1044–50° – Cans   *Courage*

Just under 100 years after a free settler, John Boston,
made the first successful attempts to brew and therefore
gave Australia its first home-produced beer in 1794,
the Foster brothers from New York started the
country's second lager brewery, the first having been
founded by two Germans in Melbourne during 1885.
The plan of W. M. and R. R. Foster was to brew and
sell a chilled lager beer which would be totally different

from the traditional English-style ales then being sold. Though it faced stiff competition from imported German beers, the first pint, pulled in February 1889, was heralded with triumph and the beer became an instant success. However, just nine months later, they sold their business to a local syndicate which, 18 years later, was swallowed up when the remaining six local breweries in Victoria amalgamated to form Carlton and United Breweries Ltd (CUB), itself owned by Elders IXL – Australia's largest brewers and now the sixth largest in the entire world, and who are expressing interest in taking over Anheuser-Busch! In the second half of 1987 Elders announced an 83 per cent rise in their net income to reach £111 million (though some sources say it is upwards of £190 million), more than twice as much as their closest rival, the Bond Corporation, brewers of CASTLEMAINE and SWAN (qq.v.), whose net profit was £44.5 million.

Having effectively carved up the Australian domestic beer market between them, both companies have been forced increasingly to turn their attention overseas during the 1980s, not least towards Britain where lager has pursued a remorseless pattern of growth over the past 20 years, from 4 per cent in 1968 to 45 per cent of all beer sold in the UK today, and rising! Thus, although FOSTER'S had actually been available in the UK since the 60s when Watneys imported a modest amount of the authentic stuff annually, it really arrived in 1981 when Watney Mann and Truman negotiated a licence to brew the draught and, later, canned lager. Then, in 1985, Elders tried to storm the UK brewing scene by buying Allied Lyons. However, the bid was aborted by the worldwide equity market collapse. But that didn't stop them from snapping up Courage from the Hanson Trust for a mere £1.4 billion just six months later. This, coupled with Grand Metropolitan who launched the brand here in 1981, gives FOSTER'S a massive 11,000 outlets for the amber nectar, which is more than any of its rivals, though it is still only the fifth best-selling lager on the market. Not bad, eh? Not bad, but not good enough for Elder's Chairman John Elliot who harbours dreams to 'Fosterize' the globe! Plans are already drawn up for its European invasion, and its first significant exports there are scheduled for early 1989. I say 'export' because that's exactly what they intend to do, using their facilities at Courage as the source to cater for the market. European brewing itself is still a long way away, although, no doubt, it is next on the list as they already have operations in Australia, Canada and the UK, each serving its own global region. The exception to this is the United States which is still supplied via Australia as American beer-drinkers demand 'authenticity' from their foreign brews. This in itself is quite unusual, considering the reputation of American lager beers throughout the globe, which, to put it kindly, is not good. Personally I wish that we had more of the authentic stuff ourselves which, at the moment, is only available in the bumper 750ml cans, and they can prove difficult to find. Things might have been a lot different if the same sort of advertising and promotion which they have now had been put behind the imported lager when Watney was the sole outlet some 20-odd years ago. That advertising bill now runs to a cool £12 million per annum and is handled by a team of three at top London advertising agency Boase Massimi Pollitt, whose groundbreaking campaign, featuring Aussie superstar Paul Hogan, has proved a great success, and for the consumer is one of the more memorable campaigns to run on the box for the past few years. This is all very satisfactory, as not only are the creative standards extremely high but the importance of advertising cannot be stressed enough in a market where journalist and lager afficianado, Matthew Gwyther, stated that 'people don't choose the product, they just drink the advertising'. If this is true, then FOSTER'S has it made because the campaign, with the slogan 'Foster's – the amber nectar', originally devised by advertising agency, Hedger Mitchell Stark, is one of the most popular on television, being mentioned by 47 per cent of consumers in a spontaneous ad awareness study. A lot of that success is down to Hogan, as people believe they could actually bump into him in the local pub, despite the fact that he is a multimillionaire film star. In that way Hogan is one of the strongest-ever brand personalities of all time. Yet Aussie lager was always bound to be a major success in the UK. After all, they have the perfect credentials to qualify for admiration with the standard British drinker. They have a tough, macho image, and because of their legendary drinking we believe they know their lagers, and to many British drinkers they are more like us than any other nationality. Fosters and Hogan have become synonomous with Australia, and the adverts reinforce our belief that the 'amber nectar' is a wacky, innovative and in-touch lager when, in truth, fresh from Mortlake, it is considerably weaker in alcohol than the Aussie original. The draught version, which they are brave enough to label a session lager (which it is, but it isn't good for the image), isn't a bad tipple by British-brewed standards.

The imported canned version, however, is different, and as a premium lager it competes strongly with anything else on the market. It has a malty, full body with a mild sweetish taste and is not over gassy. Actually, I quite enjoy the imported Foster's and it is usually the brew I'll select to take to a party or something. It's strong and refreshing with a clean, crisp bite. It's guaranteed that if you take half a dozen of these giants to a party and dump them in the fridge they'll all be gone when you go back for your second – surely the true sign of a great lager!

Thus, we are happy to announce that Foster's does come recommended and though not as highly as some of its German rivals, it and its whole operation have to be admired – not only for its advertising but for what it promotes. It is through Foster's that we've been able to have a look at some of their more specialized sports, like Aussie Rules Football, whose teams they even bring to this country to play exhibition games. As a fan of baseball, I know just how hard it is to follow a sport that you can never see or play, and therefore I think this is a great thing as there are undoubtedly many thousands of expatriot Diggers and followers of Aussie Rules in this country. Not only are Fosters also continually giving away money, beeny hats, towels, umbrellas etc. with their ring pulls but, more recently, they are even stepping in to bail out truly British events with their sponsorship, the most recent of which is their bid to promote the English Football Association Cup, offering to pay £20 million just to have their name put in brackets after the official titles: FA Cup (Foster's). The deal would last four-and-a-half years, and although a third of the world's population watch the event it is not that big an advertising spot, some of those countries don't yet sell Foster's lager and there is no opportunity to put forward an image to accompany the name. Not only that but the adverts on the teams' shirts will be seen throughout the entire game whereas the Foster's logo would probably only be seen here and there when the score is flashed up.

So, all in all, Foster's lager is a massive worldwide operation; the biggest in Australia, third biggest here, available in 80 different countries, the world's number seven exported brand, one of the top ten imported beers in the USA, etc. Whether or not people really do just 'drink the advertising', there is no doubt that an operation cannot grow to this size if there isn't something in the product. But what is also true of an operation this size is that quality must suffer somewhere down the line, even if only partially, and allowing the British to brew their own must be viewed as a terrible mistake for they must be about last in the league table when it comes to brewing palatable lager. Ales? Yes, and plenty of them. Stout? Naturally, a lovely pint. But lager? Who are we kidding? Think about it. Although brewers Down Under recommend their beers are served at 5.6°C (42°F) they are often served at brutally low temperatures, even as low as 2.2°C (36°F) – which I think is too low to actually appreciate the taste of the stuff. If they were to be served as we serve them, albeit more conducive to the taste buds, your actual Aussie would probably bathe in the stuff. OK, so I've established that there is a world of difference between us and them, despite the fact that the advertising is selling us *them*.

FRISK   UK

OG 1030–34°   *Vaux Breweries*
Draught

FRISK was launched by Vaux Breweries throughout their outlets in the north-east in 1979. Vaux have brewed some good beers in their time, though personally I doubt whether this is one of them. When one looks at the original gravity (1030–34°), one automatically thinks that it was introduced to meet the demand for a 'throwing' lager. I haven't sampled this one myself so your reports would be welcome.

FRYDENLUND NORWEGIAN
PILSNER BEER   Norway

OG 1042°
Bottles 35cl

I've never been to Norway and I doubt I ever will. 'Why?' I hear you asking. 'The Northern Lights are beautiful,' you say. Well, it's a long story, so why not open a bottle of FRYDENLUND and make yourself comfortable.

When I was younger, a *lot* younger, I was thinking of going. I'd heard that the Norse women were beautiful, very beautiful, and I'd heard they were all blonde and that blondes have more fun.

Needless to say I started saving, *desperately*! I had a milk-round and two paper-rounds to do before school. During school I had a busy 'Dinner Money Extortion Racket' to run, as well acting as the Mars Bar 'fence'. After school I had another two paper-rounds to do as well as managing all the other kids in a popular 'Car Wash' company. Then, before bed, there would always be an opportunity to beg/steal any loose change my dad had on him as he tried to relax with the evening paper. Things were going all right. On a good week I could turn over about £3. 7s. 6d which seemed good to me then (it still does!), but it just didn't seem to be making a dent in the vast sum required to book a flight to Oslo. Anyway, to cut a long story short I didn't make it to Norway but stayed at home and discovered something altogether more satisfying. *Pubs.* Yes, the subtle dark ambience of pub life, a warm friendly world where one can pull up a pint of one's favourite and talk to people and learn the history of the world and the culture of other countries ... like Norway. And I was devastated ...

Some areas of Norway are completely dry, in other areas you're forbidden to buy lager anywhere apart from the special state shops of which there are 100 for the *entire country*! My dream shattered, died and slipped away. No wonder they show naked women on your everyday, household, television chocolate commercial. No wonder they are continuously romping playfully on their rugs in front of their huge open fires in their snowbound log-cabins. No wonder they are watching the Northern bloody Lights every single night of the week! No wonder ... there is nothing else to do! 'Why don't they just go to the pub?' I hear you asking fearfully. 'Like any other normal, self-respecting person?' Well, the answer to that one is: *Find one!* See, it's not that the Norwegians don't like their beer, indeed, they love it! And home-brewing has been at the heart of Norwegian life for over 600 years. But as for pubs, forget it! Having shocked you with that (open another bottle now!), the Norwegians, as I have already said, take great pride in their brewing and they brew a different strength for every occasion – births, christenings, Christmas, marriages, deaths, and even for the different seasons of the year. During the 70s over 25 million pints were brewed at home each year, and all with *natural* ingredients. In fact, much the same as

Germany, Norway had strict pure-beer laws until the
EEC struck and forced them to open their gates and
allow in all the vulgar, cheap, chemical-packed beers
the likes of Britain could produce.

Norway's 16 breweries still follow a non-competitive
agreement ratified over 50 years ago, in which sales
outside the breweries' immediate territories are
arranged by quotas. For this reason FRYDENLUND's
availability in this county is extremely limited. One of
only three breweries in Norway's capital, Oslo, it was
founded in 1859 and prides itself on its totally pure
ingredients, all of which are from Norway, and on its
quality. Acknowledging the fact that it most certainly
isn't the world's largest brewery, it can afford to let
this delightful pilsner beer brew for three long months
as opposed to the two or three weeks practised by
many of the world's major, competitive breweries. Although one of the more blatant commercial beers of
Norway, it is extremely pleasant and light with a
strong hoppy taste. It's even capable of rekindling
dreams of travelling around all those small towns of
Norway, sampling the local home-brews and hoping
that all the blondes don't spoil one's appetite!

As if!

FÜRSTENBERG ANTONIUS   West Germany

OG 1054°   *Fürstenburg Importers Ltd/*
Draught   *Scottish German Beer Importers*
Bottles 50cl, returnable

The first pint of FÜRSTENBERG was drunk more
than 500 years ago yet the noble family of Fürstenberg
can be traced back to far earlier times. Their ancestors
were the Counts of Achalm and Urach who were large
landowners residing in the south-west of Germany
during the eleventh and twelfth centuries. In 1218

Count Egino V of Urach inherited the major part of the lands of Zahringen whereupon he transferred his family seat to the present residential city of Zahringer and called himself Count of Freiburg. When the inheritance was divided after Egino's death, his youngest son, the Duke Heinrich of Freiburg, took possession of the estates in the Black Forest in the region called Baar. For a home he moved into the spacious Fürstenberg Castle near Donaueschingen where the family ancestral estates are still to be found. Henceforth Heinrich called himself Count of Fürstenberg and it is with him that the story of Fürstenberg lager begins.

In 1278 Count Heinrich assisted his cousin Rudolf of Hapsburg on the battlefield 'Marchfields' near Vienna to defeat his rival King Ottokar of Bohemia. Their victory secured the ascent of the Hapsburg family to imperial power which lasted until 1918. Reward for his assistance and loyalty followed swiftly – land, castles, lakes, etc. – yet most important of all he granted Heinrich the licence to brew beer! The Counts of Fürstenberg naturally set great store by the quality of their lager and they were anxious to improve the skills of their brewery staff. For this reason their chief brewer, Anton Stofermann, was sent to Prague in 1591 where another Fürstenberg taught him the Bohemian methods of brewing. By 1705 the then Count, Anton Egon, decided to increase the commercial activities of the brewing business and by 1739 a bigger brewery had to be built in Donaueschingen to cope with the demand. Modernized, this brewery is still in use today! During the business year 1779/1780 the Fürstenberg Brewery sold 660,000 litres of beer yet just twelve years later this had soared to a massive 165 *million* litres! Today the entire drinks output of the brewery is in excess of 950,000 hectolitres and is exported to many nations; the USA, France, Italy, Switzerland, Australia, Japan, Australia, South America, and the UK, to name but a few.

Launched here in 1982 by the Falkirk-based Scottish

German Beer Importers, most of their efforts behind the brand were concentrated in Scotland, where a large proportion of its sales are through free trade distribution. Talking of which, during the seven years SGBI have handled FÜRSTENBERG they became embroiled in a protracted and bitter distribution battle with the mighty Guinness brewing group, but in 1987 they finally secured the distribution rights to the UK market and a new company was formed to handle it, Fürstenberg Importers Limited. (On my last annual visit to the wonderful pubs and clubs of Ireland I noticed that FÜRSTENBERG was available just about everywhere and is an extremely popular pint amongst those somehow not addicted to the black-and-white holy drink of Ireland.) Fürstenberg Importers are now keen to establish the brand south of the border in both the on- and off-trades and the line has already been tested in some Oddbins outlets. Unfortunately, however, at the time of going to press the results of these tests were unavailable.

Brewed to the strict German 'Purity Laws' of the 16th century, ANTONIUS is imported and delivered to the customer no later than 7–10 days after bottling in order to keep it as fresh as possible. To maintain quality the lager is also unpasturized, which is a bonus for real-ale buffs and (dare I say it?) may tempt one or two of them away from their traditional ales. ANTONIUS does actually have this potential as it is a strong, dark lager with a firm malty bouquet as well as a rich malty flavour. Unusually for a lager of this strength, it is surprisingly smooth and refreshing with an aftertaste that only a few might find unpleasant, and I stress the word *few*. In Scotland over three million pints of the FÜRSTENBERG range were greedily guzzled in 1987, and it'll be interesting to see how the brand develops in England and Wales now that the importers have opened new offices in Warrington, Cheshire. A good, clean, crisp lager, it deserves your lips and has the potential for growth.

Your round!

FÜRSTENBERG EXPORT   West Germany

OG 1049–53° – 5.6% ABV   *Fürstenberg Importers Ltd/*
Draught   *Scottish German Beer Importers*
Bottles 50cl, returnable
Cans 44cl

Although only launched in England and Wales in
March 1988, FÜRSTENBERG EXPORT was introduced in Scotland in 1982 where it enjoyed a spec-
tacular rise to fame and is now established as a market
leader. Quite rightly Fürstenberg Importers are quick
and proud to point out that EXPORT is the genuine
German article and most definitely isn't another in the
long line of foreign-sounding 'brewed over here under
licence' lagers. Indeed, it is brewed, matured and
bottled at the huge Fürstlich Fürstenbergische Brewery
in south-west Germany which belongs to an exclusive
group of successful brewers of high quality beers. The
importers tell us that it's one of only six 'premium
beers' produced by the country's 1800 breweries and
it's the only 'premium beer' made in the south-west.
Although called EXPORT it's actually not brewed for
export, but is exactly identical to the lager that the
Germans consume with relish on their own home
patch. It's the most popular of the three FÜRSTEN-
BERG brands available here, accounting for 85 per
cent of their overall sales – the other 15 per cent is
split virtually evenly between ANTONIUS (*q.v.*) and the
PILS (*q.v.*).

The brewery is situated in Donaueschingen, just 20
miles from the Swiss border and in the heart of the
Black Forest, and this is where the water used in the
brewing process is to be found. It is obtained from one
of more than 30 natural springs to be found in the park
that surrounds Fürstenberg Castle at Donaueschingen
and the soft composition of it is ideal for brewing. This
water is more than just a contributing factor to the

purity and quality of the lager, and it needs no modification before being used. Interestingly, the Black Forest region is the same geological age as the Scottish Highlands and the waters in both locations are extremely similar. The rest of the ingredients are dictated by Germany's 'Purity Laws' of 1516 in that only barleymalt, brewer's yeast and hops can be used. However, it is worth noting that there are some German brands, including some well known in Britain, that do, in fact, contain various 'environmental impurities'. This is not the case with FÜRSTENBERG. An independent analysis commissioned by the importers from the chemistry lab of Stirling University proved that FÜRSTENBERG was uncontaminated by trace metals, PCBs, pesticide residues or industrial waste. The analysis went on to say that the lager 'contained fewer impurities than household tap water'!

Once again, as with the other FÜRSTENBERG brands, EXPORT is a strong lager and tastes as such. Free from all additives and unpasturized, it has a relatively dark golden colour and a crisp, full-bodied bite. It is exceptionally good, and I heartily recommend that you give it a try should you fortunately stumble across it in draught or bottled form. It's both refreshing and full tasting, both qualities very much in demand from the discerning lager buff, of which, I'm proud to say, I am one. Join me.

FÜRSTENBERG PILS   West Germany

OG 1047°   *Fürstenberg Importers Ltd/*
Draught   *Scottish German Beer Importers*
Bottles 33cl & 50cl,
    returnable

In 1886 the Fürstenberg Brewery took on a new chief brewer, one Josef Munz who immediately introduced a new golden-coloured FÜRSTENBERG beer. This brew was enthusiastically welcomed throughout Germany, and notably by the then Chancellor of the Reich, Otto von Bismark. Otto's doctor, Professor Schweninger, was even moved to declare the new beer to be 'The beer of beers!'

Yet this wasn't the only contribution made by Munz to brewing, as he once again delighted his contemporaries with a new beer towards the end of the century. This time it was a type of lager brewed in the style of that from the famous Czech town of Pilsen. Emperor Wilhelm II went to see his friend Max Egon, the Count of Fürstenberg, on April 26th 1900. Max, being the owner of his own brewery, was naturally the perfect lunch partner as all the lager was free, which proves that the Emperor wasn't stupid! Anyway, needless to say, over bratwurst and the like, Bill and Max enjoyed a few bottles of Munz's new pils. The Emperor was so pleased with it that he declared it immediately as the 'dinner beverage of His Majesty the Emperor', which is a bit like the Queen's logo here, and for the Fürstenberg Brewery was a huge marketing boost.

This lager of great tradition has satisfied several generations of eager and demanding drinkers, and today Munz's brew is known as FÜRSTENBERG PILS. Crisp and clear, it has a fine, light malty bouquet, while retaining a quite dry quality. The palate, however, is stimulated by its sharp bite that is extremely pleasant. I really do feel that pils drinkers shouldn't be obsessed by brand loyalty and I'd encourage them wholeheartedly to give this one a chance. It's actually an extremely fine brew. What else could you want for your money?

GAMBRINUS PILSEN　Czechoslovakia

OG 1048–54°　　　*BB Supply Centre Ltd*
Bottles 500ml

Gambrinus is one of only two beers actually brewed and bottled entirely in the town of Pilsen, Czechoslovakia, a town that is surely synonomous throughout the world with quality lager beers. Pilsen is in Bohemia in western Czechoslovakia, an area famous for its brewing skills since as early as the 11th century. The name itself was derived from Gambrinus, the Duke of Brabant and Flanders who lived between 1251 and 1294, – a man who wisely favoured beers from that area. In 1869, when the present brewery was founded, it was decided to honour him by naming not only their premium beer but also their entire brewery after him, which is possibly the highest honour bestowed upon man – I look forward fondly to the day my great-great grandchildren will be able to hold up with pride a pint of Daft Lager before their friends and drink a hearty toast in my name.

Like BUDWEISER BUDVAR (*q.v.*), GAMBRINUS also takes Bohemian hops from Saaz as well as the local natural spring water as its ingredients. It is also given an equally long fermentation period, which results in an alcohol by volume content of 4.5 per cent. With a full-bodied aroma, GAMBRINUS possesses that distinct, characteristic Czech flavour in a beer, not too bitter to leave you with an unpleasant aftertaste. Light and honey-coloured, it is a worthy representative of the famous town and is joyfully available in full half-litre bottles. I strongly suggest that you pop down to the nearest off-licence and, after carefully nursing it home and allowing it to chill, crack it open, sit back, and enjoy a real quality lager. Personally, I believe it to be one of the best lagers I have ever had the pleasure to drink. A relatively new product on the import

GERSTEL 95

market, you should really pester your local off-licence to stock the stuff. Its beautifully balanced flavour, rich bouquet, and deliciously smooth taste goes down well at any time of the day. Beautiful.

GERMANIA
West Germany

OG 0.5% ABV
Bottles 33cl
GB Vintagers

The fact that this particular low-alcohol lager is from the famous Dortmunder Union Brauerei of West Germany is enough to arouse the interest of all genuine lager buffs worth their salt. With nationwide distribution it shouldn't be that difficult to find, though if you do venture to look for it, I can promise I won't be accompanying you.

Another low/no-alcohol lager with little to distinguish it from it's competitors.

GERSTEL
West Germany

0.8% ABV
Bottles 33cl
Courage

Yes, just when you thought it was safe to go back into the pub with a packet of Capstan Full Strength dangling from your bottom lip, Courage have introduced yet another low-alcohol lager. Interestingly enough, however, GERSTEL is a German brand brewed in Frankfurt by Henniger-Brau (the local Henniger was my favourite for the two years I lived in Frankfurt). In Germany, like everywhere else, the low-alcohol lager market is expanding at a frightening pace and now accounts for nearly two per cent of the market.

Naturally, we're assured that GERSTEL is brewed *just like any other lager* ... but then the alcohol is extracted! Shock! Horror! However, we're not told just how it is removed, and it makes one think of the famous hoover of Australia's SWAN LIGHT. I couldn't really recommend this to the punter as all the low/no-alcohol drinks seem to have a taste unique to themselves.

GILDE EXPORT   West Germany

Bottles 33cl

Hanover, like most German towns, has a rich and proud brewing tradition that spans centuries, and although there are many fine and upstanding lagers brewed there, GILDE EXPORT, I'm afraid, isn't one of them. Brewed and bottled by the Lindener-Gilde Brauerei I found it so bitter as to be offensive, and it left a ghastly aftertaste. As a rule it's a policy of ours to encourage all lager buffs to try whatever they can get their hands on, but with GILDE EXPORT we also recommend that you have a lighter lager on hand should you need to wash the taste away with something.

GILDE PILS   West Germany

OG 1044–50°   *Baron von Ritter/*
Cans 50cl   *New England Wine Co.*

Again brewed and canned by the Lindener-Gilde Braue-rei GILDE PILS is a little lighter and crisper than GILDE EXPORT (*q.v.*). However, it is by far a preferable brew to EXPORT. Still bitter, we feel it's an acquired taste even for a lager of such common strength. An original taste then, but unpleasant for some.

GILDER West Germany

Introduced to the UK in early 1988 GILDER is currently being test marketed in the pils sector in Scotland where it faces extremely stiff competition from the five major and established pils brands: HOLSTEN, SATZENBRAU, KALTENBERG, LOWENBRAU and LAMOT (*qq.v.*). Both HOLSTEN and SATZENBRAU are already imported by Dunn & Moore, but they've been looking for their own pils brand because of the runaway success of pils in the sector north of the border and GILDER is as good a choice as any because it enjoys a strong following by the discerning drinkers of its homeland. Although they won't reveal with exactly *whom*, Dunn & Moore are currently holding talks with a regional brewery to gain national distribution. Their sales director said, 'Gilder has tested very well here and the German brewer is aiming for a national launch.' So, for all us south of the border, in search of a pub that is open and a quality lager to quaff once inside, we'll just have to hope that they can knock back enough to convince the powers-that-be that we all like a good pils. In our opinion, GILDER should do well in Scotland despite the five major brands. Quality, you see, is in constant demand.

GIRAF Denmark

OG 1060–66°
Bottles 33cl
Giraf (UK)

There's no knowing how sales of GIRAF (translated that means giraffe) are going in the UK, for in late 1988 it has only been on the market for a couple of months, mostly through the up-market shops of our golden-paved capital, London. Retailing at around the 85p mark, it's certainly not a cheap lager, but then with such a high gravity what do you expect? GIRAF doesn't quite make a super-strength lager, although it is no 'premium' either. It rather awkwardly sits between the two. Good. Because GIRAF is a very good buy. Slightly thick with a rich bitter taste, it's certainly more drinkable than super-strength and gives a good deal of the pleasure one derives from a premium. It's a quality product definitely reserved for the discerning drinker; therefore you should stick your neck out and grab a bottle!

GOLD FASSL PILS   Austria

OG 1049–52°   *Continental Lager Distributors Ltd*
Bottles

Produced by Ottaklinger, the second largest brewery in Austria, GOLD FASSL PILS has recently been made available nationally.

This one should find many supporters in the pils-drinking fraternity. With an original gravity of 1049–52°, it is slightly spritzy, but dry tasting and easy to drink. Recommended.

GOLD FASSL VIENNA LAGER   Austria

OG 1049–52°   *Continental Lager Distributors Ltd*
Bottles

Again from Ottaklinger in Austria, this one is certainly different from GOLD FASSL PILS (*q.v.*), but comes equally recommended. With an original gravity of

1049–52°, a deep golden colour, and a slightly malty taste, VIENNA is definitely a lager to be savoured. Well worth badgering your local off-licence for it.

GOLD STANDARD   UK

Nurdin & Peacock PLC

If this lager was the standard of all beers, in the same way that gold is the standard of all currency, then believe me, house bricks would be the world's favourite jewellery. Enough said?

GOLDEN EAGLE   India

OG 1042°   *Continental Lager Distributors Ltd*
Bottles 32cl

For some the Jewel in the Crown of the British Empire was India. For others it was the breweries of India. One such jewel is Mohan Meakin, founded by the plucky English entrepreneur and pioneer, Edward Dyer, who set up the first ever brewery in India in 1855 at Kasauli. But Dyer wasn't a man to stop there and other breweries followed at Solan, Simla, Murree, Rawalpindi and Mandalay. It was shortly after this that yet another plucky English entrepreneur and pioneer arrived in the shape of H. G. Meakin who bought both the old Simla and Solan breweries from Dyer before adding another half-dozen himself. It was when these two breweries merged after the First World War that Dyer Meakin Breweries was formed. But what of Mohan?

Well, in 1949 a Mr Mohan took over the management of the company and such was the increase in assets and profits under his leadership that in 1967 the name was changed to Mohan Meakin Breweries. The 'brewery' was dropped in 1982 as the company is now involved in a variety of interests.

GOLDEN EAGLE lager beer falls into the premium sector and is brewed and bottled in Madras, drawing on 130 years of experience. Pure Himalayan spring water and specially grown barley ensure a lager of some quality. Soft, yet relatively lively, GOLDEN EAGLE is without doubt a perfect accompaniment to Indian cuisine. Indeed it is a fine drink on its own.

GOSSER EXPORT   Austria

Bottles 33cl   *Caxton Tower Wines Ltd/*
                                 Winter & MG Imports Ltd

Gosser is one of Austria's top three brewing concerns
and its headquarters can be found resting snugly in
the foothills of the Alps at Leoben, Styria. The lager in
question, GOSSER EXPORT, has been brewed since
1860 with water from the numerous mountain springs
of the region, as well as other equally fine ingredients.
Unusually, GOSSER EXPORT is aged for a minimum
of four months, but this seems well worth the trouble
because it results in a hearty, light-coloured lager beer
with a well-balanced hop flavour. Certainly a robust
brew, GOSSER travels well and is Austria's number
one export lager, being shipped to every continent on
the globe. It is also currently being exported in a 50cl
bottle, but at the time of going to print we couldn't
ascertain if it was available in the UK, so for now
you'll just have to buy the three smaller 33cl bottles
instead of two of the larger ones. A fine brew that is
often enjoyed in my favourite bar – the front room!

GRAF ARCO EXPORT LAGER   West Germany

OG 1047°   *Gibbs Mew PLC*
Draught
Bottles 33cl

Introduced to the UK in June 1987, it's rather unfortunate that this fine Bavarian lager is only made available
through Gibbs Mew's pubs, which are basically within
a 30-mile radius of Salisbury. Lucky for the locals, yes,
but it always saddens me to know that there's a lager
about that I might never get close to. Thus I advise

you lager lovers of Salisbury to get out there and enjoy; after all, it's been laid on especially for you. *You lucky people!* And while you're at it send me a few crates.

THE GREAT DANE   Denmark

OG 1042–48°   *Danish Bacon Co. PLC*
Cans 1 litre and 50cl

Some 140 metres below the Faxe Brewery, Denmark's largest independent, is a subterranean coral reef (seriously), and from this reef pure fresh water is produced that literally gushes out at the surface. It contains no iron nor manganese, but it is rich in valuable salts and minerals. It's this water, as well as the secret Faxe recipe and the brewery's own know-how, which combine in the brewing process to produce what is a fine lager beer. Therefore it is not surprising that Faxe refuses to pasteurize its lager, instead it has through many years of research developed another secret, a special cooling and filtration technique which ensures a long shelf life and preserves the lager's delicate flavour.

The GREAT DANE is produced in Denmark as a draught lager, and each daily batch undergoes 320 analysis checks throughout the brewing and canning process in the upkeep of quality. The Danish Bacon Company (seriously) are quick to point out that this is 'an entirely different' GREAT DANE from the version previously handled by Allied's now defunct Worldwide Beer Importers. In fact the bottled GREAT DANE was introduced to the UK in 1984 but was withdrawn just eighteen months later.

You should have no trouble spotting Faxe's GREAT DANE in the can as it is decorated with a very lively, though clean and Danish, early 1970s pub scene, and

I can't decide whether I like it or not. With the lager I'm a little more decided as I've always found something odd about canned draught. Faxe's GREAT DANE, however, isn't actually unpleasant, in fact it's extremely refreshing. It's just that it tastes a bit thin and over carbonated, which certainly isn't the case, for with a 5 per cent alcohol by volume measure the GREAT DANE is actually a pretty potent brew. One should be careful not to make the mistake of treating it as a session lager despite its deceptive texture.

Try one.

GROLSCH PREMIUM LAGER Netherlands

OG 1044–50° – 5% ABV *Grolsch UK Ltd*
Bottles 45cl
Cans 44cl

In its native Netherlands, GROLSCH enjoys a position second only to HEINEKEN (*q.v.*) in its level of success, and with its distinctive pot-stoppered swing-top bottle, it has attracted a great deal of attention in the UK in a relatively short time. There are better-known Dutch beers available here, although some of them are produced under licence in the UK, but GROLSCH, not being a mass-market product, is exactly the same in Britain as it is in its homeland.

GROLSCH takes its name from the country town of Groenlo, originally Grol, in the east of the Netherlands close to the German border. The Grolsch Beer Brewing Company still has a brewery at Groenlo as well as one in the nearby textile town of Enschede. The family who own and run the brewery today are called de Groen and they can trace their enterprise back to 1676. At that time their forebear Peter Cuyper, which appropriately means cooper or barrel-maker, was Master of the Guild of Groenlo brewers. The 1660s are known as 'The Golden Age' in the Netherlands through the likes of Rembrandt and Frans Hals, whose art was made possible by the national prosperity which derived from trade in tobacco, spices, tea and, naturally, beer! The sobriquet 'The Golden Age' may not have referred to the colour of their beer, but this was certainly the period in which the foundations were laid for the country's present importance as a brewing nation. GROLSCH was, and still is, at the very heart of the Netherlands brewing industry, and the region in which it is brewed has close affinity with the brewing traditions of Flanders and the mighty Germans.

Sold through some 26,000 outlets including most of the major brewers and a great number of regional brewers and wholesalers, GROLSCH is expanding at three times the market rate by volume. Ideally served at 8°C (45°F) it has a lightly fruity character with a rich, flowery bouquet. Blessed with a slightly hoppy bitterness in the finish, it is soft in texture and has a fresh palate. This is possibly due to a three-month lagering period and the fact that it comes to us unpasteurized. Brewed with water from its own wells, two-row malting barley, German Hallertau aroma hops and its own strains of yeast, GROLSCH is most certainly a lager of distinction. Well worth sampling if you haven't already done so.

GRUNHALLE   UK

OG 1037°   *Greenhall Whitley*
Bottles
Draught

Brewed in Warrington, Cheshire, by Greenhall Whitley, GRUNHALLE is yet another sheep in lederhosen!

Yes, it's another British-brewed lager pushed onto the British market with a German name.

It was introduced to the UK through Greenhall's outlets in 1971, and is apparently based on an 'original German recipe', the name of which is GRUNHALLE! Surprise, surprise! Especially when you consider that *Grunhalle* means Green Hall!

GRUNHALLE's marketing man, whose efficiency is severely hindered by his apparent inability to answer letters, and his aversion to talking on the telephone, told me during the course of an unenlightening telephone conversation that 'people don't care that much about the purity of lager over here'.

Well, thanks for a great quote, but as for your lager . . .? You can keep it. GRUNHALLE is another insipid British-brewed 'session' lager that should be avoided.

HACKER PSCHORR EDELHELL EXPORT   West Germany

Bottles

This lager has been brewed since 1417 and HACKER PSCHORR is one of the most highly esteemed names in Munich's brewing industry. The name is the result of the two breweries merging into one, and it was recently swallowed up by the huge Paulaner Brewery. However, Hacker Pschorr continue to produce their own lines and their strikingly robust lager can now be found over here, where its dry, full-bodied flavour is much appreciated. Reasonably widely available (try Sainsbury's), this one should most certainly be sampled.

HANSA   UK

OG 1036°   *J. W. Cameron*
Draught
Cans 44cl
PET Bottles 2 litres

The original HANSA is a West German lager from the
famous city of Dortmund. This version, however, comes
to you direct from breweries in Hartlepool and Cleve-
land. It was introduced to the market in 1981 and as
yet still isn't available nationally, only to be found in
Yorkshire, East Anglia and Tyne Tees. The simple red
and white can which gives the beer a rather cheap
image, actually carries the logo of the Dortmunder-
Actien Brauerei, which unfortunately adds prestige to
what is a very common, if not unpleasant lager that
somehow sells approximately 100,000 barrels per
annum. Recommendation: put the kettle on.

HANSA SPECIAL EXPORT   UK

Draught   *J. W. Cameron*
Bottles 33cl

Introduced six years after HANSA (*q.v.*) HANSA
SPECIAL EXPORT was an attempt to cut a slice of
the premium market on the back of the success of its
sister brew. With sales already in the area of 8,000
barrels a year, SPECIAL EXPORT is available
'almost' everywhere in England and Wales. The Scots,
however, don't get to see a drop.
   '*Taxi!* Heathrow airport!'

HARP   UK

OG 1030–34°   *Harp Lager Co.*
Draught
Cans (440ml)

Created in 1960 at Dundalk in the Republic of Ireland, Harp was the first national 'pilsner' to be launched in this country in 1961, being introduced by a consortium including Courage. However, although Guinness Brewing Worldwide Ltd claim to have created 'the authentic taste of the Continental product' this particular little beverage has about as much in common with Europe as a double-decker bus, or, as one passing tippler remarked, 'Continental? More like incontinental!' In fact HARP, described by Europeans as 'poison', would be difficult to sell in Germany, for not only is it laced with additives but it has a gravity of only 1030–34°, which would put it outside the alcoholic drinks class for some people! Perhaps this is the reason why £4 million has been spent on an advertising campaign for this nasty liquid run by top London advertising agency DFS Dorlands Ltd, the forefront of which has been the TV commercials including Jonathan Ross. Dorlands and Guinness are so desperate to try and push HARP as 'modern' and 'stylish' that in their press release they even describe the can as 'cool and refreshing'!

The truth of the matter is that HARP was a first-generation lager in this country and should now, possibly, be scrapped. It is weak, and tasteless, and I can assure you that in blind tests virtually no one could tell the difference between it and other first-generation lagers. And that just about sums it up!

HARP EXTRA   UK

OG 1041°   *Harp Lager Co.*
Draught

HARP (*q.v.*) had been around for over a quarter of a
century and it was known throughout the length and
breadth of Britain as a low alcohol lager that could be
drunk all night without doing any real damage –
except to the punter's pocket. Harp was known. Harp
was popular, but then again, so was *lager*. The market
was expanding in leaps and bounds, and it seemed
that almost every day saw the launch of a new brand.
Suddenly Harp wasn't that popular. Suddenly there
was a choice and quality became important. People
just couldn't go on drinking the advertising. Then, on
October 3rd 1987, three-and-a-half million pounds
changed all that.

Although such a *massive* sum of money invested in
advertising is not unusual, that is how much Harp, 75
per cent owned by Guinness, was willing to pay to
recapture their now flagging share of the market. The
advertising strategy employed may well have been
called a pincer move in military jargon as the money
was invested not only to maintain the mass market
appeal of Harp Lager but also to develop a strong
premium market. HARP PREMIER, KRONENBOURG
1664, SATZENBRAU (*qq.v.*) and HARP EXTRA are
these premiums, and for PREMIER and EXTRA a new
£2.5 million brewery was built at Morrell's lager brewery in Oxford, while £7 million was invested in an
extension to London's Park Royal site. There were new
can designs, new font designs, and massive promotions.
Fair enough, but what about the lager?

The 'extra' in the title doubtless refers to the extra
alcohol in this version of Harp lager as it is slighly
stronger than the stuff that was first introduced. However, with a gravity of, 1041 EXTRA is struggling to

be promoted from the standard lager market into the premium sector, but it simply just doesn't make it. In fact there aren't many nice things I can say about EXTRA. I could say that it has no unpleasant after-taste, but this is probably because it has no foretaste either. Highly carbonated, it emerges from the tap with a thin head that soon disappears. There is no firmness of texture to give it a full-bodied feel. Yet despite this it's a more qualified brew than the original and, as a session lager itself, can still be drunk all night without too much affect. I realize fully that there are people out there who like HARP EXTRA, love discos and eat their 'E' additives with relish but, I'm proud to say, I'm *not* one of them! Supposedly 'based on' an original German recipe, it's like calling the great British banger a bratwurst!

HARP MASTER LAGER   UK

8% ABV   *Harp Lager Co.*
Cans 44cl

'Aaah! Isn't it cute! The *baby* of the book!' Yes, HARP MASTER LAGER is the youngest beer in the book as it was only launched in September 1988, and even then it was only available in its Lancashire test-market area. Therefore there is no information on sales or on what the punters think about it. This doesn't stop Harp though. Remember how I told you that for the normal Harp brand their promotional material called their can 'cool and refreshing'? Well, here's another. We're into the second week of September 1988 as I write this and the promotional bumpf, which I received some weeks back, already flagrantly boasts, 'In test market, total super-strength sales increased significantly'. It was *only launched* in September! Still, you might be interested in

some other information: HARP MASTER LAGER
was rated best-tasting super-strength lager (Independent Product Research – of course!) and 78 per cent of
trialists said they'd buy again. That's about it then. At
the time of going to press we hadn't been able to get
our hands on a can, but the brewers assure us that it's
brewed to have less of a sweet taste than other super-
strengths. I look forward to finding out for myself, as
I'm sure you do.

Anyway, we should give Harp a round of applause.
They've got the set! HARP (*q.v.*) for the session market,
HARP EXTRA (*q.v.*) for the standard/premium sector,
HARP PREMIER (*q.v.*) for the specialist market, and
now HARP MASTER LAGER for the super-strength
drinkers. Well done, Harp! Oh no! No Pils! There's no
Pils! Oh, my god! Clear the decks for another seven
billion quid launch. *DA-DA-DAAH! HAAAAARP PILS!!!*

HARP PREMIER

OG 1045° – 5% ABV   *Harp Lager Co.*
Bottles 33cl

Although HARP PREMIER has been exported to the
United States since the late 60s where it now enjoys
the honour of being the biggest-selling exported British
lager, it wasn't introduced in the UK until 1987, and
even then it wasn't launched nationally until early
1989. It is undoubtedly the finest of the Harp range
and, not only that, PREMIER is actually a great lager
in its own right. Packaged in a very classy, slim pale
green bottle with a short neck and a thin, simple,
wrap-around label, HARP PREMIER is clean, sharp,
smooth, strong and very refreshing. Its only problem is
with existing Harp drinkers in that it is totally different
to the other two brands, i.e. it is enjoyable. It is full-
bodied as opposed to thin, and it is not a session drink,

therefore a lot of Harp drinkers will find the change too much to take. However, we shouldn't let that put us off and at last I can recommend a Harp product to the discerning drinker with total honesty. HARP PREMIER has won four Monde Sélection medals for product excellence, even the eye-catching bottle has won an award! Find it, buy it, chill it and enjoy it. I have, on several occasions, and will go on doing so till I drop.

HARTSMAN LAGER   UK

OG 1035°   *McMullen & Sons*
Draught
Cans 44cl

It is not often that one can genuinely recommend a British-brewed session lager, so steady yourselves against the shock and take note. HARTSMAN LAGER, brewed in Hertford by McMullen and Sons, was launched in the UK in May 1984, and although initially only available within roughly a 30-mile radius of Hertford, it is now spreading throughout the country – and I'm not surprised! From these small beginnings just a handful of years ago, it can now be found also in London and the northern home counties. I hope that given a few more years this fine, pedigree lager will be found in every county and town in the country. Full of the finest Bavarian hops, HARTSMAN is known endearingly to the enlightened as 'Hoppy Hartsman' and in 1987 it cheekily walked off with the Monde Sélection *Gold* medal in Brussels. For those of you who live in the aforementioned districts I proudly recommend that you catapult out there and sample a few, after all it *is* a session lager. For those of you that live outside these towns, my advice is . . . don't worry! It'll be heading your way any day now.

HEINEKEN   UK

OG 1031–35°   *Whitbread*
Draught
Bottles 25.5cl
Cans 27.5 & 44cl

I know for a fact that the gold medals proudly displayed on the can have got nothing whatsoever to do with its contents. HEINEKEN is brewed in the UK by Whitbread, under licence from the world-famous Heineken Brouwerijen of Amsterdam, and it is Whitbread's biggest-selling brand. Originally the agreement between Whitbread and the Dutch brewers meant that the brew was imported from Holland and it first began arriving at British ports in 1961. A very fine lager, it goes without saying that it was an immediate success – which was usually the case, no matter which country it went to. However, it was such a runaway winner that by 1968 sales were so high that the terms of their agreement were changed and Whitbread began to brew it here – and thus began the demise of a great name in the brewing world and a great lager to boot.

It was in the early 1970s that the advertising copyline 'Heineken refreshes the parts that other beers cannot reach' first emerged and 18 years later this famous campaign is still as effective as ever. Indeed, this brilliant advertising campaign has probably been one of the most influential in the whole of the lager sector. Personally, I believe that it is this campaign, which covers not only TV but also cinema, radio, posters and the press, which has kept HEINEKEN as the second largest brand in the country for so long. My own research has proved that the majority of people buy HEINEKEN simply because of the fact that they are familiar with it, and also its price – which is cheap. Not one person who was questioned mentioned the taste as an incentive; in fact it was only when we

asked them about the flavour that they responded
virtually unanimously with the uncontentious 'it's all
right', though we should add here that none found it
unpleasant – they wouldn't have been buying it if
they did! The small 27.5cl can is apparently often
bought for parties (they bring *their* HEINEKEN then
drink *your* BUDVAR (*q.v.*) until it's gone – then they
drink their HEINEKEN while you leave!) and these
sales of 88,000 barrels account for a respectable 4
per cent of the total take-home standard lager sales.
HEINEKEN currently holds a 54 per cent share of
this market with a volume three times that of its
nearest competitor in the year ending March 1988,
according to Stats MR's retail audit for England and
Wales. It should also be noted that in 1988 lager's
share of production at Whitbread rose from 46 per
cent to 51 per cent.

As regards the draught HEINEKEN, I'm afraid it has
deteriorated as much as the canned version. At the end of
the 70s I lived in Amsterdam and Nijmegan, in the south
of the Netherlands, for two-and-a-half years. I drank
HEINEKEN virtually consistently on draught while I
experimented with other brands in the off-trade sector.
HEINEKEN draught was light and refreshing, a most
enjoyable lager, a repeated gold-medal winner. When I
returned to England the first thing I bought was a pint of
HEINEKEN. It was one of the few pints I've been unable
to finish in my life. It is thin, over-carbonated, tasteless,
sugarwater, and it is twelve degrees lower in alcohol
than the original. I know it's a session lager but this is no
excuse. HEINEKEN, as brewed by Whitbread, is quite
simply awful and I don't have one good word to say
about it. Once again, though, the punters of Britain
prove me wrong. A brand leader in the off-trade and
a close runner-up in the on. There's an old saying
that goes something like this: 'Eat sh*t. Twelve billion
flies can't be wrong.' If this maxim were applied to
HEINEKEN, 'Drink Heineken. Four million punters
can't be wrong', I'd take my money to Ladbrokes. No,

HEINEKEN is not recommended – not that that will make any difference.

Anyway, I've always liked the ads.

HEINEKEN EXPORT	Netherlands

OG 1046–50°/4.8% ABV   *Whitbread*
Bottles 33cl

Not surprisingly HEINEKEN EXPORT has greater sales outside its own market than any other beer in the world. It is the Netherlands' most famous export and it's not unusual to bump into a bottle just about wherever your travels take you. Although Heineken didn't actually become Heineken until the middle of the 19th century, its origins can be traced back virtually 450 years.

It was the jobless 22-year-old Gerard Adriaan Heineken who started it all way back in 1864 when, using virtually every penny he had, he bought a failing Amsterdam brewery called 'The Haystack', which was some 300 years old. It seems that under his guidance, for there is no man as determined as he who is driven by hunger, the brewery began to pick up and he was able to move his plant to its present site after just four years. It was shortly after 1864 that the famous 'Heineken A' yeast cell was isolated. It is that cell that gives HEINEKEN EXPORT its unique taste and the success that was to follow is largely attributable to this asset. After 10 years he opened a second brewery in Rotterdam. Although Heineken began exporting his lager in 1876, the brand's first *major* foray abroad came with the repeal of prohibition in the United States of America where, and I don't mean this derogatorily to Heineken, they'd drink anything that didn't make them go blind. It was the first brewery in the world to make this move and it was met with some success as today HEINEKEN is America's leading imported brand and the Americans are, fortunately for themselves, not allowed to brew it under any licensing agreement.

For those who must drink HEINEKEN (*q.v.*) on draught in the pubs you unfortunately have no choice but to buy the far weaker and inferior British brand, but those who consume it from the bottle are rewarded with the far superior Dutch-brewed version. There is no real comparison between the two versions, and I, without the slightest doubt, wholeheartedly recommend the Dutch HEINEKEN – and not just over the British version but also as a lager in its own right. HEINEKEN EXPORT is a smooth, crisp, light and lively lager in the pilsener style, with a somewhat fruity and spritzy finish. You should hunt it out from amongst the millions of cans of the wretched British version, for if you do, I believe there's a pretty good chance that you'll never buy British-brewed Heineken again unless, that is, you're skint and need a cheapie. Basically, it's the difference between a gutter on Skid Row and a suite at the Ritz.

HELDENBRAU   UK

OG 1030–34°   *Whitbread*
Draught
Cans 16fl. oz (45cl)
PET Bottles 2 & 3 litres

Originally developed as a regional draught lager for the north-west, which is still the only area where it's available from the tap, it has, in fact, enjoyed far more success in the take-home sector where it is available nationally. Whitbread increased HELDENBRAU's national off-licence distribution in 1983, and on their

promotional brand data leaflet the phrase 'and it is
currently the leading PET lager with a market share
of over 20 per cent' has been inked over. Unfortunately
I wasn't able to find out whether or not this meant it
was but now isn't, or wether it never was and they'd
jumped the gun – difficult to say without confirmation.
One thing I can tell you, however, is that *Heldenbrau*
literally means 'Hero's Brew' – *hardly!* It's a little more
palatable than many other British-brewed lagers in the
1030–34° gravity range, but this certainly doesn't mean
that it comes recommended.

HEMELING	UK

	Bass
4.1% ABV	
Draught	
Bottles	
Cans	

'Are you drinking? ... No, I'm Hemeling!' That was
the advertising copyline for HEMELING when it was
introduced some time ago as a lite lager. I think what
Bass meant by 'lite' was that it's lower in carbohy-
drates (which are fattening!) than your average
lager.

I didn't even know it was still available until I spoke
to the brewers last year, who informed me that it can
be had in draught, bottled and canned form throughout
England and Wales.

Well, it certainly feels light as it goes down, but it
does have a somewhat decent, fully-brewed taste to it
that goes some way to redeeming its watery character.

In my view not bad, but then again not too *good*
either. Certainly preferable to some lagers in the same
strength bracket, but not one that I would choose personally.

HENNINGER KAISER PILS   West Germany

OG 1043–47°
Bottles 27.5cl

During the early 80s it was my good fortune to live in
the district of Sossenheim, Frankfurt AM, for some
two years, an opportunity I certainly didn't waste
outside the city's famous bars. Indeed, of an evening
I would usually catch one of the sparklingly clean
underground trains into town before I wandered into
Sachsenhausen for the night. I often think that all
German cities must have a district like Sachsenhausen,
an area dedicated to upgrading the social ethos of
drinking, a place where entire streets are made up of
bars – a heaven on earth, a paradise. Many a long
night was spent in these bars, sampling the hundreds
of German beers available. But, as time wore on, I
became very German myself and soon began to develop a fiercely regional patriotism when it came to
lager. The Germans have no real 'national' brand,
and regional drinks abound. Frankfurt is the home of
Germany's largest brewer, Binding, and this is the company that produces what soon became my firm favourite HENNINGER KAISER PILS. Binding produces
an impressive output of about one-and-three-quarter
hectolitres per annum, which was just enough for
me!

Binding produces an enormous range of lagers yet
one of its principal products, and the one to which I
owed my loyalty, HENNINGER KAISER PILS, is a
premium lager, marketed in brown bottles so as to
protect its contents from harmful supermarket lighting.
It is full-bodied and lively, with a light hoppy flavour
and bouquet. Introduced originally to the UK by Courage it still keeps its brown bottle, which is adorned
with a stylish black and gold label. It was made available through Courage's many outlets. Even for export,

Henninger brew under all the strict regulations of the Reinheitsgebot and, although not the greatest German lager, it is very easy to drink and is refreshing, with a taste that quite simply grows on you with every fresh bottle. HENNINGER KAISER PILS is most certainly a lager you should look out for.

HENRI FUNCK PILS	Luxembourg

OG 1047° – 4.8% ABV	*Euroimpex Ltd*
Draught	
Bottles 25cl	
Cans 33cl	

Just because we used to beat Luxembourg at football by scores of 10–nil and the like (weren't those the days!) there are a lot of British people who rather ignorantly look at the little Grand Duchy and its half-million people as if it were irrelevant. They couldn't be more wrong. Like the Netherlands, it has no real heavy industry producing goods for the world, and so it settled for banking and finance instead. In this fashion, both countries have flourished and Luxembourg has one of the highest standards of living in Europe. We would do well to learn a few things from it (even soccer these days!): the art of lager brewing, for one. I've said it before, but I'll say it again, Luxembourg is among the top 10 nations of the world when it comes to consumption. So what drives so few people to drink so much? The quality of their lagers has something to do with it, so it is always nice to see one or two cross the Channel to be tested by the British palate.

In 1980 the Grand Duchy's new ambassador was HENRI FUNCK PILS, a name that doesn't exactly roll off the tongue without embarrassment after a couple

too many! The brand, manufactured by Brasseries
Réunies, and exclusively imported by Euroimpex, at
last began to show substantial signs of growth in
1988. Brewed with natural spring water from an original recipe that dates back to 1825, it is matured
under permanent temperature control for two months
before being twice filtered. HENRI FUNCK, therefore,
is a lager that should be sampled in all its forms,
though the cans and bottles are more readily available
than the draught version which, unsurprisingly, is
only housed by landlords with a discerning taste for
lager.

Perhaps the reason the Luxemburgers always lost
10–nil is because they drank so much. Well, who
wouldn't?!

HERFORDER PILS   West Germany

OG 1046–50°   *Jenks International*
Bottles 33cl

Born at Herford in 1867, the proud father being one
Brauerei-Felsenkeller, HERFORDER has remained
firmly in those hands since. Indeed, Brauerei-Felsenkeller is one of Germany's largest family-owned breweries. Herford is in northern Germany, close to many
bases of the British Armed Forces stationed there, and
therefore it is not surprising that HERFORDER came
to our shores in 1977. It has gained a considerable
reputation in the opinion of thousands of servicemen
that travel back and forth between the two countries,
and rightly so.

With a wholesome, clean character, HERFORDER
is a refreshing, full-bodied lager in the pilsner style.
For a lager in the premium sector, it is delightfully
light with a mild palate. Available only in the off-trade,

it comes in two handy pack sizes: a 3 × 33cl sleeve and a 10 × 33cl bottle case. The 10-bottle case is fitted with a sturdy cardboard handle and is therefore known in the trade as the 'suit-case', and known in my house as a 'godsend', as it is an easy way to carry your windfall of HERFORDER home. By 1988 its sales had begun to show signs of substantial, if not outstanding growth. Which is only fair, as such an admirable and impressive lager needs rewards. I encourage you all to give it a go.

HOBEC	Netherlands

OG 1048°   *Allied*
Bottles 44cl

Introduced as recently as 1986, HOBEC already enjoys national distribution and, although not one of the Netherlands' more famous lagers, it is a fine brew with nothing but success ahead of it.

For starters, I should say that HOBEC is packaged in one of the most attractive bottles on the market. A simple green, embossed, squat bottle is stoppered with an air-tight plug to keep the lager fresh when not in use, and is decorated minimally with the word Hobec in red with a white surround. Once the stopper is removed your nose is instantly greeted with a beautiful full hoppy bouquet. Extremely refreshing, this golden-coloured lager is both crisp and lively with a pleasant slightly bitter aftertaste. Indeed, overall it is a fine lager that is a must for any buff or punter. Yet although HOBEC is available nationally it is still quite difficult to get, as the majority of off-licences only stock the country's major brands in a bid to make a sizeable profit. Thus, depending on where you live and the quality of your local 'offy', a lot of you will experience some difficulty in obtaining a bottle, but don't let this put you off. Tell the off-licence manager to order some, for, I assure you, HOBEC is a quality premium lager that you should seek out and destroy.

HOFFMAN'S
UK

Guinness

Launched originally in Limerick, Ireland, in mid-1983, HOFFMAN'S is a light-coloured lager with an unnecessary amount of carbonation, which should be served very cold. This all sounds very session-lagery but, as discovered in Ireland's own expanding market for the brand, its alcohol delivery is deceptive. For all the world tasting like a session lager, and indeed a good one, HOFFMAN'S packs a little more punch. Three or four of them later and, believe you me, you'll know!

HOFMEISTER
UK

OG 1034–38°
Draught
Bottles 10fl. oz
Cans 44cl

Courage

Originally a product of the famous Henninger-Brauerei of Frankfurt AM, HOFMEISTER is yet another German brand being destroyed under licence in the UK. This time the culprits are Courage who introduced the brand in 1977 and now brew it at the Berkshire Brewery in Reading. Despite my animosity towards the brand, it evidently has a great appeal to the British lager drinking population, and in a little over a decade it has grown into one of the top five brands in Britain.

Around 15,000 outlets push annual sales up to three-quarters of a million barrels.

Even as an out and out session lager, there is not much I can find to say about the brew itself. It is weak, tastes thin, has no aroma to speak of and is highly carbonated. On a scorching hot Saturday afternoon, it can be refreshing, but then again isn't any other cold session lager? Or even lemonade, come to that? It is very frothy and in my view can only really be enjoyed when you are thirsty, and I mean desperately thirsty. HOFMEISTER was the lager laid on free of charge when I appeared as a Lager Consumer at the Bristol Power Boat race in 1983. It was *that* hot day we get every two years and, unfortunately not having any money that weekend, I had to stick to HOFMEISTER throughout the day. At its peak, the temperature soared into the low 30s (Celsius) and my head was so red that upside down I looked like a thermometer. Anyway, desperately trying to slake a man-sized thirst, I can tell you with all honesty that I drank more than *a couple of pints* of HOFMEISTER, as one does when it's free. And I was still thirsty! So, with nothing good to say about the lager, which will probably never win an award in its life, I move onto the advertising, which most definitely has.

It was in 1983 that Courage decided to make a major financial commitment to the brand and the first of the now famous and highly popular 'For Great Lager Follow the Bear' TV commercials was launched. Although initially a harrowing decision to take, Courage's huge investment began to pay dividends almost instantly as 'George, the Hofmeister Bear' commercials generated an unprecedented rise in the brand's sales. The lager is a loser with me, but the adverts and promotions? The adverts took a Silver in the Campaign Series Award at the British Television Advertising Awards in 1985 – the advertising industry's premier Oscar ceremony – and the promotions took a Gold in the 1985 Institute of Sales Promotion Awards.

Courage doubtlessly believe it is worth it and in the 1987–88 financial year they spent £5 million on TV advertising. I'm sure that in years to come their new commercials will pick up an award or two throughout the world, but as far as the lager goes ... forget it.

HOLSTEN DIAT PILS West Germany

OG 1044–50° – 5.8% ABV *Holsten Distributors Ltd*
Bottles 27.5cl
Cans 44cl

Although not the case today, Hamburg was once described as Germany's beer-house. Famed for their exports, it was the mighty brewers of this town who first realized the preservative qualities of the hop and they became pioneers in its use. In the Middle Ages the north German port had over 500 independent breweries! To this day the Holsten Brauerei is the city's major exporter, shipping its products to over 80 countries worldwide and, in this country, HOLSTEN DIAT PILS is its most famous brew. Indeed, not only famous, HOLSTEN has achieved a staggering degree of success since its introduction to the UK in 1948, and today it is the brand leader in the pils sector with 65 per cent of the market. Not only that but HOLSTEN enjoys a 33 per cent slice of the premium-packaged lager market in the on-trade and 25 per cent overall; and, lest we forget, this premium-packaged market is worth £800 million plus, and is growing at 16 per cent per annum in an overall market that's stagnating at around 39 million barrels per annum. Lager, with just over a 40 per cent share of the overall beer market, is expanding at the expense of Britain's traditional ales and stouts. Beer, that is including *everything*, accounts for 85 per cent of all alcoholic consumption in Britain, and 80 per cent of this is consumed in public houses. It could even be said that the culture of the British pub is the most dominant culture of all.

It is due to this success that HOLSTEN can spend a staggering £6 million on advertising in 1988 alone, and it is famous within the business as being one of the most consistent heavyweight spenders of them all. There's no doubt that their award-winning black-and-white Griff Rhys-Jones TV commercials, produced by the talented agency Gold, Greenless, Trott, are hugely successful, and research has proved that a good percentage of the population can recall them. Indeed, HOLSTEN has been called, and wants to be called, a 'lifestyle brand'; basically that means Perrier, Filofax, 501s, Benetton, Swatch, etc, all products indicative of the character that consumes them. But why am I telling you all this? Maybe it's because I don't think HOLSTEN is so great. Maybe it's because I think you're drinking the ads, consuming the lifestyle. Indeed, research carried out on behalf of the rival pils SATZENBRAU (q.v.), who hold a piddling 2 per cent of the pils sector, makes interesting reading. Blind tests proved that 64 per cent of those tested preferred the taste of Satzenbrau to HOLSTEN's 34 per cent. There is something about HOLSTEN that's too bitter for me, and although the taste is very dry, there's something sweet about its texture. It tastes strong, which it is, but this isn't necessarily a good thing as it certainly isn't a refreshing drink. Interestingly enough it was originally brewed for diabetics, but a lot of weight-watchers drink it in the belief that the advertising copyline of 'most of the sugar turns to alcohol' means that it is a slimming aid, but with alcohol being more fattening than sugar the high calorie count of this Diat Pils is not recommended for them. There's nothing really unpleasant about HOLSTEN, but I find it difficult to drink more than one bottle whereas the people of Britain obviously don't. In fact, there's no point in telling you what it tastes like as, judging from the statistics, it looks like you've all had a go anyway!

HOLSTEN EXPORT West Germany

OG 1044–50° *Holsten Distributors Ltd*
Draught
Bottles 64cl
Cans

The Black Knight that's visible in the red seal displayed on all the products of the Holsten Brauerei is in honour of the late Duke Adolph III of Schleswig-Holstein who, in the 12th century, conferred the brewing rights of the 'Freie und Hansestadt Hamburg' (the Free Hanseatic State of Hamburg). It was this approval that led to the city's subsequent rise to its position as one of the world's most important brewing cities, and today Holsten is the biggest German exporter to the UK. It was in Adolph's honour that the Holsten Brauerei adopted his symbol as their own and today he looks out over the brewery from the weather-vane, high above the main complex.

Although nowhere near as popular as the brewery's DIAT PILS (*q.v.*) the name itself, as well as the fact that it is available on draught, makes it a relatively popular pint. However, it should be pointed out that in early 1988, while Grand Metropolitan were renewing their existing contract with Holsten for the exclusive rights to package and distribute their Diat Pils, they also secured an agreement to allow them to brew, package and distribute HOLSTEN EXPORT in the UK until 2003. The agreement also gives Grand Met the opportunity to introduce new Holsten products – though nothing as yet has been confirmed. The last attempt to launch a Holsten product was a total failure; this was the powerful 1067–69° 'bock' type lager, Holsten Urbock, in 1985, which never achieved national distribution after its test marketing in the Granada area. It was phased out completely in 1986. HOLSTEN EXPORT, on the other hand, was launched in 1976 with some degree of success, though it was brought in primarily as a draught product. Indeed, with a full-bodied texture EXPORT is a refreshing lager in the premium sector. Personally I prefer it to the DIAT PILS and recommend that you give it a try next time you bump into it.

HURLIMANN STERNBRAU   UK

OG 1043–47°   *Shepherd Neame*
Draught
Bottles 33cl
Cans 44cl

The lagers of Hurlimann of Zurich are famous in their homeland of Switzerland for their light, dry and lively finish, and Shepherd Neame, who have brewed it under licence here in the UK since 1968, can hold their heads up proudly for capturing all the qualities of the original Continental brew. In fact Shepherd Neame are indeed proud of their lager and they've stuck religiously close to Hurlimann's pure malt and hops Swiss recipe as well as importing the original brewer's own specially cultivated yeast. Unfortunately for us, despite its 21-year life span, STERNBRAU is still only available on draught in southern England and Wales. The cans, however, have made it national and therefore I'll direct myself to those.

The can itself is an attractive package, being gold with a red band in which sits a five-pointed gold-and-white star, and it is not only the can that is gold! The lager itself is a light, golden blond with a slightly sweet and firm bouquet. Initially the lager tastes very strong, although it's only in the premium sector. It leaves a pleasantly bitter taste in the mouth for some minutes. In fact, once you've worked your way through half the can the texture of the lager seems quite heavy, and its mature, full-bodied flavour is slightly sweet. We found it to be an entertaininingly pleasant lager that we would recommend for the occasional tipple, although we're not yet decided as to how one would feel about the taste after a few. Shepherd Neame have done a good job here and it's a lager well worth looking into.

IRONHORSE MALT LIQUOR Canada

OG 1051°　　　　　　　*Continental Lager Distributors Ltd*
Bottles 34cl

Research has proved time and time again that when it comes to lager, or anything else for that matter, the average British consumer thinks that Canada and Canadians are *bor-ring!* Yet when it comes to your Aussies, down there in the desert, well they're the bee's knees – your *bona fide* lager-swilling macho-men: men that live only to drink; men that *can* drink; men that can take the heat of the dustbowl and laugh it off; men that sunbathe on the beach on Christmas Day, fer God's sake!

Let's look at Australia in another way. In that heat wouldn't you drink all day?! If we were on a beach, if we still *had* a beach, wouldn't you drink all day? I mean, what sort of dobber lives in a desert anyway when it's three or four hundred miles to the local? A big one, I'll have you know. See, many Aussies drink because they've got nothing else to do, and being long

lost Brits, they can't take the sun for longer than 10 minutes without needing a drink.

The Canucks, on the other hand, are a completely different ball game. What influences the average lager lover in favour of the Aussie when it comes to producing lager is the fact that Australia is hot and Canada is cold. But that doesn't stop your Canadian from prospecting for gold, now, does it? No way! He's hard, he can take it. Fighting grizzlies all day, driving a pack of dogs before him. Chopping down a forest before breakfast, and warding off man-eating, hunger-crazed wolves with nothing else but a pencil. Now *that's* your Canadian! He drinks because he's earned it! And that's why a lot of Canadian lagers are good, because if any self-respecting publican served up a bad one after your Canadian had earned his pint then it'd be curtains. Take your IRONHORSE MALT LIQUOR – now doesn't *that* sound like a man's pint?

It is brewed at the Old Fort Brewery at Prince George,

which is some 500 miles *north* of Vancouver in the Rockies. The nearby Mount Cariboo, with its tall Douglas Fir trees, makes Prince George an important lumberjack base. As you'd imagine, strong, quality lagers are in demand there, as they were a hundred years ago when half the world flocked up the Yukon Valley just north of there in search of gold. Tons of it! I'm sure that IRONHORSE would have pleased them all as it has a good clean bite to it; it's a strong premium beer with a firm, full body, a strong malty character and a lively finish. IRONHORSE MALT LIQUOR is certainly a refreshing change from your average Continental and we fully recommend that you give it a go. It might give some of you Aussie-idolizers a pleasant surprise.

J.K. LAGER   UK

OG 1037°   *King and Barnes*
Draught
Bottles 10fl. oz

A genuine UK lager this one, no imitations, no licences, nothing. It's the product of the small independent Sussex brewery, King and Barnes. They decided to name their lager J. K. after James King, the founder of the brewery and the great-grandfather of the present chairman. At present the brewery is turning out 3,000 barrels per annum and they claim it's the only lager currently being produced in Sussex.

King and Barnes are naturally proud to reveal that a genuine German yeast is used in the brewing, together with English 'Challenger' hops. During an impressive five-week fermentation and lagering period in new purpose-built conical fermenters and conditioning tanks, they strive to achieve an individual and well-balanced harmony between the flavours of malt, hops and yeast. Whether they succeed or not, a lot of you will never know as it's only available through King and Barnes' pubs as well as some free houses in the area. This area constitutes an approximate 50-mile radius around the town of Horsham, West Sussex. J. K. is a pleasant enough lager but it's very much a middle-of-the-road pint, however the brewery does make a fine pint of bitter based on 130 years of experience. Perhaps after an equal length of time King and Barnes' J.K. LAGER might rival some of the finest lagers in Europe ... but don't hold your breath!

JENSEN   UK

OG 1030–34°
Cans 44cl

JENSEN is another cheap insipid lager that, in my view, you should most definitely avoid. Thin, character-less and weak, this stuff really is diabolical.

JEVER   West Germany

Ruddles

JEVER is an excellent product from a subsidiary of the great Hamburg brewery Bavaria-St Pauli. It's an honour to have such a fine lager in the house, and its dry, golden, full-bodied and extremely well-hopped flavour should most certainly be sampled at the first opportunity. Well worth seeking out.

JOHN SMITH'S LAGER   UK

OG 1036°   *Courage*
Draught

Launched in Yorkshire in 1982, JOHN SMITH'S
LAGER has gradually crept into other regions of northern England, Wales, the West Country and even parts
of southern England. It's a typical session lager, only it
has a slightly more bitter aftertaste which imposes
itself somewhat unpleasantly on the palate. One thing
this brew isn't, is a great lager. Traditionally aromaless,
it's over gassy.

John Smith's should stick to bitter: after all lads,
home is where the heart is.

JUPILER   Belgium

Edwin Cheshire

The bars, brasseries and cafés of Belgium are arguably
the best-stocked bars in the world, such is the variety
of their lagers, ales, stouts, pales, bitters, etc, on sale.
The regular café brew is, of course, a pils, but exactly
which pils is entirely up to you. JUPILER is one such
pils and it enjoys huge sales throughout the country,
which is not too common with a regional Belgian
brew. Not only nationally but *internationally*, for Edwin
Cheshire now imports it into the UK. A light, well-
balanced pils with a good character, it should be
consumed on sight.

K 2	**UK**

O G 1040°–4.7% A B V	*Fuller, Smith & Turner*
Draught	
Cans 16oz	
PET Bottles 2 litres	

In 1856 Captain T. G. Montgomerie, an officer of the British Survey of India, approached the Karakorum mountain range in northern Kashmir. There, just a few miles from its base, he saw what Sir Francis Younghusband was later to describe as 'a mountain unbelievably higher than anything I had imagined'. A mountain that would later be assessed by Wilhelm Bittorf who said, 'It may resemble the Matterhorn, yet it would take forty-one Matterhorns to assemble the amount of rock from which K 2 is constructed.' Captain Montgomerie recorded the peaks, using the K of Karakorum – K1, K2, K3, etc, although K2 is also known as Godwin-Austen and 'Chogori'. One hundred and thirty years after this discovery Fuller's was to sponsor a team in their bid to conquer this legendary peak, a bid that would claim the life of Alan Rouse, a climber of great skill and determination, but not before he had stood heroically at its summit – the first Briton ever to do so.

However, some say a bad, and some say a distinctive, can design makes the product look like yet another ghastly British brew when in truth it disguises a lager inside with a full body, and we can be proud of Fuller's for creating a lager up to the German 'Purity Laws' of 1516, for this one contains nothing artificial at all. Being a standard lager, it contains no overwhelming aroma as such, but gives off a light hoppy bouquet which my wife described as 'lovely'. Indeed, K2 is a very good lager with a honey-colour, and is well-balanced leaving no unpleasant aftertaste, and it goes down the hatch very nicely. It's tasty, thirst-quenching and makes an ideal session lager.

Admittedly, it's an unusual name, though it rolls off the tongue with comparative ease. This was just one of the things Fuller's wanted to achieve that day back in 1985 when the board huddled around their table to take a unanimous vote to brew their own new lager. A brave move, for they could have licensed a foreign product, but a wise one in that it gave them exclusiveness, individuality and flexibility. And it was not until February 1986 that Fuller's decided on the name K2 to tie-in with an expedition to the peak.

Fuller's proudly market the beer as 'All British' — the can even carries a Union flag. Everything now ready, K2 was launched onto the UK market in April 1987, and the result?

Truly a great British product!

KALIBER UK

0.05% ABV *Guinness*
Bottles

The UK's second favourite low-alcohol lager (so Guinness claim) was launched in Ireland in May 1983, and within two years it was totally dominant, capturing 90 per cent of the nation's alcohol-free beer market. It was this success that tempted Guinness into the export market and in January 1985 it landed in New York, and by October it was flooding into the USA. In fact, 1985 was a good year all round for KALIBER as they also won the Gold Medal in the non-alcoholic beer category at the prestigious Monde Sélection of quality goods in Lisbon.

So in just three years KALIBER has grown to be the second most popular drink in its market, and a very close second at that. Some even see it as taking the top spot within the next two years.

It's first brewed and fully matured as a premium

quality lager, we are told, but then the alcohol is removed through a special secret vacuum evaporation process (it's worth noting at this stage of the book that nearly all the brewers of low/no-alcohol lagers seem to have a 'secret vacuum process' of some sort) which retains the full flavour and 'bite' of a premium lager. As far as the taste goes: if it were a premium lager I wouldn't drink it. It's very coarse and sweet with a foamy, unpleasant texture. Recommend you try a nice orange juice . . . or a premium lager?

KALTENBERG BRAUMEISTER   UK

OG 1035.5° – 3.6% ABV   *Boddingtons*
Draught

Boddingtons itself is already a famous name with the discerning drinkers of the UK, and therefore it should come as no surprise that they are extremely proud to be brewing their own authentic Bavarian-style lager. This is KALTENBERG BRAUMEISTER, a fine draught lager pitched at the session drinker.

The Kaltenberg Brauerei GmbH is situated in Kaltenberg Castle, Geltendorf, the ancestral home of Prince Luitpold of Bavaria, whose family ruled the state for over 700 years, until it became a republic in 1918. Needless to say, this isn't the only family of royal blood in Germany involved in brewing, as beer has been a central part of Bavarian social and political life for centuries. Bavaria is the very heart of the German brewing industry, if not the planet's, for it contains one fifth of all the world's breweries, and can even boast the highest consumption of beer per head.

Beer has been brewed at Kaltenberg Castle for hundreds of years, but until 1871 only for domestic and local use. After 1871, however, Kaltenberg's range of fine beers were at last brewed commercially. The brewery now produces seven beers, plus special brews for festivals, etc. Kaltenberg is best known in the UK, though, for KALTENBERG DIAT PILS (*q.v.*), which was introduced here in 1979 by Whitbread and rapidly rose to second position in the market. Boddingtons watched this rise with some interest, bearing in mind that the biggest sector of all in the UK beer market is draught lager and, when the time was right, they made their move. Thus, in August 1986, Boddingtons began to brew KALTENBERG BRAUMEISTER, under licence from the Prince himself, at the Higson Brewery, in Stanhope Street, Liverpool, thereby offering the drinkers of the north-west an opportunity to sample a high-quality lager with a truly royal pedigree. Within two years, despite the fact that it had only 800 outlets, BRAUMEISTER was responsible for 50 per cent of all Boddingtons' lager sales! Now that's something!

Prince Luitpold of Bavaria actually travelled to Liverpool to direct the brewing himself. KALTEN-BERG BRAUMEISTER is brewed over here to the Reinheitsgebot Bavarian 'Purity Law' of 1516, and is an excellent lager. It's when you think of all the other 1030–36° mainstream lagers on the market that you realize that BRAUMEISTER is a superb, quality lager in a market full of some very sub-standard brews.

Using local water, as well as the Czech and Bavarian aromatic hops (Saaz and Hallertau, respectively), English-blend pure barley-malt and Kaltenberg imported *fresh* yeast – the only ingredients used in the brewing – Boddingtons stick religiously to the proven Bavarian method of producing KALTENBERG. Bottom fermented, naturally, it has three separate hop infusions before low-temperature fermentation and an equally low-temperature four-week lagering period. BRAU-MEISTER is not the only draught lager brewed in Britain to the German 'Purity Laws', there is also the admirable K2 (*q.v.*) lager from Fullers, for instance. K2, however, is of a slightly higher gravity and is therefore aimed at a different market. KALTENBERG is aimed

at the session market, though the term seems somewhat derisory when applied to BRAUMEISTER.
While other lagers in this range are essentially there for
'throwing' throughout the night, BRAUMEISTER
can actually be enjoyed as a pint in its own right and,
not only that, several can be enjoyed without getting
totally plastered. Only available in the north-west, KAL-
TENBERG BRAUMEISTER must be the envy of
many lager lovers throughout the nation. Well worth
sampling – if you get the chance.

KALTENBERG DIAT PILS   West Germany

OG 1044–50° – 6.1% ABV   *Whitbread*
Bottles 27.5cl
Cans 44cl

It's a beautiful summer's day in June and the sun
burns down across the fields and mountains. Its light
cascades in shafts through branches and leaves of the
forest while a man and women walk their children and
dogs to take in the clean, fresh country air. The bird-
song is sweet and gentle and the hurried flap of their
wings is one of the only sounds as they are disturbed
intermittently by the distant pop of a hunter's shotgun.
They soon settle once more, ignoring the excited barking of the dogs as they spot an inquisitive deer who
has come to take a cautious look at the strangers in
the forest. The children's laughter and joy brings a
broad smile to the faces of their parents and, as the
father glances at his watch, he throws a final stick for
the dog and calls the children to him. It's time to make
their way back; after all, they don't want to miss the
main event of the day. Eagerly the children run on
ahead, scattering rabbits into the undergrowth with
their loud yelps of fun. Then, as the trees begin to thin
on the edges of the wood, they can see the old castle

perched on the hillside where it nestles snugly within the quiet glory of the countryside, just 30 miles from Munich. Its white walls glow in the afternoon sun and its orange-tiled roofs seem almost alive. As they draw closer to this formidable sight the sounds of shouting and laughter begin to grow in their ears, and then the fanfare of trumpets cuts through the stillness, urging them all to break into a trot lest they miss the event the trumpets herald.

In a large field close to the castle a knight takes his lance as his valet makes the final adjustments to his master's horse. Then, with another blast from the trumpets, the knight ties his loved one's scarf to his wrist and spurs his mount into action. The horse pushes itself forth on its hind legs and breaks into a swift gallop. A hundred metres away another mounted knight comes thundering towards them, his lance lowered across his body and his chest hidden behind an enormous, lion-decorated shield. Just seconds later the crowd gasps as the two knights pass each other with a loud crash and one falls heavily to the ground, his wooden lance shattered and splintered and his horse galloping on, riderless. The joust over, a cheer greets the victor as he wheels his horse around and trots over to the bandstand where he comes to a halt and presents himself to the owner of not only the castle but all the land around: Prince Luitpold von Bayern, the great grandson of Bavaria's last king, Ludwig III. This is his annual costumed joust, but it is by no means the most important event of the day, for this is the Prince's beer festival and the thousands now gathered here on his land have come to drink *his* beer.

Prince Luitpold's family has been involved in brewing for over 500 years, and so it was not surprising that he chose a career in brewing for himself. In fact, it was one of the Prince's ancestors, Wilhelm IV of Bavaria, who was responsible for introducing the famous Reinheitsgebot or 'Purity Law' to Bavaria in 1516. This law states that beer may only be brewed from barley-malt, hops and water and it is still adhered to today. Although it has been modified over the years to include wheat and yeast, it is still basically there to ensure that German brewers use only *natural* products in their brews, therefore ensuring that their beers and lagers are healthy and as nutritious and good for you as food. The result of this law is that beers of an exceptionally high quality are produced, which has made Bavaria famous throughout the world. Although Prince Luitpold produces a range of seven beers, his most famous brand in the UK is his KALTENBERG DIAT PILS, which was introduced here by Whitbread in 1979.

Kaltenberg Castle dates back to the 13th century and, although the original structure was extensively rebuilt 400 years later, it still remains a classic of Bavarian culture. Today it is Prince Luitpold's home. However, the man's extraordinary good luck doesn't end there, for within the castle he has what most men on this planet wish they had in their own living room – a brewery! This makes it almost certainly the only royal residence in the world with a commercial brewery in the cellars. I, for one, am an amazingly fluorescent green with jealousy.

Whitbreads have made KALTENBERG DIAT PILS available nationally through their own pubs and the Threshers chain of off-licences, as well as through more than 30 independent breweries. After its first decade in the UK market, KALTENBERG has established itself as the second best-selling pils in that sector with a 12 per cent share of the market and more than half of these sales are through the off-trade. Equally enjoyed by all, it is particularly favoured by diabetics, as are many pils, because of its low-carbohydrate content. Weight-watchers, however, should not be deceived by its 'Diat' label because this refers to its suitability to diabetics and not 'diets'. Alcohol is more fattening than sugar and KALTENBERG is one of the strongest pils in alcohol content on the market. KALTENBERG's share of the market is growing, and Whitbreads have gone to the trouble of organizing a number of in-depth tests in public houses up and down the land. These tests have provided them with extremely positive results, for every 'blind' test they've carried out proved that the consumer preferred the taste of KALTENBERG to the market leader, HOLSTEN (*q.v.*). Surprise, surprise! But it's difficult for anyone to compete with Holsten's massive, multi-million pound heavyweight advertising campaigns produced by the talented agency Gold, Greenless, Trott. KALTENBERG is advertised with the unfortunate copyline, 'Kaltenberg Pils in Glorious Technicolour'. What this actually means or alludes to I have no idea. Frankly, I think it's a miserable, if not disastrous campaign, showing very little imagination alongside Holsten's award-winning black-and-white Griff Rhys Jones film spoofs. Personally, I prefer the taste of KALTENBERG as, although slightly bitter, it's dry with a full, golden body and a pleasant hoppy flavour. However, until they can organize their advertising I feel they'll continue to play second fiddle.

Still, don't let this put you off. I recommend that you and a few friends try your own blind tests, for you might just be surprised at the results. No cheating, now! (Let me know how you get on, as I'm always interested in the results of independent research.)

KARLSBRAU West Germany

5.4% ABV *Majestic Wine Warehouses*
Cans

From the Karlsberg (no relation!) Brewery in Homberg, and available over here through Majestic Wine Warehouses, KARLBRAU is another lager well worth spending some time with!

Crisp and light but with a full, rich flavour (note its

ABV), and a slightly malty finish, it was one of the lagers that I most enjoyed during my tasting sessions. Well worth a visit to a Majestic Wine warehouse to stock up.

KELLERBRAU   UK

OG 1032–36°   *Charles Wells Ltd*
Draught
Bottles 27.5cl & 2-litre PET
Cans 44cl

Brewed by Charles Wells Ltd, and introduced in 1977, KELLERBRAU lager has never made it out of the shires, and today is still only available in South Wales, the Midlands and the Charles Wells area around Bedford that can be measured as roughly a 50-mile radius. As it is a session lager with nothing actually unique about it, there's no need to get in your car and drive 70 miles to hunt it out. However, for those of you determined to sample every lager contained in the book, no matter what, let me tell you what it tastes like.

Lager!

KEO   Cyprus

KEO won the gold medal at the Brewing Industry International Awards World Bottled Lager Competition held at Burton-upon-Trent in March 1987. In the 5 per cent ABV sector KEO proved itself to be a lager of distinction by beating some very stiff opposition, such as HENNIGER PILS and RED STRIPE (*qq.v.*), which finished second and third respectively. To prove to you what the award means, I'll mention that losers included ALTENMUNSTER, KALTENBERG, HARP,

SAMUEL SMITH'S, TENNENT'S (*qq.v.*), among many, many others.

A nice, light, hoppy lager with a very slightly dry character, KEO is another that comes highly recommended.

KESTREL   UK

OG 1030–34°   *Scottish & Newcastle*
Draught
Cans 44cl
PET Bottles 2 litres

I've never liked KESTREL since its introduction to the market, nationwide, in 1979. It's thin and gassy, with no overall aroma or flavour to speak of. Scottish and Newcastle, however, will do anything to encourage you to drink it – they'll give you free cans, woolly scarves and even motor cars (that is, of course, if you can manage to drink enough of the stuff). Being a session lager is no excuse for not being a lager of quality. KESTREL simply just ain't good enough, and if it's a session lager you're after then there are plenty of much better ones around for you to spend your money on, which is what I suggest you do.

Then again, someone must drink it to keep them in business. I only hope it isn't you!

KESTREL in a nutshell: cheap!

KESTREL SUPERSTRENGTH   UK

OG 1080–88°   *Scottish & Newcastle*
Cans 44cl

Heavy, sticky and difficult to drink, as are most lagers of this strength, KESTREL SUPERSTRENGTH is new to the battleground, making its début in the latter half of 1987. Fortunately, it has a distribution network already established by its sister brew, the session lager KESTREL (*q.v.*). As opposed to progressing from session to standard, standard to premium, premium to super-strength in marketing strategy, *à la* Harp, Scottish and Newcastle have done it in one giant bound. Being so strong, KESTREL SUPERSTRENGTH will have its fans, though as competition in that market gets increasingly fierce, it's going to be difficult for many super-strengths to survive. However, although I don't think this brand will ever challenge the supremacy of the formidable CARLSBERG SPECIAL BREW (*q.v.*), I believe it will survive – if only because of its aforementioned sales network. As far as the taste goes, I do recommend that you give it a try, not that I believe you'll be pleasantly surprised, but because it is new to the market and to ignore it would be ignorant. For those of you put off by its unpalatable sister, just remember that it is the *complete* opposite!

KINGFISHER INDIAN BRAND LAGER
India

OG Draught – 1034°   *United Breweries International*
Bottles 33cl – 1047°

When the British marched into India and made it part of the Empire, they called it the Jewel in the Crown. The British, of course, have long since gone but the phrase remains. However, it no longer has the original meaning. Today the 'jewel' refers to India's breweries! One of these, United Breweries, is situated in the south of the giant sub-continent at Bangalore, and was founded in 1857. Although India's brewing history is relatively short by world standards, it must be remembered that the British not only took their guns when they set out on their quest for conquest, but they also took their brewing knowledge. It's all very well to talk about *tea* and all that 'Mad dogs and Englishmen' stuff, but when it comes down to it we all know that the Englishman likes his beer. When you begin to think about the ferocious heat of Hindustan, the flies, dust, and hour upon hour with nothing to do but boss other people about, then 'drink' becomes 'drinks' and breweries were born to cope with the demand. Thus, although today India's breweries are Indian owned, their heritage is deeply interwoven with our own.

Draught KINGFISHER INDIAN BRAND LAGER is the session lager of Bangalore. Born of the British Raj, it comes to us, however, in two strengths, with the bottled variety being much the stronger. This is because the bottles are imported, whereas the draught is now brewed here by the extremely competent Shepherd Neame group. The draught is very much a session lager, and as such, it is very light with a high degree of carbonation. A pleasant pint, it is leisurely sweet with a hint of hops.

The bottled variety, however, is a much more qualified brew altogether. Brewed in India using imported American malt and hops, it is fermented over a healthy two-month period in the traditional style, giving it a very pleasant and light body. This is surprising, considering that it's in the premium lager range with very much a premium lager strength. With a sweet bouquet, it is smooth and its strength is hidden subtly by a very palatable hoppy flavour that gives the lager much character. It does leave a slightly bitter aftertaste, but this is in no way unpleasant and does not reflect badly on a lager that can be described overall as mellow.

Naturally, KINGFISHER is the perfect choice to complement a complete range of spicy Indian cuisine. For vindaloo I recommend the draught – several times! However, I should point out that you don't always have to consume it just with Indian food as it is now available in many pubs and bars.

Since its launch here in 1983, KINGFISHER has quickly established itself nationwide, and by August 1988 was turning over just over three-quarters of a million pounds. Not bad considering it isn't advertised at all. There aren't that many Indian lagers available in the UK, and so given the chance you should sample them all. After all, it was our great-granddads that started it all in the first place, so now it's our turn to finish it! Several pints of it!

KINGFISHER PILS LAGER   India

OG 5.6% ABV   *United Breweries International*
Bottles 33cl

Another in the Kingfisher range from Bangalore's United Breweries International group and also marginally the strongest. Slightly darker than KINGFISHER INDIAN BRAND LAGER and KINGFISHER STRONG LAGER (*qq.v.*), KINGFISHER PILS LAGER has a very distinct sweet aroma. Heavier than the other two, it is both over-gassy and unpleasantly sticky, leaving an aftertaste somewhat akin to the one you get after licking 2,304 Royal Mail postage stamps. So I'm afraid Kingfisher haven't quite made the hat-trick. I enjoyed their other fine brands, but PILS LAGER didn't go down that well and I didn't like it, vindaloo or not. Oh well, two out of three isn't bad.

KINGFISHER STRONG LAGER   UK

OG 1043–47°   *United Breweries International*
Bottles

Sweeter, sharper and fresher than KINGFISHER INDIAN BRAND (*q.v.*) STRONG LAGER is also brewed in the UK although it is not available on draught. Very pale, it might be called 'strong' but the taste is extremely light and the carbonation a lot higher. Its major outlet is through the restaurant trade where it is very popular. It is not hard to find as there are Indian restaurants in every part of the country now, and quite rightly so! This brew is also recommended with your vindaloo.

KIRIN

Japan

OG 1043–47°

Marblehead

Bottles 33cl

Producing in the region of 25 million hectolitres of beer per annum, Kirin is the largest brewer outside America and the third largest in the whole world. Now, I wouldn't blame you for questioning the Orientals' ability to brew a quality lager that would be appreciated in the West as their tastes and customs, in fact their whole way of life, is completely different to our own. Yet you should remember the Japanese efficiency, dedication and competitiveness in all things. Thus, when they discovered lager beer they went about it with their traditional zeal. Although it was an American company which started their first brewery as an experiment in 1869 it wasn't long before the Japanese government sent a researcher to Germany to discover their methods and absorb their knowledge. By 1888 the Japanese were confident enough to go it alone and they took over the American's brewery and renamed it the Kirin Brewing Company.

The Kirin, which is not only the name of the brewery but also the trademark, is an imaginary animal that's half-dragon and half-horse, and it dates back thousands of years in Japanese folklore and mythology. It's this mythology that claims that the Kirin appeared before a Chinese peasant woman about 2,500 years ago, and stayed with her for two nights. Some time after this the woman gave birth to Confucius. According to legend, the Kirin puts in an appearance before the birth of great men and virtuous rulers to this very day. The symbol of good luck and happiness, the Kirin appears on the labels of all the company's products, and therefore makes each bottle the harbinger of happy events to come, and with KIRIN LAGER it works.

KIRIN is without doubt the premier Japanese lager

and, accounting for somewhere in the region of two-thirds of all sales in its home market, it puts all its rivals in the shade. A lager beer in the pilsner style, it uses Hallertau and Saaz hops and, as a result, has a rich hoppy bouquet as well as taste, and a full, firm body that gives it a certain robust quality that can be enjoyed almost anywhere and not just with your Friday night *sushi*. Try one at home and see.

KONIG PILSENER   UK

OG 1047–51°   *Tennent*
Draught
Bottles

A mighty lager from Tennent's that is unfortunately only available in Scotland. Slightly stronger than TEN-NENT'S EXTRA (*q.v.*), KONIG is a beautiful, full-bodied, slightly sweet-tasting lager that goes down very nicely. Well worth drinking if you live in Scotland, and well worth looking out for if you're just passing through.

KROMBACHER PILS LAGER   West Germany

Bottles 33cl   *Longmans Distribution Ltd*

KROMBACHER PILS is a typical pils, in as much as it has a dryish, smooth, pleasantly hoppy flavour, and a slightly bitter aftertaste. It is imported by the Long-mans Distribution Company of London, and I feel it could do pretty well nationally in the already crowded pils market place, were it to receive a marketing push.

Not widely available, KROMBACHER is well worth sampling, and comes highly recommended to 'pils' drinkers.

KRONENBOURG 1664

France & UK

Harp Lager Co.

OG 1043–49° Draught
    1043–49° 44cl cans
    1060° 33cl Bottles (France)

I was surprised to discover that draught KRONEN-BOURG was only introduced to the UK by Courage in September 1984, and even then only on a regional basis, as I seem to remember it from my teenage days, but I must be thinking of the original French bottled version. Courage brew their version under licence and within five years it is not only available nationally, but it has become one of the UK's leading premium lagers. This tremendous surge of interest in such a short period of time was doubtless helped not only by its quality, which always receives word-of-mouth recommendations, but also by an advertising campaign which picked up three awards.

KRONENBOURG is France's largest, most famous brewery, and was established in Strasbourg by the Hatt family over 300 years ago in 1664. Also founded, interestingly enough, in 1664 were the British Royal Marines, and it was this link that encouraged KRONENBOURG to sponsor the Marines' free-fall parachute display team. However, it is only the bottled version of KRONENBOURG that now comes to our shores from France; the cans and draught are produced here. The French KRONENBOURG is certainly dry with a light bouquet and a relatively fruity flavour that is actually quite pleasant. Unfortunately it is also rather sticky, which is really only to be expected in a lager of this strength. However, there is nothing unpleasant about it, and if served well chilled, it's a fine, strong lager. I must emphasize 'chilled' here because once the chill begins to wear off the taste does begin to change and rather more unpleasant qualities become evident, such as stickiness and a slightly bitter aftertaste. I like it, but once I open one I avoid allowing it to warm by consuming it at a fair old lick, which is what I recommend you do! But not too many – it's certainly a potent little brew.

The British version, if served under the right conditions, is as enjoyable as the original. It is not quite as strong but, believe me, it's strong enough! KRONENBOURG 1664 draught and cans are placed in the premium lager sector which enjoyed a 23 per cent expansion in 1987, making it the fastest-growing sector of the market. In the same year sales of KRONENBOURG draught and cans increased by an impressive 24 per cent. Considering its weight, it is actually quite a smooth drink, and its rich, full body retains some of the sweet fruity qualities which make the original so popular. It is enjoyed by millions throughout the country, so you'd be daft not to find out what all the fuss is about. Get your cheque book out and join in.

LABATT UK

OG 1035° Draught *Greenhall Whitley*
1045–48° Cans

LABATT is originally from Canada, where it was founded by the Irishman, John Kinder Labatt, in 1853 in London, Ontario. It is the Canadians' number one lager and, on February 1st 1988, the first pints of draught LABATT were pulled and supped in the UK. Initially it was only available in the north and Midlands through Greenhall's 1,600 outlets. It is brewed at their Warrington plant. How it will fare, only time will tell, but I don't think it will ever achieve the sort of success it enjoys in its homeland where it outsells its nearest competitor by a remarkable 2 to 1.

The reason why LABATT is sold in two strengths, we're informed, is because Greenhalls believe this strategy will enable them to sell into each region in gradual progression, and therefore, hopefully, LABATT will become one of the country's top five national brands within five years, and then the UK's leading brand, and then the *leading lager in the world! CRIKEY!*

To back up the launch there was a heavyweight advertising campaign launched in the initial sales region; if the equivalent had been spent at a national level it would be in the region of a huge £6.5 million. Now that's a lot when one remembers that the brewers of the UK spent £65 million on advertising in 1987. But the advertising, no matter how much there is of it, has to be *right*. The British drinker is acutely sensitive about the origins of his pint and if the advertising projects the wrong image of those origins it has a pretty good chance of stifling the brand at birth, *à la* BUDWEISER (*q.v.*).

The agency for LABATT is Abbott Mead Vickers, famous in the industry for researching ideas to death. Apparently, instead of just being given to one creative team, which is standard, AMV handed out LABATT to virtually every creative team at their disposal.

Well, in the end, they came up with 'Malcolm the Mountie'. Malcolm is a fine old name, to be sure, but 'Malcolm the Mountie' – I personally think they would have been hard pushed to have come up with a more clichéd image of a Canadian drinker. Remember, many Brits, and more to the point, British lager drinkers, unjustly think Canada is *boring*! 'Malcolm the Mountie' apparently 'always gets his can', but will Brits bother? How long will the campaign last? I don't know, but I wouldn't be suprised if LABATT ended up with an image problem the size of Budweiser's.

Anyway, May 1988 saw Labatt Brewing UK take its second step in world domination when they appointed J. W. Cameron to distribute LABATT throughout their outlets in the north-east. In the south the deal went to Eldridge, Pope. By June S. A. Brain, the admirable Cardiff-based family brewer, agreed to distribute LABATT in South Wales, as well as the Bristol area, and July saw the Suffolk brewery, Tolly Cobbold, sign an agreement to sell the lager in East Anglia. These five regional partnerships opened up nine different areas of the UK market for LABATT within four months of its launch.

The lager itself is a little fluffy for my liking, although it is fresh with a clean, congenial flavour. Smooth and easy to drink, it is indeed an above-average lager that deserves to do well, but whether it will or not remains to be seen. Give it a try and get your can *now!*

LA CHOULETTE   France

OG 1065–68°   *Applejack Trading Co.*
Bottles 75cl, cork-stoppered

This one was a relatively late entry to the book, and I've got my suspicions that it's not, in fact, a lager (a bottom-fermented beer), but the suppliers assure me it is, so here goes!

From a small family brewery in the Haiaut region of Northern France comes LA CHOULETTE, which is a traditional, full-bodied dark brew. It is made with highly-roasted malt which gives it its depth of colour and a rich, almost caramel flavour.

LA CHOULETTE is described as a bottle-conditioned lager which has been filtered but which may still throw a slight deposit. As it is bottle-conditioned the contents will continue to work in the bottle for some time and will improve with age, almost like a wine. Its final strength should end up somewhere around the 7 per cent alcohol by volume measure. The end result is a drink of quality for the discerning lover of lager. Is that you? Why not try a bottle and find out?

LAMOT PILS   UK

OG 1043–47°   *Bass*
Bottles
Cans

Darker than the draught LAMOT STRONG LAGER (*q.v.*),
PILS has a slightly sweet bouquet, a full body, and a
typically dryish taste.

On the whole not bad at all, but not one of my
favourite pils on the market.

LAMOT STRONG LAGER   UK

OG 1045–49°   *Bass*
Draught

LAMOT STRONG LAGER is brewed in the UK
by Bass, though from what I can remember from my
time spent in Belgium, it's a pretty well-known name
over there.

The advertising copyline is 'Seek out the lager of
Lamot', so I did! Eventually I found it at the Samuel
Pepys pub in Mayfair.

It's not a bad drink at all. Available only on
draught in south-east England, it's got a good hoppy
nose and a nice golden colour. Smooth and slightly
hoppy with a pleasant aftertaste, it's well worth seeking out!

LCL PILS   UK

OG 1034–38°   *Federation Brewery*
Draught
Bottles 27.5cl & 33cl
Cans 44cl

Voted Supreme Overall Champion at the Brewing Industry International Awards World Bottled Lager Competition for the best lager in the range of 1030–40°.
Twenty-eight breweries from 13 different countries
entered 45 lagers in this competition, only to be
thrashed into insignificance by this plucky north-east-
ern lager from the working-men's Federation Brewery.
Naturally, its promotional material now carries the
copyline 'The Best Bottled Lager in the World'. Knowing this, I was eager to sample it – wouldn't you have
been?

Let's start at the beginning. The Federation Brewery
seems famous not only for its proud, working-men's
heritage, but also for its virtually unrivalled bad taste in
graphics, as LCL PILS' ugly green can, nobly wearing
its gold medal, proves. This is enough to put you off, but
please, please don't let it. Inside is a light-coloured pils
with an unusually sweet, manure-like bouquet. Despite
its 5 per cent alcohol by volume measure, it is im-
pressively smooth and goes down very well. It is surprisingly light and, if one were blindfolded, this characteristic might well make one think that it's far weaker in
alcohol than it actually is. It's definitely the best lager
from the Federation's portfolio and is highly recommended for parties, pubs and picnics, as well as just a
quiet drink on your own with the TV. Dry and lightly
carbonated, LCL PILS is an excellent brew and one
you should definitely sample. Cheers! Here's to a great
British lager!

J. W. LEES DIAT PILS   UK

OG 1048°   *J. W. Lees & Co.*
Bottles
Cans
Available only in the Manchester/North Wales areas
this one from Lees is a relatively hoppy lager and was
only introduced to lager land in 1980. It's a good pils
with a very short history, and you're advised to look
into it further.

LINDENER LAGER   West Germany

OG 1030–34°   *Baron von Ritter*
Cans 44cl

Brewed and canned by Lindener Gilde-Brau AG of
Hanover, LINDENER LAGER is another natural
German brew – in its importers words it is 'additive
and preservative free'.

It is certainly full-tasting and slightly sharp, and its
body certainly belies its original gravity.

All in all, not a bad lager, though I feel personally
that a bottled version might be even better. Now there's
a statement that's going to get me crucified by many of
the world's brewers!

To sum up LINDENER LAGER, then, it's a very
palatable drink that you could enjoy all night without
falling over, and I hope you do ... enjoy it, that is.
If only more British-brewed session lagers were like
this.

LINDENER SPEZIAL West Germany

OG 1049° *Baron von Ritter*
Cans

Another admirable product from the Lindener Gilde-Brau AG, based in Hannover. LINDENER SPEZIAL is a fair bit stronger in alcohol than its sister brew LINDENER LAGER (*q.v.*), and shows it initially in its deeper, more golden colour. Rich in taste, and with a nice bite to it, it's a good smooth lager that goes down easily.

LION South Africa

OG 1044° *Continental Lager Disbributors Ltd*
Bottles 34cl

A little dark and ale-like for my taste, LION, produced by the huge South African Breweries company, is nevertheless a sweetish lager that I'm sure will find supporters in this country. We can again thank Continental Lager Distributors for bringing it to our attention, palates and bellies. Well worth trying if your conscience lets you.

LONE STAR USA

OG 1042° *Associated British Liquor Distributors*
Bottles 35.5cl
Cans

Brewed by G. Heileman Brewing Company (now a part of the huge Bond International Brewing Company) in San Antonio, USA, LONE STAR has long been known

as 'the national beer of Texas'. It was first brewed in
1940 by one Peter Kreill, a German graduate of the
Weilhenstephan Brewers Academy in Texas.

Although only available in the UK in the standard
bottle and canned form, the Lone Star Brewery has also
developed a glass can (yup, really!), that I'm sure will be
most welcome in specialist bars throughout the country.

Served well chilled (they recommend 40°F) LONE
STAR is indeed a most enjoyable drink. Light, spritzy
and slightly sweet, it is well worth your time. *YEEE-
HA!* Round 'em up, Joe!

LONG LIFE   UK

Cans   *Allied*

Apparently the first beer (it was only renamed 'Lager'
recently – I wonder why?) that was brewed for the
can, for the fridge. Personally I don't like it! It is thin
and weak tasting, and there are many other real lagers
available that you should stock *your* fridge with.

LOWENBRAU PILS   UK

OG 1045–49° – 6% ABV   *Allied*
Bottles
Cans 44cl

Allied take-home switched production of its LOWEN-
BRAU PILS brand from West Germany to Wales in
the summer of 1988. New cans were introduced which
excluded most references to either Germany or to the
brand's German heritage. By brewing it in Wales,
Allied's managing director pointed out that it gives
them 'more flexible control over production'. But

whether this meant quantity-wise or quality-wise, it was not made clear. The original German-brewed LOWENBRAU PILS has won eight gold medals – ranging from Antwerp in 1885 to Brussels in 1958. These gold medals have been retained in a way, on the new can design, though they are now basically gold circles containing barley, hops, mash tuns and German steins. While you may think this practice to be a little unethical, it's downright honest compared with the way that the canned HEINEKEN (*q.v.*), which is brewed in this country, displays the many medals won by its Netherlands-brewed namesake. And that's about all it is, a namesake.

But what is LOWENBRAU DIAT PILS like? It is a light yellow, almost blond straw colour, and has a deceptively light, sweet bouquet with a trace of hops. Sharp and initially spritzy, it's a little sweet tasting and leaves a lingering, bitter aftertaste, though this certainly isn't unpleasant. LOWENBRAU's strength is clearly evident, but the initial 'bite', nice as it is, and its slightly foamy texture, prevent it from going down as smoothly as it might. Now that the water used in the brewing process has been changed, it doesn't seem to be quite as clean as the traditional German brew.

Still, for all I've said, it's certainly not unpleasant, and it's one that I might just buy ahead of the other pils on the market. Not bad at all.

LOWENBRAU SPECIAL EXPORT

West Germany

OG 1052°	*Allied*
Bottles	

Now this one has been around for a long time – ever since I was tall enough to peer over a bar!

In its distinctive foil-topped green bottle with the pale blue label, LOWENBRAU SPECIAL EXPORT is the real McCoy in as much that it is brewed and packaged in Munich before being lovingly consumed over here.

Light, hoppy and spritzy, its taste belies the hefty original gravity of 1052°. So be careful! A lovely little lager that in our view makes for ideal summer drinking! Recommendation: your round!

LOWENBRAU STRONG LAGER	Wales
OG 1044–50° – 5% ABV	*Allied*
Draught	
Bottles	
Cans	

Probably the most famous of the Munich breweries. Lowenbrau has a huge beer garden which 10,000 people can squeeze into on a crowded day. Although not the city's largest brewer it exports at least a quarter of all it produces and Lowenbrau is one of America's favourite imported brands – although it should be noted that the Lowenbrau generally available in the United States tastes distinctly different from that available in Germany.

Since its launch in 1987 the Welsh-produced version of LOWENBRAU STRONG LAGER has 'surpassed all expectations', as far as Allied are concerned. It has a pleasant, light golden colour with a slightly sweet, lightly hopped bouquet, topped off by an attractive, frothy head. Dry, with a distinctive malty flavour, it leaves a not unpleasant mildly bitter aftertaste. Not over carbonated, LOWENBRAU STRONG wins with a smooth texture and it has a definite premium quality that's a pleasure to drink. It has a good, firm character with a bite significant enough to slake a mighty thirst. This is one not to turn your nose up at when offered. I would certainly drink it quite happily, were it offered to me! (Case in the post, please, to *Daft About Lager*, Sphere Books Ltd, etc.)

MACCABEE   Israel

O G 1047°   *Continental Lager Distributors Ltd*
Bottles

Kosher lager? MACCABEE is all on its own, being the only Israeli lager in the book.

Though currently available in a small dumpy bottle, as are many French and Belgian lagers, it is soon to be relaunched in a more elegant, slim, foil-topped bottle.

When it was first brewed MACCABEE was based on the American BUDWEISER (*q.v.*). Now, though, it has gone its own way. It has a rich golden colour and a full body that goes down well.

The Maccabee Brewery was taken over a couple of years ago by the huge Tempo Industries. This certainly doesn't seem to have impeded the quality of the brew, and indeed, with the new packaging and financial muscle behind it, I can see MACCABEE receiving a major sales push worldwide in the near future. And why not? It's a pretty good lager.

MAES PILS   Belgium

Bottles

Cooled in open vats with a painstakingly slow, chilled fermentation period, MAES is a fine Belgian lager still faithful to the pilsner tradition in as much as the brewers use as many Saaz hops as possible. The result of this three-month lagering period is a gentle, medium-dry, slightly fluffy lager with a distinctive hoppy flavour that is both appetizing and pleasing to the palate. As a principal beer in Belgium, a country renowned the world over for its pride in its beers, it should be welcomed to our shores enthusiastically. Highly recommended.

MALT MASTER LAGER   UK

OG 1030–34°
Cans

Yet more cheapo lager-flavoured water to avoid at your local supermarket. With the familiar low original gravity, this one is apparently brewed with the 'finest English barley and hops'. Well, I don't know if it's the water they're using or what, but basically something's gone wrong! To be avoided . . .

MARKSMAN   UK

OG 1039°   *Mansfield Brewery*
Draught
PET Bottles
Cans 16oz

Well, lager lovers, ever fancied a journey on British Rail? No? Is it the thought of the two dozen unpopular brands of lager they stock that'll accompany you throughout your journey? I can imagine many of you screaming 'Yes!' However, British Rail actually seem to have made efforts in this area of customer service in the last couple of years. Indeed, amongst others, they now sell GROLSCH (*q.v.*) . . . well, that's not bad! Anyway, get yourself a ticket to Mansfield – return, you certainly shouldn't drive home! – or anywhere else between the boundaries of Hull, Leicester and Lincoln.

On arrival at your destination, you can sample the dynamically named MARKSMAN lager. But why all the expense of train tickets and the hours of lost drinking time? Simple: MARKSMAN is only available in the Mansfield Brewery trading area, the dimensions of which I've listed above.

Is it worth the effort? *Pfff!* Isn't a drink always worth the effort? Seriously though, without national distribution there's no other way you'll get to taste the stuff unless Mohammed goes to the mountain. So when you're in the area why not take time off from the 'usual' and discover the delights of what your fellow countrymen have been keeping to themselves all this time? After all, you know as well as I do, it's not just the bitter man that can enjoy the produce of hundreds of small breweries throughout the length and breadth of the land, for those very same breweries more often than not create their own bottom-fermented lagers as well these days. Thus, in the words of ye balding pale one, with the in-set dark eyes. 'Lagermen of England, *get on yer bike!*' With MARKSMAN it's well worth it: a lively, hoppy-nosed little lager that's certainly worth a try.

MARKSMAN EXPORT UK

OG 1045°   *Mansfield Brewery*
Draught
Bottles

An interestingly named lager, this one. After all, my research tells me that, like its sister brew, MARKSMAN LAGER (*q.v.*), this slightly stronger tipple is also only available in the Mansfield Brewery trading area. This may seem unusual for a self-proclaimed EXPORT lager; however, those of you that have ploughed your way through the whole book will know that 'export' is a tag that many brewers add to a product that is stronger in alcohol than their standard brews.

Regarding what I've said about its sister brew, while you're in the area you should give it a whirl. I mean, it'd be pretty daft to take my advice about MARKSMAN and then not sample the entire range while you're at it. This one won't let you down either. While retaining the light and hoppy qualities of MARKSMAN, EXPORT has a little more bite to it. Well worth seeking out on your forays into the lager-producing regions of old England! Remember, as the great man said, 'One pound eighty in the hand is worth two in the pub!'

MARSTON'S PILSENER LAGER UK

OG 1036–40° *Marston, Thompson & Evershed*
Draught

Introduced to the market in 1977 as Marston's Pilsener Lagerbier (the bier was dropped from the title in 1987), this is a fully developed British lager from the much respected brewers Marston, Thompson and Evershed, of Burton-on-Trent.

Only brewed at Marston's brewery, it is generally available in the Midlands and North Wales, although it is delivered as far north as Penrith, and also as far away as Southampton in the south.

As you can see from its original gravity, MARSTON'S PILSENER is a mite stronger than many domestic lagers, and this is reflected in its fuller body and richer taste.

To sum it up, MARSTON'S PILSENER is a superior domestic lager that's well worth sampling. However, as it's by no means available nationally, you might have to get on your bike again to find it! Happy cycling . . .

MARY ANNE JUBILEE PILS   Channel Islands

OG 1061°
Draught
Bottles (half-pint)

Little is known about this strong Channel Islands brew except by legend, and not the legend of gods either, but those of returning holiday makers stunned by a few pints of what they expected to be yet another 'session' lager. Wrong!

This is one of the strongest lagers available on draught and should therefore be treated with some respect. As you might expect, it's a little heavy and sweet, but nevertheless goes down a treat! You've been warned! It's not all yellow water in the Channel Islands!

To sum up then, MARY ANNE JUBILEE PILS is a competent lager that I feel would do well in the UK market were it distributed by a major company. However, its high quality is due to its exclusivity for it's that small brewery mentality of pride in the product that makes it an exceptional little lager well worth trying . . . in moderation!

MAVERICK   Belgium

5% ABV
Cans 440ml

A full-tasting, well-hopped golden lager that produces a fine head when poured from the can. With a smooth texture, and a slightly bitter, but by no means unpleasant, aftertaste, it comes recommended.

MAYFIELD LAGER   UK

OG 1030–34°   *Batleys Wines*
Cans
PET Bottles

This is brewed somewhere in Blighty (sounds ominous!), and is supplied by Batleys Wines of Huddersfield.

Available in cans and PET bottles and with an original gravity of 1030–34°, it's again a lager that you should, depending on your tastes, either look out for or avoid.

MAYFIELD PILS   UK

5% ABV   *Batleys Wines*

Ah! The great unavailable MAYFIELD PILS! Unavailable, that is, to me, because I live a life of sumptuous luxury in the most expensive part of London, where it's not available, and also because the suppliers were unable to send me a case. Shame!

So what can I tell you about it? Not much, I'm afraid, apart from the fact that it's got an ABV of 5%. Well, that's not bad, but what does it taste like? I'm afraid you'll have to tell me that one! Answers on a postcard to Sphere Books, 27 Wrights Lane, London W8 5TZ.

McEWAN'S LAGER   UK

Draught   *Scottish & Newcastle*
Cans

Like all good things, and bad things come to that,

there is some discussion as to who was first in the UK when it comes to lager. Was it Scotland? Or was it Wales? And does it matter? Yes, of course it does! But, as clear documentation is not available as to the answer it's probably best simply to press on with the point that I intended to make in the first place, which is that the Scots have been enjoying lager for a lot longer than those of us living south of the border (but not necessarily west of it!) and should therefore know a little more than us Anglos. The Scots know what their favourite lager is (and it's not McEwan's!), but one thing is crystal clear: McEwan's need to learn a thing or two about describing their product.

There were two weeks in May 1988 when nobody knew whether McEWAN'S was lemonade or alcohol! 'No', you might protest. 'We all know it's beer!' Well, *we* might know, but the *law* doesn't! What am I going on about? Sit back, crack open a can of McEWAN'S pop/lager . . . and read on.

Two cases in as many weeks were dismissed by the Dundee Sheriff's Court when the Crown found itself in a position where it could not establish that the contents of a can of McEWAN'S were alcoholic. The Sheriff ruled that because a can of the tartan lager didn't carry a full description of the alcoholic content by volume, there was no evidence that the lager was alcoholic! I mean, come on! You'd think the daft old legal gentleman would've just drunk the stuff, then he would have known! But no, and when the procurator fiscal asked the prosecuting cop if he knew the lager he mumbled that he did but he wouldn't touch the stuff! It was at this point that the solicitor for the accused, a Mr Ul-Haq of Dundee who'd sold two cans of it to a minor, pointed out that legislation ruled that if the container didn't carry a full description, including the percentage point of the alcohol, or an analysis of the contents, then the accused must be aquitted. Which the Sheriff duly obliged by doing. Thus, for Mr Ul-Haq and his mates it looks like there's a killing to be made.

After all, at less than a quid a can virtually any five-year-old and up can afford one! It's no wonder the Scots know more about lager than we do! Aye, it's been said before and it'll be said again: there's many a strange story in your lager.

Pop or not, McEWAN'S is still a firm favourite with many a punter both north and south of the divide – as well as west – though its stronghold in draught form is most definitely in Scotland and the north-east. It's no silly gimmick that has drawn the punters in as it has been firmly established on the market for several years. Not that that would stop them giving away *something*! Let's face it, they all do, and Scottish and Newcastle are no different with McEWAN'S LAGER. For instance, in February/March of 1988 the simple purchase of a 12-pack would earn you a *free* pop-video at the point-of-sale. Thus we can see once again at which market the on- and off-sales trade is aimed – the 18–30 age group. And why not? It's nothing to be ashamed of. After all it is *business*, and it's a long time since the large breweries would brew anything for pride alone.

'But what about the lager itself?' I hear you say. Well, it's not bad, and is certainly preferable to many on the market. Not one of my personal favourites by any means, but it's a good honest pint produced by a company with a fine brewing tradition. Lightly carbonated and therefore relatively easy to drink, it's . . . well, it's not bad!

METEOR PILS   France

OG 1047°   *Majestic Wine Warehouses*
Bottles

From the Alsace region of France, as are many great

lagers, METEOR is brought to us by Majestic Wine Warehouses, who certainly know their wine. They're not doing so badly with lager either, as METEOR is a pleasant drink. Produced by the Brasserie Meteor, in Hochfelden, this lager has a rich dark colour, and a beautifully full, hoppy nose.

With its smooth, malty, and slightly fruity flavour, METEOR is highly recommended.

MICHELOB	USA

| OG 1049° – 5% ABV | GB Vintagers/ |
| Bottles 33cl | Global Beer Co. Ltd |

Some say the name MICHELOB was 'adopted' by Adolphus Busch (the Busch in Anheuser–Busch) in 1896, from the town of the same name in Bohemia – in much the same way, some people claim, that he took the name BUDWEISER (*q.v.*) – for his own American brew 20 years earlier. However, where the original Czech Budweiser had been famed since 1531 for its popularity in the Czech court of King Ferdinand, the MICHELOB brew was named after the home of the great Viennese brewer Anton Dreher, who by the mid-1800s owned one of the biggest breweries in the then Austro-Hungarian Empire, being second only to that at the now 'holy' town of Pilsen. Therefore, knowing that it had such historical ties, the British public looked forward to MICHELOB's launch with mouth-watering anticipation, which was finally fulfilled when it was introduced to the UK in 1985. It became available nationwide shortly after.

MICHELOB, like most American beers, offers a refreshingly different taste from the more traditionally produced lager that we're used to, in that it uses ingredients which would no doubt shock the average

British punter, were they more widely known! For instance, although many American beers have corn as a basic ingredient MICHELOB, along with other Anheuser-Busch brews, uses rice! In fact it's the 25 per cent proportion of rice in MICHELOB that gives it its very light colour as well as its delicate flavour and snappy bite. Its sweet aroma and palate are produced by a complex blend of at least eight different strains of hops – and they are *real* hops, as opposed to a hop-extract. These two principal influences, along with the now famous fining over beechwood which the Americans claim imparts a clean character, and a fermentation period of between 32–40 days, all add up to produce a very delicate but full-bodied, extremely drinkable lager beer. And so it should be as MICHELOB is promoted as Anheuser-Busch's prestige, 'super-premium' beer, where the discerning drinker will find that the additional strength produces more flavour and character. Popular in America, there is no reason why it shouldn't achieve some success in this country despite the stubbornness of Britain's lager drinkers who seem to me to be more obsessed with some sort of brand-loyalty death-wish than the desire to experiment and enjoy the God-given lagers of the world. To the guilty among you who read this book, I suggest you stop me and buy one (I mean buy *me* one – and one for yourself too): if you don't like it then what've you lost? Go on, it's better than Budweiser and at least it's brewed in the land of the free!

MILLER LITE   UK

OG 1030–34°   *Courage*
Draught
Cans 440ml

Brewed under licence in Berkshire from Miller of the

USA, by Courage, MILLER LITE, we are told, is the result of a special brewing process in which most of the sugar turns to alcohol. Now I've heard that somewhere before!

This *special brewing process* 'creates a clean, light product which consumers describe as smooth and easy to drink'. Hmmm? Where do they find these consumers?

Anyway, it was launched in the States in 1973, and claims now to be the second best-selling lager. No guesses as to who number one is! MILLER LITE was therefore one of the first 'lites' to appear in America. There are now many of them, including 'Bud Lite' which I'm sure will be appearing over here some time in the future – though hopefully not with the tedious and much abused bull terrier Spuds McKenzie.

Anyway, to put it in a nutshell, MILLER LITE is a flimsy, weak-tasting lager of little character that's certainly not recommended.

MOLSON Canada

OG 1045–51°	*Molson Breweries UK Ltd*
Bottles 33.5cl	*Marblehead*
Cans 33.5cl	

Imported by Molson Breweries UK Ltd and Marblehead, this is North America's oldest brewing company and the largest in Canada. Founded in 1786 by the British-born John Molson, the brewery now claims to produce the leading Canadian beer to be exported to the United States.

Brewed and packaged in Canada, MOLSON is now available in the UK, and the company boasts that it sells 'over one and a half million bottles a day', therefore snatching a staggering 3 per cent of total consumption at a growth rate of 10 per cent plus per annum. However, I personally find this a little difficult to believe.

As usual, MOLSON is 'brewed from the finest ingredients' God can provide by a 'master brewer'. For a premium lager with a high gravity, it's surprisingly light and clean with a crisp, refreshing taste. Indeed, MOLSON is an extremely pleasant lager which I have drunk myself in America in between quaffing their admirable micro-breweries' products: ROLLING ROCK and Jamaican RED STRIPE (*qq.v.*). Therefore I was delighted to see it make its début in the UK and I wish it all the best. (Shame about the advertising, though – the ever-lonesome and unpopular 'Jim Dunk says "Don't drink it".' Big deal!)

MORAVIA PILS West Germany

Bottles

Moravia, in Bohemia, was granted its licence to brew at the same time as those legendary Czechoslovakian brewing towns Pilsen and Ceské Budéjovice. King Wenceslas actually interceded for his lager-loving folk against a Papal Edict that prohibited brewing on pain of excommunication in the mid-1200s. However, this didn't mean that huge, billowing, chimney-land breweries immediately sprang up all over the countryside – far from it. It simply meant that *every* man had the right to brew and sell his own beer within a one-mile radius. So, for the tipplers of the aforementioned towns, King Wenceslas's intervention was truly a timely and perfect Christmas gift!

Still, MORAVIA the lager isn't brewed in Moravia the place; it is brewed in Luneberg by Holsten where, in their words, it is 'a super-premium product from a very modern subsidiary brewery'. Its pale colour reflects its light body, which is accompanied by a rich, strong hoppy bouquet. It has a very pleasant dry, hoppy taste without any of the sweetness one might well imagine for such a light beer. You should most certainly sample it alongside other lagers until you discover the brew most suited to your taste. For me personally, it wouldn't be my number one choice to accompany a Sunday lunch, but I certainly wouldn't turn my nose up at it on any other occasion.

MORETTI   Italy

Bottles

One of only three Italian lagers in the book (*see also* PERONI and VON WUNSTER CLASSICA), MORETTI seems to be becoming much more widely available as many restaurateurs seek an alternative to the dominating PERONI.

This one is probably my favourite Italian, with its light and clean taste. The bottle also displays one of my favourite labels, a wonderful moustachioed old man holding a huge foaming glass of his favourite.

Well worth sampling.

NEW ORLEANS BEST   USA

Cans 35.5cl

Brewed by the Royal Brewing Company of Louisiana, NEW ORLEANS BEST arrives in the UK as a pretty ugly ambassador of the United States. The gaudily designed can, which is most definitely unpleasant to look at, is gold with a red flash, and displays an interesting silhouetted logo of a man in Yukon clothing standing next to what appears to be the remains of his motor car after a 90mph crash into a tree! Oh dear, many people these days seem not to care what contains their lager.

NEW ORLEANS BEST is not the appropriate title for this lager as it is unfortunately a sub-standard American brew. It is light and watery and, being almost tasteless, there's no chance of any unpleasant aftertaste! Not unless you hate thin air! The only thing you can taste is a slight sweetness. Pale in colour and thin, it's not as highly carbonated as a number of other American lagers I could name, but all in all it's a very disappointing brew. One really does expect more from a town famous throughout the world for its culinary expertise. A great disappointment!

NEWQUAY DRAUGHT STEAM LAGER   UK

OG 1042°   *Cornish Brewery Co.*
Draught

Though not quite as strong as its bottled sister brew with the lengthy name of NEWQUAY REAL STEAM LAGER 'NATURAL STRONG' (*q.v.*), NEWQUAY DRAUGHT nevertheless fully lives up to the reputation and standards of the steam range. Indeed, it's one of the excellent British lagers from the Cornish Brewery Company. The only disadvantage to drinking the draught is that you won't be able to participate in the 'ritual' – *see* NEWQUAY REAL STEAM LAGER 'EXTRA STRONG'. Then again, who knows? Perhaps they'll invent a glass with a flip-top stopper! I wouldn't put it past them. A great lager!

NEWQUAY DRAUGHT STEAM PILS   UK

OG 1042°   *Cornish Brewery Co.*
Draught

Another lager from the ever-expanding Newquay Steam range. This draught pils was only introduced to the market during the summer of 1988 – on, I believe, a Tuesday afternoon in August! There's no reason to believe that this new lager won't be as successful as the company's bottled range (*see* NEWQUAY REAL STEAM LAGER 'EXTRA STRONG' and 'NATURAL STRONG') and, if it is, it might well appear at your local before too long. At the moment, it's only available within Devenish's 170-pub estate in the south-west. This brash, go-ahead company, however, is always looking towards expansion, so keep your nose to the ground.

Again, like its sister brew 'NATURAL STRONG' LAGER, NEWQUAY DRAUGHT STEAM PILS is in the classic Continental style. With a high gravity, it's competing directly in the premium lager category where I'm sure its delicately hopped flavour and clean dry taste will be very much appreciated.

NEWQUAY REAL STEAM LAGER 'EXTRA STRONG' UK

OG 1080° – 9% ABV *Global Beer Co. Ltd*
Bottles 45cl
      50cl
      55cl

On July 4th 1987 the Cornish Brewery Company, part of J. A. Devenish PLC, declared that it was 'the first brewery in the world to produce a complete range of beers with no artificial additives, preservatives or colourings'. Now, that's what I call a claim! I'd certainly like to be a fly on the wall when the Cornish Brewery Company's head brewer, Tony Wharmby, has his office full of enraged Germans and Czechs.

The CBC people are placing their bets on the 'lifestyle phenomenon' with this new range; they've chosen the name Newquay after an old Cornish town to exploit the image of naturalness and traditional quality, and the bottle's back label carries a signed statement guaranteeing that the contents are produced with only pure Cornish water, malt, hops, and fermented with yeast. They're even trying to promote the pouring of the lager as a 'ritual', as if it's the only lager available with a swing-top stoppered bottle. Still, 'ritual' fits in with 'traditional' and I'm quite sure that there are enough of the 'lifestyle brigade' out there to ensure that it succeeds.

Indeed, the British Bottlers Institute awarded the Cornish Brewing Company two silver medals and a diploma, and the British Institute of Packing, as well as the Labologists Society, also threw in some awards. These are all people who enjoy a good old traditional ritual! The brewery appeals to the retailer to give the lager to the customer in the bottle, enabling him to participate in the ritual, and he certainly has! Within a year of its regional launch NEWQUAY REAL STEAM LAGER 'EXTRA STRONG', as well as its sister brew NEWQUAY REAL STEAM LAGER 'NATURAL STRONG' (q.v.), were nationally established brands. The company is now preparing to refurbish its 170-pub estate in Cornwall to the tune of £6 million. Another £7 million is to be spent on new equipment and facilities at the Steam Brewery in Redruth. That's success for you!

It should be pointed out, I feel that the word 'steam' has absolutely nothing whatsoever to do with the lager. It is brewed at landlocked Redruth in Cornwall, and steam *is not* used in the brewing process. The word 'steam', as the CBC use it, is simply there to exploit a marketing opportunity.

Steam beers were actually quite popular in San Francisco during the 1800s (*see* ANCHOR STEAM) where steam was used in the brewing process. Today, it refers to a way in which to climb on a bandwagon. Even the label shows an 'old' paddle-steamer alongside a dockside warehouse. Newquay has probably never seen a boat like it in its entire life, being a former pilchard-fishing centre! Then again, to put pilchards on your label would hardly be a wise marketing move.

Let me assure you that I don't want to put you off the C.B.C.'s products. I actually really like them.

As you'll gather throughout the book, I'm not really a fan of super-strength lagers as I usually find them just too overpoweringly strong to make drinking them a pleasure. With NEWQUAY STEAM 'EXTRA STRONG' LAGER, however, this is slightly different. Brewed over a three-and-a-half week period – there are no enzymes used to speed it up – it has a full body that although certainly heavy, isn't too sticky and is therefore quite easy to drink. Clean and smooth it is an absolute pleasure to consume. It has a distinctive taste and, once again, its super-strength category doesn't destroy its flavour. Now that it is available nationally, I wholeheartedly recommend that you all try it, as I can honestly say that I don't think you'll be disappointed.

My only reservation about the CBC's products are that they're not more widely available in their native Cornwall. I must have asked for 'Steam' in every pub in St Austel, only to be occasionally offered TUBORG (*q.v.*), which is the 'official steam' in Cornish surfing circles. Now that's a great shame for a great local product. Probably the best super-strength lager on the market! Cheers!

NEWQUAY REAL STEAM LAGER
'NATURAL STRONG'   UK

OG 1046° – 6% ABV	*Global Beer Co. Ltd*
Bottles (*see* EXTRA STRONG)	

For the background to this classic lager in the Continental style see NEWQUAY REAL STEAM LAGER

'EXTRA STRONG'. This is a fine palatable lager full of character. Subtly dry and mildly hopped 'NATURAL STRONG' is in the premium sector and, as the title implies, you shouldn't throw it about. Far more palatable than its bed-mate, the 'Extra Strong', its beautiful, clear body carries not only a distinct taste but also a strong kick in a long finish. One of the very best lagers on the market, this is one you should definitely make an effort to try, as I'm pretty sure that once you've sampled it you'll be queuing up for more.

NIKSIK   Yugoslavia

OG 1045–50°   *Vitkovitch Brothers*
Bottles 500ml

In the last 17 years NIKSIK has won an incredible 15 gold medals in as wide a field as from London to Plovdiv, Brussels to Vienna, and Paris to Madrid. As is obvious from the many medals it has won, NIKSIK is a popular lager with many different palates around the world, including mine!

On pouring it from the bottle, the first thing you notice is a definitely sweet aroma. Behind this hides a thick, full-bodied beer with a strong, yeasty taste and a delicious malty accent. As an occasional lager I really like it but I think that four or five of them would be a little too heavy and sweet for my personal taste. However, don't let that deter you as it is by no means unpleasant and from a reasonably strong lager one has to expect a slightly sticky aftertaste. NIKSIK is blessed with a clear, golden colour, in contrast to its vigorous rustic flavour that is every bit as strong as you would imagine in a beer of this high gravity. Definitely recommended to you all, and I can only hope that you enjoy your first bottle as much as I did.

NOCHE BUENA   Mexico

OG 1058°   *Maison Caurette Ltd*
Bottles 35.5cl

The question is: is it a lager or isn't it? After all
NOCHE BUENA is dark brown! Then again it's
brewed using a bottom-fermented yeast, so in my book
it *is* lager! By the strength alone you can see for
yourselves that it's a powerful, very full-bodied brew. It
has a very strong malty and hoppy flavour, and although it's heavy, its slightly sticky character doesn't
by any means ruin it.

It's a Christmas drink brewed specifically for the
occasion. The name NOCHE BUENA means Christmas Eve. Therefore, lager lovers, get into the Christmas
spirit and wake up on January 4th! WHOOPS!

Another great lager that we should feel proud to
have on sale in this country. Well worth sampling –
within reason!

NORSEMAN   UK

OG 1030–34°   *Vaux Breweries*
Cans 27.5 & 44cl
PET Bottles 2 & 3 litres

Have you ever noticed in the supermarket or off-licence
that crowd of gaudily-decorated lager cans stacked to
the roof alongside Heineken, Hofmeister, Kestrel and
Carlsberg? They're usually labelled 'Please Buy Me'!
You know, they are priced at about 50p for a 12-pack.
You see them at parties as well.

Well, NORSEMAN is one of these. The lager was
launched in 1971 and the packs have a very long shelf
life. Indeed the stack of them just never seems to get

smaller. How can I describe it to you? Lagery? No. Hoppy? No. Full-bodied? No. A little bit of a bite to it? Don't make me laugh! How about, thin, characterless, very gassy, or, in a nutshell, cheap and horrible? You've got it!

OBERNAI VILLAGE France

OG 1047°   *Continental Lager Distributors Ltd*
Cans 1 litre, resealable

The French certainly know a fair bit about the brewing of lager. In fact, they have a long and extremely proud brewing history, and lager lovers throughout the world have a lot to thank the genius of Pasteur and his brewing innovations for! 'Why do they drink so much wine then?' I hear you yelling from the other side of the book. Well, their wines are probably the best in the world. I mean, what would you rather drink: a bottle of Château Petrus or a pint of Carlsberg? For you Philistines out there I realize Petrus doesn't have a head on it and doesn't even look like lager, but nevertheless it's a king amongst drinks of any type.

It's possible that when the first 'new' lager beers were originally brewed a few hundred years ago, the yeast cell used might have been a refugee from wine!

OBERNAI VILLAGE comes to our shores with a fine brewing history behind it, and it shows. It has a light and fruity taste, which goes down a treat. It is also presented in an attractive 1-litre barrel-shaped can that is resealable, though why you'd want to reseal it unfinished is beyond me!

OKOCIM   Poland

OG 1048–51°   *Grandmartin*
Bottles

Ah . . . OKOCIM . . . and on to one of the most helpful
and pleasant secretaries I've ever had the pleasure to en-
counter.

Thanks to Claire Lawrence, for that was her name,
I'm able to tell you that OKOCIM is marketed as
'smooth, light, and strong, the full light OK beer from
Poland'. And OK it is with me. Smooth? Definitely.
Strong? Definitely. But light . . . ? Hardly! I'd describe it
as a robust lager that shouldn't be trifled with! With such
a high original gravity, it's certainly up there with the
best of them in the strength stakes. It's a lager with a
character of its own that should definitely be sampled.

PS OKOCIM has one of my favourite bottle labels!

OLYMPIC GOLD PREMIUM LAGER   UK

OG 1045°   *J. W. Cameron*
Bottles 33cl

Brewed specifically for the Olympic Games by J. W.
Cameron, part of the Ellerman brewing group, a quid
was donated to the British Olympic Appeal for every
case sold, and if the number of cases sold was in any
way related to the quality of the lager, they should
have raised a few pounds. Smooth and clean tasting,
in my view it's a shame that this lager is no longer
being produced. Now that the games are over, so
indeed is the lager, but you might still find it cropping
up here and there (rather like Sebastian Coe). Therefore, for all you plucky lager lovers out there, you'd
best get your spikes on for this one.

ORANJEBOOM   Netherlands

Draught   *Allied*
Bottles

The 'Orange Tree' or ORANJEBOOM is a regional
Dutch lager from the Rotterdam area. However, like
several other local beers in the Netherlands, OR-
ANJEBOOM is known internationally, particularly in
the UK. Interest in this sort of lager is usually precipi-
tated by a visit abroad where the taste of the local
brand grows on you as time goes by. ORANJEBOOM,
however, could be enjoyed without ever visiting Holland, as it's a good, clean pint with a wonderful golden
body, although possibly a little over carbonated, depending on your taste.

It has a good full-bodied character as well as an
invigorating freshness. Not a pint you'll find everywhere. Its subtle strength and keen flavour should be
enjoyed whenever the opportunity is afforded! Also an
'ORANJEBOOM DE LUXE' (Allied's description) is
available on draught at 'De Hems' in Macclesfield
Street, London W1.

PACIFICO   Mexico

Bottles   *Continental Lager Distributors Ltd*

Now I'm sure that I drank this one years ago at
London's Mexican Café Pacifico, but apparently it's not
currently available over here, or so its old importers
tell me, due to 'trademark' reasons. Could this have
anything to do with the aforementioned establishment
in which I drank it?

If you find PACIFICO, you've found a typical

Mexican lager. Pale and lightly hopped, it's ideal served well chilled during a heat wave.

PATRIZIER EXPORT GOLD   West Germany

OG 1050°   *Continental Lager Distributors Ltd*
Bottles 33cl

The Patrizier group, centred in Nürnberg, owns several breweries in surrounding towns, producing typical Bavarian lager beers of which EXPORT GOLD is one. Although Patrizier traditions have been adhered to, since their founding in 1468, and Patrizier exports are high around the world, EXPORT GOLD is nothing to write home about. It's good, yes, but as I say, it's also typical. A run-of-the-mill German lager, which incidentally is nothing like a run-of-the-mill British-brewed lager (i.e. it is quite good!). (*See also* PATRIZIER PREMIUM PILS.)

PATRIZIER PREMIUM PILS   West Germany

OG 1045°   *Euroimpex Ltd*
Bottles 33cl

Fortunately for us, the soil in the Nürnberg area is unsuitable for the growing of vines and thus beer is the beverage they concentrate on. Indeed, like all Germans, they take the brewing of it very seriously – so seriously, in fact, that Nürnberg passed its own 'Pure Beer Law' in the early 1300s, some 200 or so years before the Bavarian Reinheitsgebot. However, it wasn't until the mid-1900s that the local brewer Georg Lederer became involved with the famous brewers Sedlmayr and Dreher and their pioneering work on creating lager.

PATRIZIER PREMIUM PILS is a slightly bitter, dry, full-bodied lager with a classic German flavour. Though well balanced, it's not the greatest German lager beer, although it is one that definitely should be sampled. After all, it's backed by a five-centuries-old brewing tradition, and that's something that commands respect. Once more Patrizier claim that their lager is brewed to the Ordinance of Purity of 1516, which forbids the use of any chemical ingredients or artificial additives. I think you'll like it, but I can't see it becoming your regular tipple.

PAULANER 1634   West Germany

OG 1049–53°   *Marblehead*
Bottles 50cl
Cans 33cl

The Paulaner Brewery is the biggest in Munich, a city that takes great pride in its brewing, and a city famous throughout the world for its October beer festival, which is a must for all lager lovers!

With over 300 years of brewing experience behind them, it's no surprise that Paulaner offer an extensive range of good lager beers. Before the 'new-style' coloured lagers were first produced, the Germans were happy with their dark beers, or Alts (old) as they are known today. In fact the term Münchener, when applied to beer, usually means dark, and Paulaner produce one of the finest in the land. Named SALVATOR, it's extra strong, and the first barrel of it is traditionally tapped by the Mayor of Munich at the beginning of spring.

Another admirable brew from Paulaner, and one that it now available in the UK, is their export-style 1634, a full-bodied, smooth lager with an original gravity that means business! However, on tasting it, I thought it by no means representative of the quality of Paulaner's other lager beers. 1634 unfortunately has a slightly acidic flavour, and an aftertaste that's bitter enough to be classed as unpleasant. By all means make an effort to sample one, but don't be surprised if you quickly turn to something else.

PELICAN   France

OG 1045–51°   *Marblehead*
Bottles 1 litre

This monster bottle is the product of the Pelforth group's brewery of the same name just outside Lille, which is often regarded as the beer-drinking heartland of northern France. Although by world standards, hardly a brewer of substantial magnitude, Pelforth is still the second largest brewing group in all France.

It is not only PELICAN's 1-litre swing-top bottles that make it stand out from any other lagers on the market. The content itself is of a high quality – full-bodied and smooth. PELICAN is indeed a palatable brew.

It is a beer that's well worth seeking out. When in London you might like to try one in the comfortable surroundings of the Pelican Brasserie in St Martin's Lane. Don't forget your chequebook though!

PERONI – NASTRO AZZURRO   Italy

OG 1048–52°   *Marblehead*
Bottles 33cl
Cans

Need I point out that the Italians are dragging up the

rear with one of the lowest rates of beer consumption per head in western Europe? Tsk-tsk! And it's not just a one off; oh, no, it's a regular thing. Even though they've increased their consumption by nearly 500 per cent over the last 30 years, they're still guilty of merely sipping their lager!

Birra Peroni was founded in Lombardy in 1846; then in 1866 it moved to Rome which at that time was not the capital of Italy. Once there, the company began expanding like it had never done before. Today it is Italy's largest brewer, holding some 25 per cent of the lager market to itself. To do this it uses five breweries situated in Rome, Naples, Padua, Udine, and Bari, which is the southernmost brewery and deep in hostile wine-lake land! Between them, their cellars can hold up to 630,000 hectolitres of lager, which is more than you'll ever see at any Christmas party! Annually Peroni brew around a massive 4·25 million hectolitres.

PERONI – NASTRO AZZURRO was introduced to the UK in 1975 by Peter Boizot, the founder of the Pizza Express restaurant chain. From a few hundred cases a year in those far off days, Peroni has expanded rapidly until today it sells the dizzy-making figure of just under 10 million bottles per annum – and that figure is rising *all* the time! NASTRO AZZURRO is no longer only available in Pizza Express restaurants and in Italian establishments; far from it, both Tesco and Safeways, as well as Oddbins, Peter Dominics, Threshers, and Augustus Barnett, to name but a few, all stock it and report good, profitable sales.

NASTRO AZZURRO is a well-balanced pilsner, though I personally find it a little thick in body for my liking, though it certainly isn't disagreeable. Reasonably light in colour, it has a mild hoppy flavour and produces a long-lasting head when poured from the bottle. It is not difficult to get, and you should definitely have a look at one next time you grab a pizza. If you like it enough it's easy to obtain and therefore ideal to keep as a lager for home consumption. However, I keep my fridge filled with something else.

PILSENER URQUELL	Czechoslovakia

OG 1048°
Draught
Bottles 33cl and 65cl

R. H. & M. Victuals

When it was poured from the bottle, the first thing I noticed about PILSENER URQUELL was its beautiful, bright and eye-catching golden colour. On tasting it, you'll soon find out, as I did, that PILSENER URQUELL is a fine, full-bodied brew with a pleasantly bitter, hoppy flavour that quickly reminds you that its original gravity is not far off the 1050° mark.

Initially brewed in a specially constructed brewery in the town of Pilsen, Czechoslovakia, in 1842, it was famous throughout Europe by the mid-1870s. Indeed, such was its fame that when other breweries began to brew their own bottom-fermented beers they called them 'Pilseners', thus the Pilsen brewery added the word *Urquell* (original source) to the name of their product. From a mere 3,600 hectolitres produced in the first year of brewing, this figure had risen to a mighty one million hectolitres by 1913. Today, capacity has been stabilized somewhere in the region of 1·5 million hectolitres per annum.

PILSENER URQUELL has won a number of awards, as well as Papal approval (*see* MORAVIA PILS), and it is now exported to over 90 countries, one of which is fortunately the UK! Perhaps the secret of this tremendous lager lies in the brewing which, to this day, is unprecedented in the entire world and cannot be copied successfully by any other major brewery. Nine kilometres of cellars have been cut into the sandy rock beneath the brewery, and these provide the perfect temperature for maturing the lager in hand-made oak barrels. Not only that, but the water used in the brewing is unique in that it has an extremely low grade of hardness at 4° – normal drinking water is 30°!

PILSENER URQUELL has a rich, dense, foamy head and an inimitable bitter, vigorous flavour that to me at least, is very pleasant. Unfortunately, the British have been slow to appreciate this fine lager; therefore it is available in only a few select places, which is a great shame as I rate it very highly indeed.

One of the best lagers in the world!

POLAR BEER   Iceland

OG 1050°   *Continental Lager Distributors Ltd*
Bottles 35cl

Lagerless since 1915, Iceland must be one of the saddest countries in the world. The country's 250,000 inhabitants have been drinking what is known as 'near beer', a sort of crude, vaguely lager-like drink brewed within the confines of their law which forbids any beer containing more than 2.25 per cent alcohol by volume. Therefore, the country's two brewers have been restricted to brewing 'real lager' for the export market only, and one of their products is the well-made, strong and full-bodied POLAR BEER. Iceland's sad predicament will change in March 1989, when the government will allow sales of ales, but only through its state-owned liquor stores. Meanwhile, POLAR BEER will continue to be available in the UK and, believe it or not, it is actually a good-quality lager powerful enough to have the entire country of Iceland licking its lips. Next time you crack one open spare a thought for them that made it, because, believe me, they're thinking of you!

PORT ROYAL   **Honduras**

OG 1045°   *Continental Lager Distributors Ltd*
Bottles 35cl

Although this lager is available in a green bottle, which is not the best colour for the promotion of one's product, I must say that I was instantly attracted to this one by the label. Red, blue and gold, it contains a beautiful summery picture of what I take to be one of the brewer's many refrigerated ships, in which PORT ROYAL is exported. White, but red below the plumb line, the vessel is steaming happily up a thin river, the banks of which are alive with green and, on the far bank, a little hamlet of white houses is visible. It really is a nice label and it speaks volumes about the lack of quality and thought that goes into the packaging of so many other lagers. It's precisely labels like this that make the casual consumer take the bottle from the shelf, purchase it and take it home.

The very instant that the compass-decorated top is popped a potent, yeasty smell erupts from the bottle and, on pouring, we can see that the lager is very pale. I found this quite surprising on thinking about it afterwards, because the lager itself is full-tasting, with a pleasant malty body. Crisp and clean, it goes down very easily, becoming more pleasurable with each mouthful. With its high original gravity, which, incidentally, is not specified on the bottle, it's a pilsner-style lager in the premium sector.

Despite the fact that it contains a little bit of novelty value, in as much as it's Honduran, I strongly recommend that you give it a try when the opportunity arises. Indeed, the South Americans treat this lager with great respect, not only the brewing of it but also in its transportation. To keep the temperature of the brew constantly cold it is transported in a fleet of specially refrigerated ships. The Hondurans are right to take such pride in their product as it leaves many other premium lagers in the shade. (Shade, by the way, is one thing you don't see on the label!) One definitely not to be missed.

PRIMA   France

OG 1046°   *Applejack Trading Co.*
Bottles 33cl

PRIMA is produced by the Brasserie Semeuse near Lille, and is currently only available in London and the south. So I'm afraid it's on-your-bike time again if you're a northern lager lover.

Packaged in a dumpy bottle it certainly looks

typically French. What does it taste like? Well, some might say typically French! Light, smooth and with a touch of malt, it's a perfectly adequate little lager.

PROHIBITION LOW ALCOHOL LAGER   UK

Another NEWQUAY STEAM (*q.v.*) beer, though this one has no alcohol. 'Ritual' or not, there's nothing traditional about this but for the way that I'm going to ignore it.

RATSKELLER EDEL-PILS   West Germany

OG 1049–50°   *Baron von Ritter*

From the Hanoverian Lindener Gilde brewery's extensive range of finely brewed beers comes RATS-KELLER, a premium, full-bodied, hoppy lager, brewed with the distinct and world-famous Saaz hops. Pale gold in colour, this one has a good yeasty character. Though, unfortunately, not widely available. RATS-KELLER EDEL-PILS should always be purchased on sight as it might be the last time you'll see a bottle for quite a while.

Another fine German lager.

RAVEN   UK

Barking Breweries

I was having lunch quite recently with a certain head brewer friend of mine at the splendid Uxbridge Arms, an artists' bar of sorts, in London's fashionable Elephant and Castle. During the course of our black-pudding sandwiches, the conversation wandered to the topic of lager beer, as it usually does in these cases. However, knowing each other well, we were already aware of each other's loves and hates and, after discussing additional contents such as corn, rice, fish and whale parts, we decided to probe each other on just *what* contents would be unacceptable. Thus, the case of RAVEN lager was placed firmly and squarely on the table.

It appears that a consumer in Dagenham, Essex, reported that a can of his favourite 'cheapie' lager tasted off, despite the fact that it was still within the sell-by date. The council's environmental health department therefore sent samples of the lager to a public analyst for examination. He duly reported back that the 'off' taste was due to 'bacterial bloom'. On hearing this, the London Borough of Redbridge environmental health and standards officer pointed out that this was not an isolated incident. Indeed, he went on, his department had 'become aware of a similar complaint concerning the same brand of lager in another borough'. In short, it was alleged that an unspecified amount of cans of RAVEN lager had been contaminated with bacteria.

Although we weren't drinking RAVEN, we instantly looked at our pints in horror. It is precisely this sort of incident that gives the entire brewing trade a bad name. All it takes is one rotten apple (much the same as the Austrian glycol affair). At the time of writing the result of the RAVEN case is not known to me, though by the time the book is published it should be common knowledge. Therefore, in my eyes, Barking Breweries must remain innocent until proven guilty. If indeed they are innocent then my heart bleeds for them as their name will be dragged through the slops. Yet, if they're found to be guilty then they will deserve everything they get, and more, much much more, for dragging the good name of the brewer's art with them.

My advice to the public is that if your tipple must be one of the 'cheapie' brands, which surely your tastes should be above, anyway, then select your lager carefully. That doesn't necessarily mean buying an established brand, as this would prevent any fine new lager from breaking into the market. Simply choose one from a brewer you trust. If this is beyond you, then I recommend that you not only consult your copy of *Daft about Lager*, but that you also encourage your friends to buy their own copy, lest they wake up blue.

RED DEVIL PREMIUM LAGER   UK

OG 1038°   *Team Advance*
Cans 44cl

Another flimsy 'footy' lager from Devenish, this one for Manchester United fans. We don't even know if it will be available at the time of publication – the supplier's are keeping that fact under the hat on their head. As it's exactly the same drink as all the other 'footy' lagers, *see under* EVERTON and SUPER REDS 'footy' lager for details.

RED STRIPE   UK and Jamaica

OG 1043–47° – 4.4% ABV   *Charles Wells Ltd*
Draught
Bottles 27.5cl
Cans 44cl

RED STRIPE has its roots in the Caribbean, where a smooth, refreshing lager is the number-one priority to get a person through the heat of the day, and RED STRIPE fulfils that function perfectly. Originally from Kingston, the first RED STRIPE brew was marketed in Jamaica in 1928, although the lager beer that we are familiar with today wasn't launched until 1934. You'd think that such a relatively short brewing history might possibly impair the quality of such a lager, but you'd be wrong. In 1986 RED STRIPE won its fourth successive gold medal for excellence at the La Monde International Brewing Festival. This consistent success undoubtedly establishes it as one of the foremost premium lagers in the world. The opinion of the independent brewing experts is certainly endorsed by the consumer, as sales are increasing all the time – in excess of some 100,000 barrels in 1988.

In the UK RED STRIPE is brewed, under licence from Desnoes and Geddes of Kingston, by Charles Wells of Bedford to the original Jamaican recipe, using American yeast and hops, choice grade malt, and corn. These ingredients, along with the method of brewing, culminate in a lager which is light, smooth and clean, as well as distinctly refreshing. In 1978, distributed by H. P. Bulmer, RED STRIPE was launched in the UK and is now available nationally.

Also worth keeping your eyes peeled for is the imported Jamaican brew. Although there's very little difference between this one and the UK-brewed version, I personally think that the water used in Jamaica makes for a slightly lighter drink.

On a lesser note, RED STRIPE was unfortunately caught up in the hysteria which followed the Masham Committee's report, which called for a total ban on all alcohol advertising. A poster advertisement for the brand contained a young woman who was embracing a young man, while at the same time holding a can of the famous lager. The Advertising Standards Authority objected, saying that the advert suggested that sexual appeal can be enhanced by drinking the lager brand. Not only that, but the woman appeared to be under 21! It was thus necessary to point out to the Authorities that, in fact, the model used was 26 and women *do* drink lager! Its tail between its legs, the ASA cautioned Bulmer not to 'encourage inappropriate responses to alcohol'. Next they'll be telling us that RED STRIPE can't be described as one of the best lager beers in the world in case the truth encourages people to drink it! Which I hereby recommend you do. Instantly!

RED STRIPE CRUCIAL BREW   UK

OG 1076–82°   *Charles Wells Ltd*
Bottles
Cans 44cl

First launched in 1986 in 33cl cans and having an original gravity of 1080–86°, the new can and gravity band was introduced in 1988 as the distributors, H. P. Bulmer, believed that the consumer was more partial to larger cans. As with its sister brew, RED STRIPE, (*q.v.*) it is brewed under licence from Dessnoes and Geddes of Kingston, Jamaica, by Charles Wells of Bedford.

We have made clear throughout this book that we're not great fans of 'super-strength' lagers. However, having said that, don't let me put you off trying out this one. As you can imagine, it is both sweet and sticky, but it does retain some resemblance to a *lager*, particularly with its slightly hoppy quality. If you're having just the one, then you could do worse than have *this* one.

RESERVE DE BRASSEUR   France

OG 1062°   *Applejack Trading Co.*
Bottles 75cl – wired cork stopper

There's no mucking about with a dark lager beer like this, and its strength is immediately evident in both bouquet and taste. Of the *bière de garde* (beer to be kept) style, it was introduced to the UK in August 1988 with a limited launch that took in only London and the south-east. Though not a lager I could personally drink all evening, it is nevertheless an excellent beer, in the old style, and makes a perfect complement to a hearty evening meal! *A votre santé!*

RHEINGOLD   France

Bottles   *Continental Lager Distributors Ltd*

Brewed by the Grande Brasserie Alsacienne d'Adelshof-fen, RHEINGOLD is lovingly brought to our shores by the Continental Lager Distributors. The brewery is situated in the Alsace region of France, the home of many a fine brew, and stands on a hill, therefore making it safe from the frequently flooding Rhein, but also enabling it to use the excellent water supplied by the Rhein Valley watershed.

Adelshoffen produce a number of fine lagers, but the

one that's most easily attainable here is the fine de luxe RHEINGOLD. The name alludes to the gold particles that are still carried by the river Rhein to this day.

A strong, wonderfully smooth, full-bodied lager, it goes down well. A great little lager that should be purchased and consumed on sight! *A votre santé.*

ROLLING ROCK PREMIUM LAGER   USA

OG 1044° – 5% ABV	*G B Vintagers*
Bottles 35.5cl	
Cans 35.5cl	

ROLLING ROCK has been brewed since the repeal of prohibition in 1933 at the small Latrobe Brewery, Latrobe, Pennsylvania (incidentally the home town of top golfer Arnold Palmer!), which was once a monastery brewhouse. Today it is still the brewery's only product. In recent years it has grown from being a popular local lager beer in the coal- and steel-producing region of Pittsburgh to become one of the most sought-after and fashionable drinks in New York and the whole of the American East Coast. This is not because ROLLING ROCK has become the central point of some new trend, but is due to the fact that over the years it has built up a steady 'cult' following. On my last visit to Manhattan I spent an evening in a nightclub called 'The World' with the film actor Matt Dillon and his then girlfriend, the stunningly beautiful, top English model Emma Woolard. When I bought a round I bought Jack Daniels. When Dillon bought a round he bought ROLLING ROCK. 'It's the only lager in America', he drawled, raising those famous eyebrows. One sip later and I saw his point. It's an excellent light and refreshing brew.

It was introduced to the UK in 1984 and launched nationally in 1985. Today, although not available at every single off-licence or supermarket, it can be found in towns as far afield as Glasgow and Torquay, Edinburgh and London, Newcastle-upon-Tyne and Wallasey. Its sales have increased dramatically, in the region of 45 per cent per annum, and in 1988 sales were forecast to increase by just under 100 per cent as the 'cult' in England grows. All this is hardly surprising, however, as ROLLING ROCK is exceptionally clean-tasting. Its elegantly light style owes as much to the pure mountain spring water with which the lager is brewed as to the glass-lined tanks of the superbly kept Latrobe brewery in which it is matured. The careful selection of the finest American brewing ingredients by this small brewery ensure a flavour and quality that is always consistent. Latrobe are also proud to announce that no preservatives or additives are used in the brewing; however, a rice adjunct is used but this is in no way detrimental to the lager. Indeed, rice is a common adjunct in American lagers and, when they are brewed to the quality of ROLLING ROCK, can offer quite a refreshing change to the generally more bitter German lager beers. ROLLING ROCK is highly recommended by me, for – dare I say it – it is possibly the finest American lager beer on the market! *Hic!*

ROYAL BRITISH LEGION LAGER   UK

3.9% ABV   *Federation Brewery*
Draught

Only introduced in 1988, there are no figures yet available to judge the success or failure of the admirable Federation Brewery's (*see* ACE LAGER) latest addition to their portfolio. Proudly named after the famous ex-servicemen's clubs, where one is always guaranteed a long game of snooker, its alcohol by volume measure makes for a slightly stronger tipple than many other 'session' lagers. If Federation had taken as much care over this one as they have with some of their other products we could recommend that you give it a go – but, alas, sadly this is not the case.

ROYAL DUTCH POST HORN   Netherlands

OG 1030–34°
Bottles 50cl
Cans 44cl

'Cheapie' imports to Britain appear to have been having a bad time lately. In nine months in 1987 they only showed a 3.4 per cent growth, the reason being that the British have discovered that they can brew equally bland lager in the same gravity band. There seems to be no doubt that at the beginning of 1988 shipments of ROYAL DUTCH POST HORN, a definite 'cheapie', were falling off, yet their sales director claimed a '44 per cent increase (off-sales) in the packaged lager market'. Whichever is true ROYAL DUTCH holds around 2–3 per cent of the market share.

Brewed and canned in the Netherlands, this insipid little lager arrives in an equally bland can which, although decorated with the horn of the Dutch postal service, is nothing to blow your horn about. It has an extremely sweet nose with a slight trace of malt and a pale, golden colour. But it is so over carbonated that I feel ROYAL DUTCH must win an award for being the noisiest lager in the world! ROYAL DUTCH also manages to taste as weak as it actually is, yet maybe a small quantity might just be refreshing for someone thirsty.

Overall it seems as if no one has taken any pride in brewing this characterless, fizzy lager, and it certainly tastes like a mass-produced product.

To be avoided if possible – even at parties!

ROYAL HOFBRAU   UK

OG 1047°   *Hall and Woodhouse*

Brewed in the UK by Hall and Woodhouse, under licence from Hofbrauhaus of Munich, HOFBRAU has only recently been made available nationally through the off-trade.

HOFBRAU (literally 'court brew'), with its high original gravity, is competing firmly in the booming premium lager market. As Hall and Woodhouse's market research has shown that consumers still look on Munich as the world capital for lager, it should sell very well.

As for the product itself, it's reasonably light, slightly malty in taste, and goes down very smoothly. All in all, an excellent British-brewed lager that should most definitely be sought out.

SAFEWAYS AUSTRALIAN LAGER   Australia

OG 1044–46°
Cans 37.5cl

To celebrate Australia's bi-centenary, Safeways launched an Australian lager from the Esk Brewery in Launceston.

A perfectly pleasant, reasonably full-bodied, sweetish brew that should go down well with Aussie lager lovers. It's always nice to see supermarkets offering something apart from the ubiquitous stacks of 29p 'Snorkdorfer Viking Haircut-brau' lager, and Safeways should certainly be applauded for giving us this one. Well worth slipping into your trolley!

SAGRES EUROPA   Portugal

OG 1046°   *Vinicave Wine Importers*
Cans

Though slightly lower in alcohol content than SAGRES EXPORT (*q.v.*), EUROPA is Sagres de luxe lager.

This one is brewed, as is the Export, by Central de Cervejas, who are one of Portugal's biggest brewers. Incidentally, the name Sagres is taken from Cape Sagres on the south coast of Portugal.

Slightly lighter in both colour and texture than Export, EUROPA is a pleasant lager. A little malty and sweet, it is a pleasure to drink and should definitely be sought out.

SAGRES EXPORT   Portugal

OG 1047°   *Vinicave Wine Importers*
Cans

With a punchy original gravity, SAGRES EXPORT is a fine, smooth-drinking lager from Portugal. Although, unfortunately, I haven't been there for years, I'm told that SAGRES, with its malty taste and golden brown colour, is a wonderful ambassador for its country.

If this was sold in the Café Lisboa in London's

Golborne Road, where they sell the best cakes I've ever had, I'd find myself hard pushed to get to the pub!

SAINSBURY'S AUSTRALIAN LAGER
Australia

OG 1045–49°
Cans

Yet another lager brewed and packaged in its country of origin by the admirable Sainsbury's.

SAINSBURY'S AUSTRALIAN is a golden, full-bodied, and slightly sweet lager, that comes recommended. The only thing I don't like about it is the can design. It's predominantly silver, and really does look cheap, which is hardly complimentary to its contents.

SAINSBURY'S DANISH EXPORT LAGER
Denmark

OG 1046–50°
Cans

Another lager from Sainsbury's. This one is 'brewed and canned in Denmark, using the finest raw materials'. Well, there's a nice variation on an old theme for you!

With a high original gravity, SAINSBURY'S DANISH EXPORT is reasonably clean tasting, full bodied, and has a nice sting in it's tail!

Another reason to visit Sainsbury's.

SAINSBURY'S DUTCH LAGER   Netherlands

OG 1030–34°

What next, I wonder, from Sainsbury's? Sainsbury's Lithuanian lager? Sainsbury's Peruvian lager?

This, however, is the only one of Sainsbury's imported lagers that I didn't like. It reminded me a lot of ROYAL DUTCH POST HORN (*q.v.*) in as much as it's over carbonated and weak tasting, which isn't actually that surprising as it *is* a very weak lager.

Not recommended, but don't let me put you off going to Sainsbury's. There are plenty of other lagers there well worth your time and money.

SAINSBURY'S FRENCH LAGER   France

OG 1045–1049°
Bottles

This one is brewed and bottled in the small town of Schiltigheim just outside Strasbourg, which as you should know by now, is deep in the French brewing region, the Alsace.

Schiltigheim is indeed a prolific little brewing town; it contains no less than six breweries!

SAINSBURY'S FRENCH, is typical of the brews of the area. Light, slightly malty, and very easy to drink, it's a very pleasant tipple.

SAINSBURY'S GERMAN LAGER
West Germany

OG 1050–1054°
Bottles

Brewed and bottled in Hamburg according to the Rein-heitsgebot 'Purity Law' of 1516, SAINSBURY'S GERMAN LAGER is one of the best Sainsbury's have to offer.

Dry, slightly hoppy, and beautifully smooth, this one goes down a treat at any time of the day. Although not one of the best German lagers on the market, this one nevertheless, comes highly recommended, and it's certainly an own brand that Sainsbury's should be proud of!

SAINSBURY'S LAGER
UK

OG 1030–34°
Cans

Brewed and canned in Great Britain, SAINSBURY'S LAGER is the great supermarket's standard 'throwing' lager.

With an original gravity of 1030–34°, there's little to differentiate it from most supermarket own-brand lagers. It's pale, weak tasting, and with little character, and I suggest you overlook it and check out the other lagers Sainsbury's have on offer – Apart from SKONA (q.v.) that is!

SAINSBURY'S L.A. LAGER   UK

Yet another low-alcohol lager, this time brought to us by my favourite supermarket, Sainsbury's.

You are no doubt painfully aware that I'm not a great fan of these insipid little products. It's very easy (believe me!) to be extremely rude about all the low-alcohol lagers, but I'm going to attempt to do this one justice by comparing it solely to its low-alcohol competitors.

It smells sweet, though not unpleasantly so; it looks all right (it's got a head on it!); and it doesn't go down too badly. The taste reminded me a little of 'Supermalt', a non-alcoholic drink containing many valuable B vitamins.

To sum it up, it's one of the best low-alcohol lagers on the market, but that doesn't necessarily mean that I like it!

Sainsbury's also sell a palatable 'own-brand' mineral water!

ST CHRISTOPHER

Allied

With an extremely sweet nose, spiced with the slimmest trace of malt. It tastes blatantly artificial. It's horrible. St Christopher is the patron saint of travel, but I can tell you that this particular 'drink' is going nowhere!

ST MICHAEL PILSNER LAGER   UK

This supermarket lager idea is really catching on. We've

seen it at ASDA, Sainsbury's, Safeways and now Marks 'n' Sparks! (Maybe we'll discover a 'Corner Shop Brau' or a 'Newsagents Snorkdorfer Pils' – who knows?)

I see this sort of thing being bought in my own local supermarket as I study the shelves in search of a decent brew. However, the shelves are nearly always packed to the rafters with first-generation or standard lagers and if this isn't off-putting enough, there, crammed in the middle of the pile, is the house brau . . . and, crikey, does it sell! And why not, especially at Marks and Spencer. I mean, there are 'St Michael' people, who buy their shoes, socks, slacks, shirts, vests, knickers, cardies and suits there, and they buy their snacks, roast, veg and beer there too. They love Marks and Spencer, and St Michael is the symbol of quality to them. And you have to agree that they make a great steak-and-kidney bachelor pudding, but I do draw the line at their pilsner.

ST PAULI GIRL   Germany

Bottles   *Longmans Distribution Ltd*

This is a pale, fresh-tasting, clean lager from Bremen's oldest brewery.

With a distinctive hoppy smell the beer seems quite light and has a sort of fluffy quality that is not unpleasant. Extremely popular, from my sightings of it, on the east coast of America, it's not the best German beer by any means, but one you should definitely try.

SAMICHLAUS   Switzerland

OG 1116°   *Shepherd Neame*

On the morning of December 6th the workers scramble

early from their beds and hurry to work for the traditional brewing of what is indisputably one of the con-
tenders for the title 'The World's Strongest Beer' –
S A M I C H L A U S or Santa Claus. Then, after a hard,
backbreaking day, they can taste last year's brew. For
S A M I C H L A U S is brewed only once a year and isn't
ready until exactly the same day the following year,
and by the time it is ready it has a huge measure of 14
per cent alcohol by volume! However, not being *daft*,
by a long chalk, the Swiss keep the deep red original
to themselves while we get a rich amber version.

It is fundamentally designed as a Christmas brew,
hence the name, and I don't have to tell you just what
this beer will do to you. Let's put it this way: it
produces so much alcohol that it virtually scares the
yeast to death!

SAMUEL ADAMS BOSTON LAGER   USA

3.5% ABV   *Global Beer Co. Ltd*
Bottles

The Boston Beer Company is part of the phenomenon in
the United States known as 'micro-breweries'. At the
last count there were approximately 150 of these tiny
breweries, most of which have their own pubs attached.
It is generally accepted that the number of these breweries could grow to as many as 500 by the end of the
decade. Put together, these 'micro-breweries' account
for about 0.03 per cent of the 180 million barrels of
beer made in the US last year. Of this, S A M U E L
A D A M S L A G E R accounted for 24,000 barrels and is
by far the premier lager made by these plucky little
breweries.

It first appeared in 1985 when it immediately won
top honours in that year's Great American Beer Festival

held in Denver. Brewed from a high-gravity down to a typically American 3.5 per cent alcohol by volume, it's an all-malt brew with a very strong pilsner character. The version available over here, although retaining all the characteristics of it's American cousin, has a significantly higher ABV content. The sheer strength of the smell of hops gives one the illusion that it's backed up by a rich, full body, which in actual fact it isn't. However, this in no way makes it a poor beer and it should be sampled at all costs, if only for the smell of those hops! Oddly enough SAMUEL ADAMS, named after a revolutionary Bostonian incidentally, holds no threat to America's major brands, but imported European beers should look out, such is the Continental flavour of BOSTON LAGER.

If you have the good fortune to stumble across this one then you should certainly buy it!

SAMUEL SMITH'S NATURAL LAGER   UK

OG 1037–41°   *Samuel Smith*
Bottles 33cl

As it says in the title, this lager is made from completely natural ingredients and, unusual for a British lager, it contains no additives, much along the lines of Germany's Rheinheitsgebot, or 'Purity Law', of 1516. It is given 10 weeks to brew, rather than the usual two. It was only introduced to the market in 1986 and is still only available through the Samuel Smith's chain, and as far as I know, some Safeways supermarkets.

SAMUEL SMITH'S NATURAL LAGER is a fine brew and comes highly recommended not only for its smooth body but also for its bouquet, which is rich and where all the ingredients have a beautiful distinctive smell all to themselves. Though not excessively strong it is full-bodied and clean tasting, which is always pleasant in a lager.

To sum it up: light in colour, smooth drinking, and with a beautiful aroma. One of the very best British-brewed lagers on the market, from a company that certainly knows a thing or two about its craft. Highly recommended.

SAN MIGUEL 'ESPECIAL'   Spain

OG 1049–55°   *Lance Brown*
Draught
Bottles 25cl and 33cl
Cans 33cl

There are probably a good 20 million British people who've supped SAN MIGUEL on their holidays, as they bask on the beaches of Spain, and they'd be forgiven for thinking it was a local brew. Indeed it is currently brewed in Spain (there are three main SAN MIGUEL breweries there), but the real home of this lager is the Philippines! Spain, O sunned ones, is its very profitable second home! The same pilsner-style lager is produced in all its breweries. Rigid tests are carried out at the Spanish breweries at Malaga, Lerida and Burgos to ensure that they all produce the same quality lager.

Sold in 47 different countries, SAN MIGUEL is Spain's favourite tipple, despite the fact that it was only introduced in 1957, 67 years after the first drop dripped from the tap in Asia. That same fabulous international success it has enjoyed looks destined to be repeated in Britain with sales of bottles and cans falling just short of the 10-million mark in 1987. In 1988 sales of three-quarters of a million cases were forecast: that is an incredible 18 million bottles, an increase of some 55 per cent – a figure not be snorted at.

SAN MIGUEL has a palatably dry taste, and despite having an alcohol content of 5.4 per cent by volume, it is unusually light, enabling the practising tippler an opportunity to fit four or five in before realizing the damage that has been done! Some of you will now be able to enjoy your holiday tipple on draught, as Greenalls began to test-market it in 25 outlets in the north-west in May 1988. Their marketing manager is hoping that this humble little figure will bubble into 3,000 before too long. So, People of the North, don't deny the rest of us your good fortune, get out there and get 'em in!

SAN MIGUEL SELECTA   Spain

OG 1058–64°   *Lance Brown*
Bottles

Introduced to Spain in the mid-70s as a luxury beer, SELECTA is stronger than the original SAN MIGUEL (*q.v.*) with 6.4 per cent alcohol by volume content.

Beautifully packaged in a bottle that you can grip tightly around the waist, it's a crisp and tasty lager with a slight hint of malt, that goes down very nicely, although it does, unfortunately, possess the sticky quality that many lagers of a similar strength do. As it's available nationwide there's no excuse for not buying it! Highly recommended.

SANS CULOTTES   France

Bottles   *Applejack Trading Co.*

From Brasserie la Choulette, SANS CULOTTES is a lager that's made in the traditional manner of the '*bière de garde*' (beer to be kept).

A lightly roasted malt is used in this process, which gives it a smooth, well-rounded flavour and a delicate bouquet. As it undergoes a secondary fermentation in the bottle, it is not a lager that Philistines should drink straight from the bottle. Pour it into a glass, carefully to avoid disturbing the deposit, and savour it!

Well worth taking care over, SANS CULOTTES, which takes its name from the time when trousers

were first worn by the revolting peasants during the French Revolution is definitely a lager that should be afforded a little of your time.

SAPPORO   Japan

OG 1043–47°   *Unlimited Limited*
Cans

Established in 1876, this is Japan's oldest, but by no

means best, lager. Introduced to the UK in 1987 by Vaux Breweries, it underwent an eight-month test period in the north-east. Oliver Peyton of Rivalage – a company set up specifically to market SAPPORO – later brought it south in what was virtually a one-man operation. Fortunately for Mr Peyton, SAPPORO enjoyed a lot of media attention during its struggle to establish itself on the market. This was mainly for two reasons.

The first is the packaging: a highly original eye-catching, tapered silver can, streamlined at the base and with forceful red-and-black graphics. This is not the only unique thing about the can: there is also the ring-pull which, when torn back, enables you not only to remove the entire lid but also to either spill the contents all over yourself or use the tin as a glass.

The second thing that attracted the media was the fact that it wasn't made available to wholesalers or the general public at large, but was strategically 'placed' in *sushi* bars, private-members clubs and fashionable concept restaurants. For this reason it's available in many of London's exclusive and foppy nightspots where, research has shown, the punters like to admire their haircuts, as well as the labels on their clothes, in the reflective silver can!

Besides all this, there's nothing much of interest about the drink itself. It's an unpasteurized draught lager with little aroma, a thin texture and a rather weak taste despite its gravity. SAPPORO is simply a novelty lager. Indeed, SAPPORO is to be found at many 'novelty' bars such as the members-only London nightspot, Fred's of Carlisle Street, the home of Dick Bradsell – the world's greatest barman.

Needless to say, it's not one of my favourites, but then again, don't let me put you off trying it should you be given the opportunity – you might just like it!

SATZENBRAU UK

OG 1044–50°
Bottles 275ml
Cans 440ml

Harp Lager Co.

Breweries in Park Royal, London, and Dundalk in Northern Ireland turn out this comparatively dark, honey-coloured pils lager with a 6.3 per cent alcohol by volume measure. This ABV figure gives it a little bit of a bite and perhaps this is why in blind tests against the brand leader, 64 per cent preferred the taste of SATZENBRAU compared with the 'leader's' piddling 36 per cent (SATZENBRAU's figures, not mine!). However, the leading brand (you know what it is!) improved its stake, when in branded tests, where a participant was allowed to view the products, they jumped to 44 per cent which still left SATZENBRAU the winner with 56 per cent. If you are like me you'll be wondering just how these tests were carried out; I'm sure the blokes at Holsten (*whoops*, mentioned the name!) were wondering too!

Well, Harp were so confident that during 1988 they devised a *master plan* in which 640 'Taste-Test Challenge Nights' were held in pubs and clubs throughout the length and breadth of Britain. At the time of publication, after 1,660 people had claimed their freebie, the results were split 60–40 in SATZENBRAU's favour. Surprise, surprise!

Promising results, huh? Harp think so. They pumped £2 million into it in 1988 as well as a 'heavyweight' trade and consumer programme. This might be because after nearly a decade it still doesn't have national distribution and, despite all the Taste-Test figures Harp are willing to lay on the table, they still only hold about 4 per cent of the pils market while Holsten still has around 50 per cent.

So despite all their proud boasts the question remains – what does SATZENBRAU taste like? It's not a bad tipple at all, though there are certainly a couple of other pils on the market that I rate higher. Still, there's a lot to be said about SATZENBRAU: for instance it's won three consecutive gold medals in international competition for product excellence at the Monde Sélection Awards held in Brussels, Belgium, and that can't be scoffed at. I recommend you give it a blind date!

SCANDIA DIAT PILS   Denmark

OG 1044–50° – 6% ABV
Cans 44cl

Brewed and canned in Denmark, SCANDIA DIAT PILS has a light, golden colour and a very pleasant, light malty bouquet with a subtle hint of sweetness. The colour gives rise to the feeling that DIAT PILS might be lighter than it seems, but don't be fooled for a moment. It's strong! Lightly carbonated, it has a good pils flavour that is full-bodied with a strong, malty character. As far as the pils sector is concerned, this one is well worth checking out as I believe it offers a pleasant alternative to the brand leaders.

SCANDIA SPECIAL EXTRA
STRONG LAGER   Denmark

OG 1078–84° – 9% ABV
Cans

Brewed and canned by the Danish firm Danish Interbrau, SCANDIA SPECIAL's packaging is made unattractive by its choice of lettering and logo, and from there on in it gets worse. The bouquet alone gives evidence that what you're about to drink will be thick and sticky by its extremely sweet nose. As dark as many bitters (though that isn't always a bad thing), SCANDIA SPECIAL is, to put it bluntly, horrible. Although lightly carbonated, it has a clinging, sickly, thoroughly unpleasant aftertaste. Anything is preferable to this, even Karl Lagerfeld after-shave. It's ghastly!

SCHLITZ	USA
Bottles 33cl Cans	*Allied*

As a rule many Americans are derisive about their own beers and look to the European fatherland for their quality brews despite the fact that America is the world's largest brewing nation with a fine brewing tradition all of its own. The centre of that industry for many years was Milwaukee, hence the baseball team Milwaukee Brewers, and 'the beer that made Milwaukee famous' was SCHLITZ.

In 1856 Joseph Schlitz took over the Krug brewery, where he remained in control until his death 19 years later. The brewery then passed into the hands of the Uihlein family in which it remains today. Despite its history and fame, SCHLITZ is not one of America's best lagers. It is highly carbonated, lightly hopped and pale, and the kindest description I can give it is inoffensive.

SCHUTZ JUBILATOR	France
OG 1056° Bottles 275ml	*Maison Caurette Ltd*

The French have a healthy brewing history and

although they drink nearly three times more wine than beer the country is packed with loyal lager lovers, and none more so than those in the Alsace region. Here many of the brews still retain an obvious Teutonic influence. SCHUTZ JUBILATOR bears such an influence and is a full-flavoured, rich Alsatian pils of good character. Considering its original gravity, it surprisingly avoids the unpleasant sticky character that mars the enjoyment of many other lagers of this strength. One of my personal favourites from this great brewing region.

SCHUTZ LITE   France

0.9% ABV   *Maison Caurette Ltd*
Bottles 275ml

A de-alcoholized brew which retains nothing whatsoever of a true lager flavour. I really would like to be able to say that it's all right, I mean, SHUTZ JUBILATOR (*q.v.*) is a great lager, but I'm sorry, I can't. This is one of the reasons that the French enjoy their wine so much.

SCHWABEN BRAU   West Germany

OG 1044 – 47°   *Maison Caurette Ltd*
Bottles 33cl
Cans 33cl

From the smallest of Stuttgart's three breweries, with its lagering cellar and copper brewhouse, comes SCHWABEN BRAU. Initially crisp, it has a strong malty smell with a rich, slightly sweet taste. Indeed, it is a good lager in the premium range, though not a lot can be said for the marketing. The can, for instance, is an unexciting green-and-white design with the usual Germanic writing over a coat of arms, comprised of three lines and a sheaf of wheat surrounded by hops. Boring, but I must admit efficient, for the can carries its information in five different languages as well as just slipping in the fact, in tiny lettering, that it is brewed to the Rheinheitsgebot of 1516.

Another recommended lager.

SHANGHAI PREMIUM LAGER China

OG 1047° *Continental Lager Distributors Ltd*
Bottles

SHANGHAI is most definitely a novelty beer and, as such, should be sampled. It is lightly hopped in the pilsner style, and I found it a little thin for my liking, though nevertheless pleasant and refreshing. You might find it difficult to obtain but virtually all lager is worth a taste. Luckily off-licences are becoming more and more adventurous about their stock in a bid to please the ever-growing number of discerning lager drinkers.

SINGHA Thailand

OG 1053–57° *Tirrell's*
Bottles

Marketed over here as 'Thailand's favourite brew', SINGHA, from the Boon Rawd brewery, is indeed a fine ambassador for its country. Beautifully hopped, and with a sharp bitter full taste, SINGHA is a great lager that you shouldn't miss out on.

Introduced to the UK, as far as I can gather, in 1980, it is now available in many free houses throughout the country as well as the more discerning off-licences and Thai restaurants.

If you have difficulty finding it then the next time you're in London make your way to the Bahn Thai restaurant in Frith Street, W1. The English proprietor keeps an extensive list of wines, but as we people of great taste know, a good beer goes down best with Thai or Malaysian food! In my view it's one of the best lagers in the world.

SINGHA GOLD   Thailand

OG 1042–45°   *Tirrell's*
Bottles

Again from the Boon Rawd brewery and lovingly brought to us by Tirrell's of Wraysbury, Berks, SINGHA GOLD is slightly lower in alcohol content than its sister brew SINGHA (*q.v.*)

This is one lager that I'm afraid I haven't yet sampled. Though, having said that, if it is in any way at all similar to SINGHA it's got to be pretty good. Indeed, a good friend of mine who lives in Wraysbury, the scenic-artist Emma Harrison, teasingly tells me it is – but never brings me a sample. If you find it, drink it, but send me a bottle too!

SKOL   UK

Allied

In an effort to revitalize SKOL Allied Take-Home invested £8 million in a package of advertising and promotions which brought about the scrapping of the familiar world map decoration. 'Hagar the Horrible', the cartoon character famed through the *Sun* newspaper, was brought in to spearhead the new advertising campaign. But can Hagar now be *horrible* under all the new advertising restrictions on alcohol? SKOL's marketing director thinks so, and maybe he's right. I mean, Hagar might not be able to fracture quite so many craniums as he used to, but he can certainly carry on bellowing away at the wife.

SKOL is the dreaded enemy of CAMRA (Campaign for Real Ale) who, at the Great British Beer Festival in Leeds in 1988, described it as 'one of the three worst drinks in the UK' – this quote was given out minus the expletives. Personally I agree with them, I wouldn't be seen dead with a can.

SKOL EXPORT LAGER   UK

OG 1044°   *Allied*

Though a far superior brew to plain old SKOL (*q.v.*), SKOL EXPORT is still by no means a lager that I would go out of my way for.

A little over carbonated for my liking, but with a reasonably crisp character and not a bad taste, it is by no means bad, but then again it's not too good!

SKOL EXTRA STRENGTH 1080

OG 1080°   *Allied*
Bottles
Cans

There's a lot of people out there tucking a lot of this
stuff away, and they are the opposite of the low-alcohol
'lager' drinkers – the backlash if you like. It's one
extreme to the other. Personally I wouldn't go near
either type of lager as they are both pretty unpleasant.
The low-alcohol stuff gives you wind because that's all
you're drinking, and the loads-of-alcohol stuff leaves a
ghastly aftertaste. But don't let that put you off. If
you're a loads-of-alcohol drinker then the next time
you're looking for a drink give this one a try. It tastes
pretty much the same as all the others to me, but one
friend who actually likes this sort of drink said it was 'a
little sharper'. Forget brand loyalty. You should always
check out the market – you never know what you
might be missing.

SKOL SPECIAL STRENGTH   UK

OG 1044–48°   *Allied*
Cans 44cl

A light bouquet accompanies a clean, amber colour in
SKOL SPECIAL STRENGTH. It's deceptively strong
for such a clear lager and although unnecessarily
gassy, it still goes down reasonably well. Unfortunately,
although initially dry, it leaves a slightly unpleasant
sticky aftertaste. As far as SKOL goes though it is
definitely their best product and therefore the best buy.
However, I can think of several other things I'd rather
do with my money.

SKONA   UK

OG 1030–1034°   *Hall and Woodhouse*
Cans

Brewed by Hall and Woodhouse of Dorset, who really
should know better! This is another insipid lager which
is to be found in many supermarkets and bargain bins.
It really is awful!

Over carbonated and very weak tasting, it should be
avoided at all costs. Even if you do only have 23p in
your pocket.

SKOPSKO   Yugoslavia

OG 1046–50°   *Docklands Wine Brokers*
Bottles

Launched during the summer of 1988 by en-
trepreneurs in London's dockland area, this one was
originally brewed in Skopje, Yugoslavia, in 1924.

Hops and malt are taken from local farms while the
water is supplied from the mountain springs of the
Shara range, which surrounds the valley of Skopje.
This area is well known amongst Yugoslavian ski-
enthusiasts as the mountain range that retains snow
on its slopes all year round. These ingredients combine
to supply a pale light beer with a dry, bitter, hoppy taste.

Packaged in a brown bottle with a rather distinctive
silver label, adorned with pink, black and orange
arrows, it has won a bucketful of medals since its
introduction to the west. In 10 years it's picked up
three gold medals, four silvers and a gold star. You
have to admit that's impressive. This one really
shouldn't be missed.

SAM SMITH – *see under* S

JOHN SMITH – *see under* J

SOL	Mexico
OG 1040–42° – 4.2% ABV **Bottles 35.5cl**	*Maison Caurette Ltd*

Just under 100 years ago, a small German brewer decided to leave Germany for sunnier climes. And so began a journey that took Wilhelm Haase and 300 years of his family's brewing formulas and skills to the New World where he was welcomed with open arms by the Mexicans.

After searching the land for a suitable place to settle and establish a small brewery, he finally decided upon Veracruz in 1896. The site he chose was at the base of Mount Orizaba where his keen brewer's eye had noticed that the water from the mountain springs was naturally filtered through 7,000 feet of porous bedrock. Quickly, Haase set about the construction of his new plant, and after months of sweat and toil in the hot Mexican sun, the day finally arrived – Haase had brewed a beer. The locals excitedly watched as Haase proudly brought forth the first jug of his beer from the brewery's gates to share with them. The Mexicans were well pleased with the taste of Haase's new brew which, to this day, is very light, mellow and refreshing. But the thing they marvelled at more than anything was the way the clear brilliance, given to it by the perfect water, seemed to catch the dancing rays of the sun. And thus SOL, the Sun Beer, was born.

SOL was introduced to the UK in June 1985, just 11 years short of its 100th birthday, and is now available mainly in Mexican restaurants as well as a few discerning bars. Although its availability is unfortunately restricted, SOL still sells an impressive half-a-million bottles per annum. A gold-medal winner, it's an easy beer to drink, as it goes down very well. Drink it *au naturel*, or stuff a wedge of lime in the neck of the bottle – the choice is yours. An extremely pleasant little lager.

SPATEN PILS   West Germany

Bottles 33cl   *C. H. Marlow*

SPATEN PILS comes from the great Spatenbrau brewery in Munich, one of the world's most important breweries. During the 1900s Spaten's master brewer was one Gabriel Sedlmayr who handed down power to his sons. Between them their influence has crept into the way men brew their beer across the globe – refrigeration, amongst other things.

Today the brewery does its best to blend its proud history and tradition into modern brewing methods, one result of which is the very dry but pale SPATEN PILS. It is an easy-to-drink, high-class brew that should be sought out and consumed.

STEFFL   Austria

Bottles   *Steffl (UK) Ltd*

Thankfully, this beer comes to us from the Schwechat Brewery on the outskirts of Vienna, and is truly a world-leading brew.

In 1841 Anton Dreher created for the first time, a

bottom-fermented beer – lager to you and me – from this very same brewery. If only to encourage you further, let me tell you that STEFFL is a wonderfully hoppy, light lager that goes down very well. It is popular in Austria's eastern provinces, and I only hope that it becomes equally popular here. Now you can rush out and buy one.

STEIGER UK

Cans 500ml *Guinness*

In a bid to cash in on the booming success of the lager market Guinness Ireland introduced STEIGER to an already jam-packed market place in 1983 with the advertising slogan, 'The Smooth-Edged Lager'. This 'expertly' brewed beer with a 'thirst-cutting edge' is 'balanced with that uniquely Continental, smooth flavour'. Or is it?

Guinness, makers of the world's greatest pint – Guinness Porter Stout – are no strangers to brewing and have a fine, proud history. More recently they've begun to instigate or brew a whole new chain: SATZEN-BRAU PILS (*q.v.*), all the varieties of HARP (*q.v.*), etc. Apart from HARP and the dreaded KALIBER (*q.v.*) they don't do a bad job. STEIGER is not the world's best lager by a mile, but brewed by the world's greatest brewers it's the sort of drink that you should sample just to put your mind at rest! After all, imagine if Guinness were a lager! Now we wouldn't want to miss that, would we?

STEINBOCK   UK

OG 1034° – 3.6% ABV   *Shepherd Neame*
Draught
Cans 44cl

This one is brewed in the UK by Shepherd Neame under licence from the Swiss Brauerei Hurlimann. STEINBOCK was launched in south-east England in 1985, and introduced to the take-home trade in early 1988 in a somewhat gaudily designed can on which curiously entwined fish can be found.

The word 'Bock' is a term usually reserved for a strong lager beer, more than 6 per cent ABV and, which is as a rule, a lot darker than your average lager. Well, STEINBOCK certainly doesn't look like a 'Bock' to me. With a slightly sweet aroma, beneath which sits a golden body, STEINBOCK is surprisingly a rather weak tasting lager. Still, it stands shoulder to shoulder with all the other thin, tasteless standard issues and those who venture to drink it are welcome to it.

STEINGOLD EXPORT DRAUGHT LAGER   UK

OG 1042°   *McMullen & Sons*
Draught

Bit of a rarity, this chap, as it's only available on draught. STEINGOLD's sales are restricted to an area of an approximate 30-mile radius from Hertford, Herts, the home of its brewers, McMullen and Son.

STEINLAGER   New Zealand

OG 1047°   *GB Vintagers*
Bottles 33cl & 75.7cl
Cans 34 cl

I know it sounds incredible, but *more beer is drunk in New Zealand than Britain*! Ever since good ol' Cap'n Cook brewed the first bevy way back in 1773 the plucky Kiwis have been shoving it in by the bucketful! New Zealand Breweries, the largest of one of only three brewing groups in the islands, are responsible for STEINLAGER, which is their strongest beer. Well, so they tell us, but don't bet on it as, actually, it's brewed under different gravities depending on the market. For instance, the STEINLAGER in this country is marketed at 1047° but it's available in New Zealand at 1052°. So, despite the fact that STEINLAGER is brewed and bottled/canned Down Under don't be fooled for one moment that you're getting the number one thing even though it won the English 'Championship Trophy Supreme Award' as 'the world's best lager' back in 1985. This lager literally depends on where you are and therefore which brew you're getting.

STEINLAGER has a slightly bitter, crisp flavour with a not unpleasant dryish aftertaste and a mild, though sweet, bouquet. Natural spring water supplies it with a clear, golden colour that would not be unwelcome to any lager lover's home. Batch-brewed with New Zealand hops and barley, it has a lovely snappy bite, despite a light texture. Extremely palatable, it is available in 26 countries throughout the world. So, wherever you are, I suggest you try and get hold of a bottle or two. A very good lager.

STELLA ARTOIS

UK

OG 1044–50° – 5.1% ABV
Draught
Bottles 330cl
Cans 44cl

Whitbread

Originally a Belgian product with a 30 per cent share of the Belgian market, STELLA ARTOIS is now brewed in England by Whitbread, and it has proved to be equally successful here since the growth in popularity of lager. STELLA has done well for Whitbread, who now sell more lager than beer, and is thriving in the premium sector. This is very impressive when one realizes that although the bottled variety landed in small numbers before the last war, STELLA has only been brewed in England since 1971.

Whitbread insist that the British version is brewed to the identical specifications of the product brewed by their Belgian counterparts, and well it might be. However, I feel it might be the way it's stored or the way it's extracted from the keg, but somehow it tastes a little different. I personally go for the imported version everytime. Don't get me wrong though – STELLA, as brewed by Whitbread, is a good strong draught lager that should be purchased before many others when given the choice. Brewed from top-quality malt and hops, it has a longer fermentation period than most of its competitors which shows in the quality – and unfortunately reflects in the price, but not that much! Go ahead, buy it, it's worth it!

STUTTGART PREMIUM PILS MALT LAGER
France

Bottles *Maison Caurette Ltd*

Yes, you've guessed it! A reasonably dry pils with a nice malty taste to it! It is by no means widely available, but I managed to pick up a bottle in Bristol. If you enjoy a good malty brew then this could be the one for you – if you can find it!

SUPER REDS
UK

OG 1038°
Cans
Team Advance

Liverpool Football Club lager, in club-coloured cans, horrified police chiefs and Members of Parliament alike, when it appeared a couple of years ago. Many expressed concern that it would encourage under-age drinkers, who apparently already spend a staggering £212 million a year on alcohol, to drink even more.

As for the lager itself, it's a bland, highly-carbonated brew from Devenish, and one that I certainly won't be buying. Anyway, the political arguments will probably rage on for a while yet.

SUPERIOR

Mexico

OG 1040–45°
Bottles 35.5cl

Maison Caurette Ltd

Difficult to imagine, I admit, but when you think of all the Germans in Latin America I think you'll understand why Mexico is actually one of the leading brewing nations on the globe. Its first brewery was established during the early 1500s under the direction of the King of Spain and was also the first in Latin America.

SUPERIOR is a traditional Mexican beer in as much as it is a clear pilsner-style brew with a subtle taste and a sparkling finish that belies a 4.5 per cent alcohol by volume content. Best served well chilled in my view, although the Mexicans have been known to enjoy their lager warm. Several cases sent from its admirable importers, Maison Caurette, proved to me that the beer is generally consistent as well as the instigator of a great evening!

Beer in Latin America is not really seen as an intoxicant, more as a thirst-quencher and a law passed in 1931 made this official. Any beer with a strength of less than 5 per cent alcohol by volume is a soft drink! Mexico here I come!

SUTCLIFFE'S ALCOHOL FREE   UK

Sutcliffe's

You've heard the saying, 'I could murder a beer!' well now you know the meaning of 'I could murder a brewer!' And let's hope someone does! Even by low-alcohol standards this stuff has reached the depths!

SWAN PREMIUM EXPORT   Australia

OG 1042–46°   *GB Vintagers*
Cans 375ml

Swan, from Western Australia's only brewery, has been brewed for 148 years and is one of the strongest Aussie lagers available in the UK. It is also claimed to be the only 'major' brand actually brewed in Australia with 'major' distribution over here. However, despite this fact, Allied Take-Home, who recently made the can available in a four-pack as opposed to its original six-pack, are concerned that Swan can't compete with CASTLEMAINE XXXX (*q.v.*). Of course, it's not going to compete with XXXX unless it's backed by a few million pounds worth of advertising! In a bid to extend their market in the US, now that the Australian domestic market has stagnated to such an extent that experts reckon it would need an investment of £15 million to gain another 1 per cent share, Bond bought the Pittsburgh Brewing Company for £40 million in 1986, and in October 1987 the giant Wisconsin brewery G. Heileman for £1.7 billion. These purchases propelled Bond's company into fourth place in the world's top ten brewing stakes. The intention obviously is to brew SWAN PREMIUM in the States, and go in on the back of Heileman's massive and existing operation. I'm sure that if this plan goes smoothly then SWAN should meet Stateside with huge success.

Long a favourite of mine over other Australian brews, it's lively, thirst-quenching when cold and has a strong, fully-brewed flavour. A delight to the palate, it's not too gassy and its rich, slightly sweet flavour make it perfect for any time of the day. Taken as a premium lager, it's one of the best overall in the country. Like all great Aussie lagers it should be consumed in the local way (i.e., regularly!) at a very cold temperature, so make sure your fridge is big enough!

SWAN in a nutshell? *Ripper!*

SWAN LIGHT   Australia

0.9% ABV
Cans 375ml

Let's face it, you can wash in this stuff, bath, shower, shave, and you'll still be clean and sober. SWAN LIGHT is brewed as usual, we're told, and then all the alcohol is removed, leaving us with a fine brew. However, in reality it's thin, wet, and over gassy. This is one of the blandest low-alcohol lagers I've tasted, and that's saying something! Yet still sales boom! This year pigs will fly, and Tranmere Rovers will win the League and Cup double!

TAJ MAHAL   UK

OG 1046°   *Shepherd Neame*
Bottles 33cl
Cans 12fl. oz

TAJ MAHAL is another Indian lager from Shepherd

Neame's portfolio and it's available nationally through Indian and oriental restaurants. Named after that unforgettable 'poem in stone'. It is brewed in the UK by Shepherd Neame under licence from United Breweries International Ltd. The promotional blurb insists that the lager brings you the enchantment of the Taj Mahal itself, which took 20,000 men 20 years to build and is the greatest testimony of a man's love for a woman in the world – the lager, however, isn't.

On tasting, TAJ MAHAL initially comes across as a pale, clean lager with a creamy head and a pleasant malty bouquet that has just a subtle hint of sweetness. Beyond this the lager is quite thick and sticky with a tacky aftertaste. It lacks crispness and bite, and a KINGFISHER (q.v.) is probably a better wash for your curry. However, some people may welcome TAJ MAHAL as an alternative to KINGFISHER, which was for years the only widely available Indian lager on the market. Although TAJ MAHAL is not one of my favourites, I would encourage you to sample it for yourself as palates certainly can vary beneath the all-conquering, all-burning vindaloo.

TALISMAN   UK

0.9 ABV   *Charles Wells Ltd*
Draught
Bottles 27.5cl
Cans 44cl

The first draught low-alcohol lager available when it was launched in the Bedfordshire area by brewers Charles Wells Ltd in 1986, TALISMAN is now available in bottles – more's the pity! Yet another 'lager' in the low/no-alcohol sector with low/no resemblance to the real thing.

TATRA PILS   Poland

OG 1048–51° – 5.5% ABV   *Marblehead/Grandmartin*
Bottles 33cl

This strong, full-bodied pils is brewed and bottled by
the Zywiec Brewery of Zywiec, a small town set deep in
the beautiful, unspoilt Tatra mountains bordering
Czechoslovakia in the south of Poland. The present
brewery was founded in 1856 by the then Archduke
Karol Hapsburg, although Zywiec has been famous for
the production of top-quality beer since the 14th century. TATRA is a lager I've enjoyed many times at
the free-flowing Daquise Polish restaurant in South
Kensington, London, as well as all good Polish clubs
throughout the Kingdom. It has a dry but extremely
full-bodied and robust flavour that is well worth trying.
I recently bought it at a Safeways supermarket, so it
might well now be available near you. The ideal accompaniment to the filling cuisine of Poland. If your
granny can make blinis as good as my granny's then
order a case now!

TECATE   Mexico

OG 1046°   *Mexican Beer Co.*
Cans 33.5cl

From the Cuauhtemoc Brewery, the second largest in
Mexico, comes TECATE, already the USA's top-selling
imported canned beer. It was originally imported by
Continental Lager Distributors, but it is now being
handled by the Mexican Beer Import Company which
was founded specifically (surprise, surprise) to handle
Mexican products. The brewers/distributors are en-
couraging us Brits to drink the beer with salt and a

squeeze of lime or lemon juice, as it's done by some in Mexico.

In fact, the off-trade sell each can of TECATE with a sachet that contains 50 per cent sea salt and 50 per cent potassium – a lower sodium content than pure salt and a clever marketing ploy in the health-conscious 80s. The on-trade is also encouraged to provide a wedge of lime or lemon with each sale. The way to drink it is to sprinkle the salt, and then squeeze the lime, onto the top of the can before drinking. Personally I like it, but the lager itself, without the added salt or lime juice, is pretty good. Not too gassy, it is crisp with a nice bite to it! Well worth trying.

TENNENT'S EXTRA	UK

OG 1044° *Tennent*
Draught
Cans 44cl

A fine lager beer from Tennent (*see also* TENNENT'S LAGER). Full-bodied and lively with a slight malty aroma, TENNENT'S EXTRA (also known as 'Export') was introduced over 100 years ago in 1885. A fine lager with a nice bite to it! Well worth your time . . . and mine!

TENNENT'S L.A.	UK

Low-alcohol *Bass*
Cans 33cl

Launched in the south-east, the main stage of the 'lifestyle phenomenon', in October 1987, its national launch followed five months later. As far as low/no-alcohol lagers are concerned, this one, along with CLAUSTHALER (*q.v.*), in our view is one of the best. At least this one looks like lager and its taste isn't that unpleasant. If you are going to drink 'low/no lager' then you could do a lot worse than TENNENT'S L.A.

TENNENT'S LAGER

UK

OG 1036–40°
Draught
Bottles
Cans

Tennent

Sit down and make yourself comfortable, and when you've cracked open a can of TENNENT'S, I'll begin . . .

Envy over German lager beers and the history of their brewers comes to an abrupt halt when we take a good look at the Tennent group in Scotland, a country that is some way ahead of the rest of Britain when it comes to *the* important thing in life – *lager*! For Tennent, and the great city in which it was founded – Glasgow – has a rich lager history all of its own.

The Molendinar Burn, which is now little more than a sewer, was once a small tributary of the Clyde. Its small settlements eventually grew into the now proud city of Glasgow. Brewing almost certainly came to the area with the arrival of the monks of St Mungo, who founded the city. It is argued today that the monks brewed only for sale or barter to the local population, as opposed to the traditional own consumption (take your own side in this one). By the 16th century the Molendinar was liberally dotted with small breweries, one of which, by the bridge at Drygate Foot, belonged to one Robert Tennent. From around 1556 when he joined the original Incorporation of Maltmen, brewing and malting runs like a giant artery through the history of the Tennent family.

In 1740 two of the many sons of Patrick Tennent, Hugh, a farmer, and Robert, a brewer, formed the brewing partnership of H. and R. Tennent. Hugh, the farmer, had several sons, two of which, John and Robert, took over the business and formed J. and R. Tennent in 1769.

Under them the business literally boomed and the brewery was expanded in 1793 and again in 1797, absorbing, in the process, the adjacent brewhouse of William McLehose at Wellpark. It was at this time that the firm was listed in *Tait's Directory* of 1783, the first published commercial directory of Glasgow. Today, Tennent is the only firm which remains in the same business and on the same site. Now that is what I call history.

John and Robert died in 1826 and 1827 and Hugh Tennent, son of Robert, took over. When he retired, Charles Tennent, a trained and skilful brewer, inherited the brewery. Charles was not only a master brewer but also a whizz kid at management, and at the time of his death in 1864, J. and R. Tennent were the largest exporters of bottled beer in the world. After Charles Tennent died, his son, Hugh Tennent, took over in 1884.

Being a sickly lad, Hugh had spent some time on the Continent 'taking the waters'. It was while he was in Bavaria in 1881–2 that, taking somewhat more than the waters, I can assure you, Hugh developed a taste for . . . yes, you've guessed it – *lager!*

Once back home, young Hugh wasted no time in organizing the brewing of lager and the first pint was pulled in May 1885, amidst much noise and celebration from the Glaswegians. In the same year Hugh employed two Continental brewers, Jacob Klinger and Eric Westergaard, a German and a Dane respectively, as well as a gang of German coopers, in order to achieve the best qualities of the European lagers he'd been busy sampling abroad. The German coopers were needed to make giant casks tight enough to retain the carbon dioxide during 'Krausening'. This higher degree of carbonation was needed to produce the main feature of this 'new' beer. So successful was Hugh's lager beer that in 1889 he commissioned a new brewery that was not only built by a German workforce but was constructed to full German specifications. Before it was finished, however, Hugh, the great Scottish lager pioneer, died. He was the last of the Tennents to be in direct control of the brewery. Still, the new management had faith in Hugh's vision and to this day the two yeast strains he introduced to TENNENT'S LAGER, one German and one Danish, are still used.

After the First World War Tennent introduced pasteurization to ensure long-lasting products. In 1935 Tennents was one of the first breweries in Europe to introduce a 12oz version of the cone-top can. This was, however, stopped by the Second World War, as well as by its similarity in appearance to the Brasso can! In 1954 the Metal Box Company persuaded Tennent to relaunch the can since they had created a flat-top design with a new lining. This time it was a success. Following this, Metal Box tried to get Tennent to sell their lager in a 10oz can, but it proved too expensive, so, in great Scottish tradition, Tennent asked Metal Box to produce the biggest can possible, believing that this would bring total costs down as more lager could be sold in it. This size turned out to be 16oz, the norm for today's market. In the 1950s Tennent also introduced the now famous 'lager lovely' to their cans.

In 1963 J. and R. Tennent took the then highly unusual step of selling lager in draught form, therefore anticipating the huge boom in the market to come. It was the last significant thing they were to do as, in the same year, they were taken over by Charrington United Breweries, who merged with United Caledonian Breweries on the first day of 1966. The firm has since been known as Tennent Caledonian Breweries. CUB merged

with Bass in 1967 to form Bass Charrington, whose name was cropped to Bass in 1978.

With all this history behind them, Tennent now produce a range of lager beers, of which TENNENT'S LAGER was the first. It is only available on draught in Scotland and Ireland – England and Wales get TENNENT'S PILSNER (*q.v.*). The famous 'lager lovely' cans are, however, available throughout the UK

Introduced on draught in 1963, and with an original gravity of 1037.5° (the canned version was introduced in 1885! It has an original gravity of 1035.5°), TENNENT'S LAGER is slightly stronger than most standard lagers.

This is reflected in its full body and robust flavour. This extremely good pint, with over 100 years of history behind it, comes fully recommended.

TENNENT'S PILSNER   UK

OG 1033–37° Draught   *Tennent*
1030–34° – 3.5% ABV Bottles/Cans

Another Tennent product, this one is their standard-strength lager for the English and Welsh markets.

As you can see from the details above, the original gravity of draught is slightly stronger than the canned and bottled versions. Having never really drunk it before, I bumped into it at an all-night pool match in aid of the Great Ormond Street Hospital for Children. There were only two lagers available: draught HEINEKEN (*q.v.*) and draught TENNENT'S PILSNER. Let me tell you straight away that by dawn three kegs of TENNENT'S had been consumed (mostly by me, you'll be proud to note), whereas less than one keg of HEINEKEN had been swallowed up. I wasn't surprised at all as TENNENT'S PILSNER is by far the superior brew. Dry, full-bodied and with a pleasant refreshing taste, it is indeed a fine standard lager. It certainly has my seal of approval.

TENNENT'S SUPER   UK

9% ABV   *Tennent*
Cans

This lager, introduced to the super-strength market in 1971, is not one of my personal favourites. For me there is little to distinguish it from most of the super-strength lagers available. Although, having said that, I suggest you take a look at this one if you are a fan of these mind-numbing brews. A big seller in its league, and brewed by the great history-drenched Tennent Caledonian, it might just become your usual.

TESCO'S DANISH LOW-ALCOHOL LAGER

Denmark

Cans

Tesco

Yawn! Another horrible low-alcohol lager, this time brought to us by Tesco.

Brewed in Denmark, which is more than can be said for the CARLSBERG (*q.v.*) in your local, this lager is nevertheless bland in both taste and appearance. Surprise, surprise!

Tesco also sell 7-Up, fresh orange juice, mineral water and tinned Ambrosia custard. If you're not partaking of alcohol, why don't you drink one of these?

TESCO'S PILSENER

UK

OG 1038°
Cans

Tesco

The one thing that surprised me about this lager was its original gravity. I'd expected it to be firmly in the lower 30s along with most of the other supermarket brands.

Having said that, it certainly doesn't distinguish itself in any other way from your average 'supermarket lager'! It is over carbonated, thin, and has little taste.

33 DRY EXTRA STRENGTH

France

OG 1060–64°
Bottles 25cl

Copak Drinks Ltd

This lager beer is aptly described by its title: dry.

Surprisingly smooth for a lager of such strength, it is full bodied but rather heavy, with a slightly bitter character in its finish. Although launched here at the same time as its sister brew, 33 EXPORT (*q.v.*), it is a little less easily available, though well worth seeking out.

---

33 EXPORT   France

OG 1045–49°   *Copak Drinks Ltd*
Bottles 25cl

Copak Drinks launched 33 EXPORT in the opening months of 1987, yet by July of the same year they were forced to appoint two specialist companies to help individual areas of sales, such was the growth in demand BBL Marketing were hired to deal with cash-and-carries while the First Beer Company of London were asked to cover the on-trade, initially in the London area, where such pubs as the French House in Soho soaked it up. Meanwhile Copak set themselves the task of preparing a programme of consumer promotions aimed at building awareness of the product, a tough job in itself, bearing in mind how crowded the expanding market-place already is.

Despite the fact that for the French their first love is their generally excellent wine, the country produces some fine lager beers. 33 EXPORT is brewed at Lille, the heart of France's lager-drinking population, by Pelforth, the country's second largest brewers, who are equally well known for their top-fermented ales.

33 EXPORT is an extremely palatable lager that complements the provincial cuisine of northern France quite nicely. Thus, next time you fancy a nice side of frog, try a 33. Well worth loading your supermarket trolley with this in Boulogne, or Bognor for that matter.

TIGER   Singapore

OG 1046–50°   *Marblehead/GB Vintagers*
Bottles
Cans 27.5 & 33cl

The Tiger Brewery was opened in 1931 and today, although TIGER beer is without doubt Singapore's most famous brand, it is not the biggest-selling lager in its home market. It's usually stocked by most Thai or Malaysian restaurants, and its rich, well-hopped flavour is a perfect complement to their incredibly spicy cuisine. The hops used to produce this flavour are imported from the USA, and only the flower of the female hop is used in the brewing process. The malted barley is imported from both Australia and Europe. These two facts go some way, lager lovers, to showing you the pride that goes into the brewing of this lager.

In the region of 4 per cent alcohol by volume, TIGER is not so much strong as refreshing, and several mouthfuls or bottles, depending on the individual palate, are in order after a large helping of Singapore fried noodles. However, with the new popularity of imported lagers from around the world, TIGER has found itself becoming somewhat of an idol to the new lager drinker and, as such, has begun to expand from its natural home in the restaurants to some of the more fashionably expensive members-only clubs of London, to a surprising number of 'locals' throughout the country. Thus, the future of TIGER LAGER BEER, as far as sales are concerned, looks very bright indeed.

I used to drink it at around 60p a bottle with my lunch, at Melati's in Soho's Great Windmill Street, and also in a certain pool hall in St Austell, Cornwall, long before it became more widely available. In a *Sunday Times* blindfold lager-tasting session some time ago, TIGER LAGER BEER came out with the top billing, and I can fully understand why. To use their old advertising slogan from the 40s, any time of day is 'Time for a Tiger'. You'll see why for yourself when you slip out to the off-licence and buy one.

TOOHEYS   Australia

OG 1044° – 4.6% ABV   *Evelyn Wines*
Cans 37.5cl

TOOHEYS, the king of New South Wales, is the baby of the Australian lager boom, only arriving in the UK in May 1988 with a measly £1 million promotional campaign. Naturally, the point was pushed that TOOHEYS is an import from Australia, while XXXX and FOSTER'S (*qq.v.*) are brewed in the UK. SWAN PREMIUM (*q.v.*), however, has also been making this point for some time, as has BOAGS (*q.v.*).

Still, whatever the virtues of the other Australian lagers, TOOHEYS is welcome in the UK, and it's a lager well worth getting aquainted with. It has a taste that is uniquely Australian in that it is light and golden with a rich, pleasant bouquet. Full-bodied and spritzy, it goes down easily. Immensely enjoyable this *real* Australian lager comes highly recommended and makes such a refreshing change from the British-brewed Aussie brands.

TOP BRASS   UK

Cans   *Watneys*
PET bottles

'Aye, lad,' confirmed the typical northerner, his flat cap fluttering in the breeze, 'where there's muck there's brass!'

Young Timmy Higgins brushed the dust from his

eyes and peered at his pint unnaturally through the grim, grey daylight. 'Aye,' he went. 'There's nowt like brass, Bill. Nowt.'

'Aye.'

Just then Tina Pearson, the Boss's personal secretary, crossed the yard from the gym to the wages office, her long legs scissoring and squeaking noisily beneath the flimsy body-hugging, nylon boob-tube she'd somehow stretched into a dress.

Young Timmy Higgins wiped the yard-and-a-half of drool from his mouth with the back of a dusty hand and spilt his lager onto Bill's boot. But Bill couldn't take his eyes off Tina until her shadow had disappeared behind the wages office door. Then he turned on Timmy with a face tight with rage. 'Ay up, yer young bugger!' he roared, straightening Timmy's pint. 'That's yer lager yer spillin there, lad!'

'Sorry,' whined Young Timmy Higgins, emptying the last of his 2-litre PET bottle into his chipped enamel tin mug. 'I was watching Tina. She's a beau . . .'

'She's not for you, son!' laughed Bill, tilting his tweed cap to a rakish angle. 'You're just recently wed, lad. Aye, besides, a young woman like that needs a man of experience. Someone that's already been through the trials and rigours of wedlock and come out the other side with his manhood intact.'

'She was in my class at school,' squeaked Young Timmy eagerly. 'They all said that her and the teacher had something . . . well, y'know . . . that they had something . . . going.'

'WHA!' erupted Bill, breaking his lunch. 'Young Tina and that fat old bag, Missus Ogden?'

'No! Mister Arkwright,' Timmy giggled.

'The Boss's son!'

'Aye.'

Bill sighed and, cupping his unshaven chin in a large, dusty hand, looked up at the giant brass letters above the factory gates. 'ARKWRIGHT & SONS. WORK FER NOWT!' His mind wandered back over all the years he'd worked there. How he'd met Edna, a clerk in the packaging department. How they'd fallen in love and married. How the marriage had failed when he found her behind the bike sheds with the eldest of the Arkwright boys, Arthur (45). He thought of all the pain and grief it'd caused him, until he met Sharon, a girl young enough to be his daughter, from the Cleaner's department. She'd left him, of course, for another Arkwright boy, Norman (37). And now Tina. Someone he'd watched grow from a snotty kid into one of Grimsby's most vivacious women, in love with Stanley bloody Arkwright. He turned and looked at Young Timmy Higgins, desperate to erase the image of Tina Pearson and Stanley bloody Arkwright from his mind. 'What's that yer drinkin', anyway?' he asked.

Timmy looked up from his lager. 'I dunno, Bill. It was something the wife just put in the sandwich box.'

'Where's the bottle, then?' Bill said sternly, his patience thin.

'Hey, Bill!' Timmy Higgins squealed, picking the empty 2-litre PET bottle from the dust. 'It's called Top Brass! Here, that's a good name, t'ain't it?'

Bill snatched the lad's mug from his hand. 'Give it here!' he snarled. 'Let a man of experience taste it.'

Bill tipped the cool lager to his lips and spat it out again. '*Yuk!* That's muck, that is!'

'Aye,' went Young Timmy Higgins. 'But like you always say, Bill, where there's muck there's brass.'

And never a truer word has ever been said.

TSINGTAO
China

OG 1047°
Continental Lager Distributors Ltd
Bottles 33cl
Cans 33cl

After the Revolution, China began to grow its own

barley and hops and today both products are to be found in China's premier lager, TSINGTAO. It's a dry lager in the pilsner style with a light quality. This is hardly surprising as the brewery was originally founded by the Germans during the heady colonial days of 1903. The brand has long been established in the USA and, to a lesser extent, the UK, and is deservedly well respected. It is available in many Chinese restaurants, but you shouldn't just restrict yourself to it when eating out, as it goes down well at any time of the day.

TUBORG GOLD　　　　　　　　　　　　　　UK

OG 1044–48°　　　　　　　　　　　*Tuborg Lager Ltd*
Draught
Cans 10 & 16fl. oz

A far, far better lager than TUBORG PILSENER (*q.v.*), GOLD has a smooth, easy-to-drink texture and a full, pleasant flavour. A little over carbonated, though inoffensively so, TUBORG offers a clean, refreshing drink in pubs throughout the country. Well worth sampling.

TUBORG PILSENER　　　　　　　　　　　　UK

OG 1030–34°　　　　　　　　　　　*Tuborg Lager Ltd*
Draught
Cans 10 & 16fl. oz

The Danes are rightly famous throughout the world for their lagers, and apart from Germany they have probably done more than anyone else to contribute to the promotion of it. After all it was the Carlsberg laboratories that isolated the first single-cell yeast culture in 1883. Today Tuborg and Carlesberg are both run by the formidable United Breweries of Copenhagen. It is rumoured in Denmark that TUBORG and CARLSBERG (*q.v.*) are both actually one and the same drink, the only difference being the name. In the UK however, both lagers are brewed by different brewers. Although I wouldn't go as far as saying TUBORG PILSENER is a good lager, compared to many of its competitors which are available on draught, it's not that bad. I've drunk it myself a few times in the past at Young's pubs in London and, well, what can I say ...? *Burp!* Crisp and slightly hoppy, but highly carbonated, it's still popular in Cornwall where it's known as 'Steam' (though God knows why) amongst the local surfing fraternity.

Having said that, I must say how sad it is that Carlsberg and Tuborg have gone some way to destroy their reputations amongst discerning drinkers by allowing their lagers to be brewed under licence over here. In both cases their Danish-brewed products are infinitely superior.

TUCHER PILSENER   West Germany

OG 1046° – 4.65% ABV   *First Beer Co. of London*
Draught
Bottles 33cl
Cans 33 & 50cl

With a high original gravity, TUCHER falls directly into the rapidly-growing premium sector of the lager market, much to the delight of the London-based First Beer Company who launched the brand in April 1987 and who are the lager's sole and exclusive distributors. The brewers, Tucher of Nürnberg, are not exactly that popular at home these days due to the way in which they swallowed up a number of small breweries and their specialized products. However, their name is welcomed by lager aficionados throughout the rest of the world as they are a major exporter of fine German brews.

TUCHER PILSENER is one such brew and it is a classic example of the art of brewing in the pilsner style. With its subtle aroma of hops, it typifies the international pils. It is sharp-tasting as well as light and bright with a pronounced hoppy bitterness. Yes, TUCHER PILSENER is a fine brew, and although the draught version is a little light for my taste it cannot be described as anything less than a lager with a certain something extra. Sounds good, huh? Indeed it is.

Unfortunately, at the time of writing, it is still only available in the London area, yet by the time the book is launched TUCHER is expected to be available nationally. Try one now – if you can find it!

TULIP LAGER   UK

OG 1034°   *J. W. Lees Co.*
Bottles
Cans

As with all J. W. Lees lager beers and bitters, TULIP LAGER is only available in the Manchester and North Wales areas, where it was introduced in 1962. We found a subtle difference in the taste of bottled and the canned versions, which isn't unusual, as you'll find as you slowly drink your way through this book.

The bottled TULIP has a rich, amber colour with a distinguished hoppy aroma. However, its malty taste plays second fiddle to a gas content which takes a lot of the pleasure out of it. The canned TULIP, which is of a deeper honey colour, also has a distinct hoppy bouquet. Dry and light, it has a pleasantly mild taste.

The same can't be said, however, for the gas content which again is not pleasant. I'd sample it at a party if it were free, but apart from that, I wouldn't bother, which is a shame because it really doesn't taste bad – if only it wasn't so fizzy!

TUSKER
Kenya

OG 1043°
Continental Lager Distributors Ltd
Bottles 33cl

The Kenya Breweries Limited was founded by the brothers George and Charles Hurst in December 1922, and their first beer was brewed in a small copper vessel heated by *kuni* fires. It was bottled by hand, and the first order of 10 cases was personally delivered to the General Manager of the Stanley Hotel. They were in business ... but not for long. George Hurst was killed by a charging bull elephant in 1923, and it was in his memory that the beer they had created together was renamed TUSKER.

Sixty years later TUSKER is available in Britain, and lest you doubt its qualities, it won a gold medal at the Brussels World Beer Competition in 1985. The same year it picked up a silver at the British World Bottled Beer Competition. Indeed, TUSKER is a fine, light and clean tasting ambassador from the African continent. Well worth charging down to the off-licence for.

VON WUNSTER CLASSICA   Italy

5% ABV
Bottle 33cl

Considering VON WUNSTER is in every sense of the word Italian, it has an extremely un-Italian name. But then again does GRUNHALLE (*q.v.*) sound English? Having said that, however, it is unfair to mention VON WUNSTER in the same breath as a tepid English brew, for this eminently palatable lager is very agreeable indeed. I first stumbled upon it in Garcias, a Spanish supermarket on London's Portobello Road, and have recently noticed it in a number of restaurants, as well as my local Italian café. Seeming light for its 5 per cent alcohol by volume measure, its rich malty flavour makes it a pleasure to drink. It makes a most welcome change from PERONI (*q.v.*). Sample with spaghetti, taste with tagiatelle, consume with carbonara and plug one in with your pudding. You'll thank me for it!

WARSTEINER

West Germany

Draught
Bottles 33cl
Cans 33cl

Warsteiner (UK) Ltd

It all began in 1753 at the Domschanke, the cathedral tavern, where beer was originally brewed for private consumption. Yet the name of quality travels by word of mouth and in time lager was being supplied to the city of Warstein and the surrounding area. Later, WARSTEINER gradually developed into a large, nationally-distributed German brand. Today it is brewed at an extremely modern plant where, in the usual German way, 'everything functions with precision'. The Warsteiner Brewery produces only one lager beer. This, they claim, is because they concentrated at an early stage on a single lager speciality. In this fashion, along with very aggressive marketing by men 'who know what they're talking about', WARSTEINER has grown into a popular brew that is welcomed throughout the world. Sales in the decade 1975–1985 increased by nearly 300 per cent, and today fall just short of 2.25 hectolitres per annum. Typically German in that it has a slightly bitter finish, WARSTEINER is dry with a pleasant hoppy bouquet and taste. Indeed, Selfridge's of Oxford Street, London, saw fit to promote WARSTEINER during the German Food and Drink Festival in 1988, as one of the best, authentic German brands on the market. They're not far wrong.

WARTECK   Switzerland

Alcohol Free   *Calderhead Wholesale Distribution/*
Bottles 33cl   *Barton International*

In its 133-year history the Warteck Brewery has developed from a small, local brewery into one of today's leaders in the Swiss beer market. In 1975 they launched a non-alcoholic lager beer. Like all the other brewers of low and non-alcoholic beers they claim to have produced a product that thousands of independent lager-tasting experts have difficulty in distinguishing from the real thing. Some brewers have secret methods of *removing* the alcohol once their product has been brewed as a premium lager; there are freezings, vacuums, evaporations, etc. With WARTECK it's different. They claim 'Warteck non-alcoholic lager also undergoes the full cycle of fermentation and storage, whereby Warteck's *knack* in brewing is to prevent the alcoholization process' (my italics). Well, there you have it. It's in the 'knack'.

What is interesting about WARTECK is that it is also supplied as a *concentrate*! This presumably means that you can add your own water when it arrives, give it a stir, and dollop it out! Personally, I'll take the water. At least it's a natural drink!

WBC   UK

OG 1032–37°   *Wiltshire Brewery Co.*
Draught

Brewed in Tisbury, Wiltshire Brewery Company (WBC) lager was launched in Wiltshire Brewery pubs in August 1988. It should be pointed out that the people of Wiltshire, and the rest of the West Country, are not only fiercely patriotic to their region but they are also great lovers of ale. Thus, WBC is pushed as an 'all English product'. Only time will tell how this will affect sales of this light, mildly hoppy session lager.

WEIZENTHALER West Germany

0.45% ABV *Scottish German Beer Imports*
Bottles 50cl swing-top

First introduced in Scotland in 1987, WEIZEN-THALER's national off-licence launch came in early 1988. Originally the pop had been packaged in a standard half-litre bottle, but sales were a little timid. Thus SGBI came up with a wizard wheeze; they put it in a swing-top bottle! Within five months sales had increased by five times! It's the bottle that does it, I know, because the contents are on a par with most other lagers in the low/no-alcohol sector – horrible!

WICKULER West Germany

Bottles *Universal Merchandisers (Wines)*

A valuable German lager, WICKULER is, as you'd expect, light with a faint hoppy aroma. What you don't expect is that it has quite a firm body and the slightly bitter finish of a premium German lager beer. However, sales of imported lagers at this lower alcohol strength have been falling since the British learnt to do it themselves. German imports in this sector are said to have fallen by 8 per cent in 1987. This is unfortunate as their quality is far superior and so much more enjoyable than your Kestrel's etc. It would be a good idea for you to keep your eye open for it before it disappears from the off-licence shelves for ever – to be replaced by your typical Chariot, Bird of Prey, and Huge Nordic Warrior in Helmet lagers!

WREXHAM WELSH LAGER   UK

OG 1031–35°
Draught
Cans 44cl

The can proudly states that the Wrexham Brewery has been established since 1882, therefore making it the oldest lager-brewing brewery in Britain. Yet it should be pointed out that the production of lager at Wrexham has not gone unbroken in its 107-year history. Original brands, I believe, failed due to the local people's wariness of a light, Continental-style product. Now, though, WREXHAM WELSH LAGER carries all the hallmarks of success in an excellent little brew.

Being a session lager, its bouquet is a little on the weak side, although its mild hoppy nose is complemented with a subtle sweetness. This is unusual as the lager is quite dry. Although not as highly carbonated as the majority of session lagers, WREXHAM has a rich, creamy head that sits comfortably on the pale, golden lager below. Clean and crisp, with a very pleasant mild hoppy flavour, WREXHAM WELSH is one of the best lagers in the 1030–36° band on the market. Although the Welsh aren't exactly renowned for their lager brewing, this one fulfils all the demands of the discerning drinker. I recommend it highly to session-lager fans, and also to the casual experimentalist who's on the look out for something a little different. With an unusually firm body for this strength, WREXHAM WELSH has a good, honest character and not a little Continental quality. We were pleasantly surprised, as you will be on your next purchase. Delicious!

YOUNG'S LONDON LAGER   UK

OG 1035–39° – 3.9% ABV   *Young's*
Draught
Bottles 27.5cl
Cans 44cl

Introduced to the market in 1980, Young's brewery is aggressively proud of this product, while at the same time a little dismissive of many Continental brands. So you can imagine what sort of old bull-and-bush party they had when they were voted the Supreme Champion in the Brewing, Bottling and Allied Trades Exhibition just months after their launch. Another chirpy cockney knees-up was thrown when in 1983 they won a silver medal in the same class at the same exhibition. Then the barrel must have really been rolled out when LONDON LAGER took a gold at the Brewing Industry International Awards in 1987.

For you see, John Young is as British as the lager he brews, and when he set his heart on brewing a Continental drink he was determined, and I mean *determined*, to beat the Europeans at their own game. So he now has every reason to be happy. But are we? Well, considering the plethora of pseudo-Continental lagers produced by British breweries, it is extremely refreshing to see a brewery proud of their all-British product. YOUNG'S LONDON LAGER, available in the M25 area only, is a little thin and slightly over carbonated for my taste. Nevertheless, it's a tasty, well-hopped, all-British product that we can be proud of. In my mind you can never do wrong to drink a Young's brew as the company takes great pride in all its products. Cheers!

YOUNG'S PREMIUM LAGER   UK

OG 1044–50° – 5% ABV   *Young's*
Draught

Following the success of LONDON LAGER (*q.v.*) in the
session market, it was a certainty that Young's would
produce a brand to try and attract the premium
strength lager drinker. Thus YOUNG'S PREMIUM
LAGER was launched in 1985 and, unlike their session version, it contains no adjuncts and is an all-malt
brew. Indeed. PREMIUM is a far superior pint and is
extremely enjoyable, especially in the surrounds of one
of the Young's pubs, which are some of the finest in
London. It's a shame that PREMIUM isn't available
to the off-trade, yet I'm sure that with the success that
this brand is bound to enjoy, this minor fault will soon
be rectified. With a firm, full body and a bold, creamy
head, PREMUIM goes down smoothly and is refreshing enough to become my 'usual' on any visit to a
Young's house.

YUKON GOLD LAGER   Canada

OG 1044°   *Continental Lager Distributors Ltd*
Bottles 34cl

Believe it or not, Canada is extremely uncivilized when
it comes to lager, and consequently the country contains some vast dry areas. In many places advertising
is restricted, and in some areas you even have to buy
your lager through the post!

Not so, however, in the formidable Yukon, which
lends its name to this admirable lager. Brewed at
Prince George, 500 miles north of Vancouver, from
pure spring water YUKON GOLD is an authentic

Canadian lager. It's a reflection of the men that live and work in the harsh environment, being firm, clean and robust. All are qualities that add up to an enjoyable lager!

ZERO
West Germany

Non-alcoholic
Bottles 33cl
Continental Lager Distributors Ltd

ZERO is not only the name of the product, it also aptly describes its merits on a scale of nought to ten!

ZHIGULI   USSR

OG 1043°   *Continental Lager Distributors Ltd*
Bottles 50cl

The Soviet Union's brewing industry is in fact the fourth largest in the world, with about 1,000 breweries producing a healthy 72 million hectolitres per annum. This, of course, is still well short of the demand of a nation famous worldwide for its love of alcohol. Today, as the Soviet people wilt under the new restrictions and legislation on the consumption of spirits, the taste for lager drinking is increasing rapidly, causing some 80 new breweries to be built in recent years.

ZHIGULI BEER is Russia's most popular brand and is marketed over here as the everyday lager of the Soviet Union. It originated near the town of Kuybyshev on the River Volga, close to the vast fields of barley by the Zhiguli hills. Today it is brewed and bottled in a State brewery in Moscow which was established about 130 years ago. However, considering that the Soviet people have built themselves a reputation for enjoying their glycol straight, as opposed to watering it down with wine, we have to ask ourselves what are their tastes like in lager? Well, surprisingly, they're not bad.

ZHIGULI is a little sweet, but not unpleasantly so and, with a rich bouquet of barley, its medium strength body is relatively firm, though a little too carbonated for our liking. Still, it's the real McCoy from the Eastern bloc and should definitely be sampled to get an understanding of the Soviet culture. In fact, as their advertising copy-line goes, you can now grab a Russian, buy Zhigulis! Best served well chilled from the fridge, it is a pleasure to bring ZHIGULI in from the cold!

ZIPFER   Austria

OG 1048–50°   *Steffl (UK) Ltd*
Bottles 50cl
Cans 5 litres

One of the most popular lager brands in Austria,
ZIPFER, is drunk mainly in the western provinces
where a major proportion of international tourism is
concentrated. It is here that many British people got
their first taste of ZIPFER, and so popular is it amongst
them that it has created a demand in the UK, where it
is now available.

Zipf is a small town at the foot of the Alps, not far
from Mozart's Salzburg, where it nestles between vast,
rolling hills covered in mile-upon-mile of unspoilt wood-
lands, green meadows, and springs of clear, pure water.
These surroundings, combined with the brewers art,

have made Zipf one of the most important breweries in Austria. A medium-strength lager beer in the premium sector. ZIPFER is actually quite light with a slightly malty nose. Refreshing, its slightly bitter taste is not unpleasant and it is definitely a challenge to the lagers of Germany. Well worth sampling.

GLOSSARY

Alcohol by Volume ABV

The percentage alcohol in the beer, comparing the volume of alcohol with the remaining liquid, e.g. 5ml of alcohol in 100ml of beer would be 5 per cent.

Bock

Bock generally denotes a lager of higher strength than normal – around 6 per cent alcohol by volume and often higher.

Krausening

The German practice of secondary fermentation (achieved by adding unfermented wort to the beer) which increases the carbon dioxide level.

Lager

The definition which revolves around *Lager*, being the German for 'a store', is a bit hackneyed and does not really bear close examination, as many other types of beer have a history of having been stored.

In Central Europe, the beers which we now know as lagers were originally known as the 'new beers'. The 'new' method which brought about the new lager beers, was a bottom-fermentation yeast, possibly from the wine industry, slow fermentation, and secondary fermentation in the cask.

A number of things have changed since 1842 and, generally speaking, a lager is now a beer produced from a pale malt (although not necessarily) that is fermented with a bottom-fermenting yeast at low temperatures (usually less than 15°C, often between 9–11°C).

Low-Alcohol Lager

Lager with less than 1.2 per cent alcohol by volume.

Malt Liquor

A term used in the USA to indicate a beer of higher strength than normal – say around 6.5 per cent alcohol. Malt liquor produced in this country usually has around 5 per cent alcohol by volume and about half the hop rate of normal lagers.

No-Alcohol Lager

Lager with less than 0.05 per cent alcohol by volume.

Original Gravity OG

The specific gravity of the wort (*q.v.*) before fermentation has taken place. The higher the original gravity, the stronger the lager!

Pils

Generally a pale lager of around 6 per cent alcohol and around 1048° gravity. These have a low carbohydrate content which is invariably achieved by adding an enzyme (amalyse) at the fermentation stage. This breaks down the dextrins in the wort (*q.v.*) to basic sugars, which the yeast is then able to ferment to produce a higher level of alcohol than would normally be expected.

Pilsner (*also* Pilsener)

Originally the 'new beer' produced in the town of Pilsen in 1842 and distinguished from other beers of Vienna and Munich by its paleness. Now generally accepted as the standard lager prototype of around 5 per cent alcohol and 1046° gravity. However, recently the term is also being applied to very low gravity lagers – around 1030°.

Premium Lager

Originally an American term used to describe the brewers' premier product (e.g. Michelob is Anheuser-Busch's 'Super Premium' beer). In the UK, however, a 'premium' label usually refers to the strength of the lager. Though not clearly defined, a 'premium' lager usually has an original gravity of between 1042 and 1050°.

Reinheitsgebot

The Bavarian purity law of 1516 which stated that only water, hops and malted barley could be used in the production of beer. Still officially adhered to today, the Reinheitsgebot has many supporters who appreciate the purity it guarantees in German beer.

Session Lager

A lager that is relatively weak in alcohol (usually in the 1030–1038° OG range) and can therefore be consumed throughout a 'drinking session'!

Standard Lager

Basically the brewing industry's term for a lager with an original gravity somewhere in the 1030–1038° range.

Super-Strength Lager

A term used to describe the strongest lagers, generally available (e.g. Carlsberg Special Brew, Tennent's Super, etc).

Throwing Lager

An advertising agency term that is not much liked by the brewing industry! *See* SESSION LAGER.

Wort

Mash (malt and water) after it has been strained through the lauterton.

COUNTRY OF ORIGIN

Australia

Big Barrel
Boags Premium
Broken Hill
Carlton Special Light
Cascade
Castlemaine XXXX
Castlemaine XXXX Export
Foster's
Safeways Australian Lager
Sainsbury's Australian Lager
Swan Premium Export
Swan Light
Tooheys

Austria

Gold Fassl Pils
Gold Fassl Vienna Lager
Gosser Export
Steffl
Zipfer

Belgium

Duvel Lager Pils
Jupiler
Lamot Pils
Lamot Strong Lager
Maes Pils
Maverick
Stella Artois

Brazil

Brahma

Bulgaria

Astica

Canada

Ironhorse Malt Liquor
Labatt
Molson
Yukon Gold Lager

Channel Islands

Mary Anne Jubilee Pils

China

Double Happiness
Shanghai Premium Lager
Tsing tao

Cyprus

Keo

Czechoslovakia

Budweiser Budvar
Gambrinus Pilsen
Pilsener Urquell

Denmark

Carlsberg Elephant Beer
Carlsberg Export
Carlsberg Pilsner
Carlsberg Special Brew
Danish Light
Dansk LA

Giraf
Great Dane, The
Sainsbury's Danish Export Lager
Scandia Diat Pils
Scandia Special Extra Strong Lager
Tesco's Danish Low-Alcohol Lager
Tuborg Gold
Tuborg Pilsener

East Germany

Berliner Export
Berliner Pils

France

Adelshoffen Biers Brune
Fischer
Kronenbourg
La Choulette
Meteor Pils
Obernai Village
Pelican
Prima
Reserve de Brasseur
Rheingold
Sainsbury's French Lager
Sans Culottes
Schutz Jubilator
Schutz Lite
Stuttgart Premium Pils Malt Lager
33 Dry Extra Strength
33 Export

Honduras

Port Royal

Iceland

Polar Beer

India

Golden Eagle
Kingfisher
Kingfisher Pils
Kingfisher Strong Lager
Taj Mahal

Israel

Maccabee

Italy

Moretti
Peroni
Von Wunster Classica

Jamaica

Red Stripe
Red Stripe Crucial Brew

Japan

Kirin
Sapporo

Kenya

Tusker

Luxembourg

Bofferding
Clausen
Diekirch
Donkle
Henri Funck Pils

Mexico

Bohemia

Carta Blanca
Mexico
Dos Equis – Amber
Dos Equis XX
Noche Buena
Pacifico
Sol
Superior
Tecate

Netherlands

Bavaria Dutch Lager
Bavaria Dutch Pils Lager
Bavaria 8.6 Super Strength Lager
Breda
Grolsch
Heineken
Heineken Export
Hobec
Oranjeboom
Royal Dutch Post Horn
Sainsbury's Dutch Lager

New Zealand

Steinlager

Norway

Aas Bok
Frydenlund

Poland

Okocim
Tatra Pils

Portugal

Sagres Europa

Sagres Export

Singapore

Tiger

South Africa

Castle
Lion

Spain

Cruzcampo
San Miguel 'Especial'
San Miguel Selecta

Switzerland

Drikoenigsbier
Hurlimann Sternbrau
Samichlaus
Steinbock
Warteck

Thailand

Amarit
Singha
Singha Gold

UK

Ace Lager
ASDA Lager
ASDA Low-Alcohol Lager
Aston Manor Export Lager
Aston Manor Pils Lager
Ayingerbrau
Ayingerbrau SVS Lager
Ayingerbrau 'D' Pils
Ayingerbrau Prinz

Barbican
Belhaven Lager
Bergman's Lager
Birell
Bleu de Brasserie
Breaker
British Home Stores Lager
Carling Black Label
Challenge
Charger
Chaser
Edelbrau
Edelbrau Diat Pils
Einhorn
Everton Premium Lager
Executive Lager
Frisk
Gold Standard
Grunhalle
Harp
Harp Extra
Harp Master Lager
Harp Premier
Hartsman Lager
Heldenbrau
Hemeling
Hoffman's
J. K. Lager
Jensen
John Smith's Lager
K2
Kaliber
Kellerbrau
Kestrel
Kestrel Superstrength
Konig Pilsener
LCL Pils
J. W. Lees Diat Pils
Long Life

Malt Master Lager
Marksman
Marksman Export
Marston's Pilsener Lager
Mayfield Lager
Mayfield Pils
McEwan's Lager
Newquay Draught Steam Lager
Newquay Draught Steam Pils
Newquay Real Steam Lager 'Extra Strong'
Newquay Real Steam Lager 'Natural Strong'
Norseman
Olympic Gold Premium Lager
Prohibition Low Alcohol
Raven
Red Devil Premium Lager
Royal British Legion Lager
Sainsbury's Lager
Sainsbury's L A Lager
St Christopher
St Michael Pilsner
Samuel Smith's Natural Lager
Satzenbrau
Skol
Skol Export Lager
Skol Extra Strength 1080
Skol Special Strength
Skona
Steiger
Steingold Export Draught Lager
Super Reds
Sutcliffe's Alcohol Free
Talisman
Tennent's Extra
Tennent's L.A.
Tennent's Lager
Tennent's Pilsner
Tennent's Super
Tesco's Pilsner

Top Brass
Tulip Lager
WBC
Wrexham Welsh Lager
Young's London Lager
Young's Premium Lager

USA

Anchor Steam Beer
Budweiser
Colt .45
Dixie Amber Light
Dixie Beer
Lone Star
Michelob
Miller Lite
New Orleans Best
Rolling Rock Premium Lager
Samuel Adams Boston Lager
Schlitz

USSR

Zhiguli

West Germany

Altenmunster Strong Lager
Becks
Bitburger
Clausthaler
Dab
Dortmunder Kronen Alt
Dortmunder Kronen Classic
Dortmunder Kronen Pils
Dortmunder Ritter
Dortmunder Union Export
Dortmunder Union Siegel Pils
Dortmunder Union Special

Eichbaum Export Altgold
Eichbaum Lite Oak
Eichbaum Ureich Pils
Eku Pils
Eku 28
Faust Diat Pils
Faust Export Lager
Faust Pilsner Lager
Fürstenberg Antonius
Fürstenberg Export
Fürstenberg Pils
Germania
Gerstel
Gilde Export
Gilde Pils
Gilder
Graf Arco Export Lager
Hacker Pschorr Edelhell Export
Hansa
Hansa Special Export
Henninger Kaiser Pils
Herforder Pils
Hofmeister
Holsten Diat Pils
Holsten Export
Jever
Karlsbrau
Kaltenberg Braumeister
Kaltenberg Diat Pils
Krombacher Pils
Lindener Lager
Lindener Spezial
Lowenbrau Pils
Lowenbrau Special Export
Lowenbrau Strong Lager
Moravia Pils
Patrizier Export Gold
Patrizier Premium Pils
Paulaner 1634

Ratskeller Edel-Pils
Royal Hofbrau
Sainsbury's German Lager
St Pauli Girl
Schwaben Brau
Spaten Pils
Tucher Pilsener
Warsteiner
Weizenthaler
Wickuler
Zero

Yugoslavia

Niksik
Skopsko

LIST OF SUPPLIERS

A

Anglo-Australian Wine Co.
2 Waterloo Place
High Street
Crowthorne
Berks
Tel: (0276) 600930

Applejack Trading Company
43 Studley Grange Road
Hanwell
London W7 2LU
Tel: (01) 579 2963

Associated British Liquor Distributors
121–123 Evelyn Street
London SE8
Tel: (01) 692 7817

Aston Manor Brewery Co. Ltd
Thimblemill Lane
Aston
Birmingham B7 5HS
Tel: (021) 328 4336

B

Baron von Ritter/New England Wine Co.
194 Ellerton Road
Surbiton
Surrey KT6 7UO
Tel: (01) 390 2376

Barton International
52–58 Weston Street
London SE1 3QJ
Tel: (01) 407 2922

Batley's Wines
997 Leeds Road
Deighton
Huddersfield HD2 1UN
Tel: (0484) 544211

Bavaria UK Ltd
Sherwood Business Centre
Gregory Boulevard
Nottingham NG7 6LD
Tel: (0602) 620227

BB Supply Centre Ltd
91 Whitechapel High Street
London E1 7RA
Tel: (01) 247 1252
          247 6324

C

Calderhead Wholesale Distribution
14 Rushworth Street
London SE1 0RB
Tel: (01) 261 1529

Caxton Tower Wines Ltd
239 Munster Road
London SW6 6BE
Tel: (01) 381 6505

Edwin Cheshire
20 Lower Street
Stanstead
Essex
Tel: (0279) 813213

City Vintagers Ltd
47 Midland Road
London N W 1
Tel: (01) 387 2623

Continental Lager Distributors Ltd
Ashworth Estate
42 Beddington Lane
Croydon
Surrey CR0 4T B
Tel: (01) 689 9033

J. A. Cooper & Son (Glossop) Ltd
58 Surrey Street
Glossop
Derbyshire S K13 9A J
Tel: (04574) 2596
     (04574) 64906

Copak Drinks Ltd
12 Eton Street
Richmond
Surrey T W9 1EE
Tel: (01) 940 9594

D

Danish Bacon Co. P L C
Parkway
Welwyn Garden City
Herts A L8 6N N
Tel: (0707) 323421

Docklands Wine Brokers (U K) Ltd
Unit 3
Mulberry Business Centre
Quebec Way
Surrey Docks
London S E16 1LB
Tel: (01) 252 0314

E

Eichbaum (UK)
48 Fore Street
Seaton
Devon
Tel: (0297) 23734

Euroimpex (UK) Ltd
Little Hatfield
Hull
HU11 4UZ
Tel: (0964) 532234

Evelyn Wines
204 Evelyn Street
London SE8 5BX
Tel: (01) 692 4422

F

The Federation Brewery
Lancaster Road
Dunston Industrial Estate
Tyne & Wear NE11 9HR
Tel: (091) 460 9023

First Beer Company of London
204 Evelyn Street
London SE8 5BX
Tel: (01) 692 4422

Fürstenberg Importers Ltd
Unit 42 Melford Court
Hardwick Grange
Woolston
Warrington
Cheshire WA1 4RZ
Tel: (0925) 827227

G

GB Vintagers
430 High Road
Willesden
London NW10 2HA
Tel: (01) 459 8011

General Atlantic Ltd
38 Evelyn Gardens
London SW7 3BJ
Tel: (01) 835 1207

German Lager Importers Ltd
86 Roding Road
London Industrial Park
Beckton
London E6 4LN
Tel: (01) 511 3116

Giraf (UK)
42 Camden Square
London NW1 9XA
Tel: (01) 267 1222

Global Beer Co. Ltd
Unit 80
Storforth Lane Trading Estate
Chesterfield S41 0SN
Tel: (0246) 33777
             76242

Grandmartin Ltd
10A Northgate
Oakham
Rutland
Leicestershire LE15 6QS
Tel: (0572) 57099

Grolsch UK Ltd
Savoy Chambers
London Street
Andover
Hants SP10 2PA
Tel: (02645) 5777

H

Holsten Distributors Ltd
30–34 New Bridge Street
London EC4V 6BB

J

Jenks International
Castle House
71–75 Desborough Road
High Wycombe
Bucks
Tel: (0495) 33456

L

Lance Brown
International House
174 Three Bridges Road
Crawley
West Sussex PH10 1LE
Tel: (0293) 543855

Longmans Distribution Ltd
26 The Highway
Wapping
London E1
Tel: (01) 488 1661/2

Luxembourg Wine Co Ltd
80 Northend
Batheaston
Bath BA1 7ES
Tel: (0225) 858375

M

Maison Caurette Ltd
228–232 Waterloo Station Approach
London SE1
Tel: (01) 928 4851

Majestic Wine Warehouses
421 New Kings Road
London SW6 4RN
Tel: (01) 731 3131

Marblehead
Macleod Building
Lovat Place
Queen Elizabeth Avenue
Hillington
Glasgow G52 4TW
Tel: (041) 950 1234

Mexican Beer Co.
Mexico House
Kirkintilloch Industrial Estate
Birdston
Glasgow G66 1SY
Tel: (041) 777 6464

Middlemas of Kelso Ltd
Pinnaclehill Industrial Estate
Kelso
Roxburghshire
Scotland TD5 8DW
Tel: (0573) 24471

Molson Breweries UK Ltd
4 London Wall Buildings
London EC2M 5NT
Tel: (01) 628 5799

N

Nurdin & Peacock PLC
Bushey Road
Raynes Park
London SW20 0JJ
Tel: (01) 946 9111

R

R. H. & M. Victuals
52 Charles Street
London W1X 8DT
Tel: (01) 409 1671

S

Scottish German Beer Imports
Unit 3/4
Lochlands Industrial Estate
Larbert
Falkirk FK5 3NF
Tel: (0324) 558894

Shepherd Neame
17 Court Street
Faversham
Kent ME13 7AX
Tel: (0795) 532206

Steffl (UK) Ltd
2 Lionel Street
Birmingham B3
Tel: (021) 233 3336

T

Team Advance
Unit E
Eastway
Hackney
London E9
Tel: (01) 986 5233

Tirrell's
39 Ouseley Road
Wraysbury
Berkshire
Tel: (0784) 812793

U

United Breweries International
17–21 Sunbeam Road
London NW10 6JP
Tel: (01) 965 2400

Universal Merchandisers (Wines)
1 Craignish Avenue
London SW16
Tel: (01) 679 5325

Unlimited Limited
13 Seymour Place
London W1
Tel: (01) 724 1207

V

Victon Ross
Wickham House
2 Upper Teddington Road
Hampton Wick
Middlesex
Tel: (01) 977 9568

Vinicave Wine Importers
Unit 3
1 Elkstone Road
London W10
Tel: (01) 969 9771

Vitkovitch Brothers
Little Mostar
Virgil Street
London SE1 7EF
Tel: (01) 261 1770

W

Warsteiner (UK) Ltd
City Gate House
399–425 Eastern Avenue
Gants Hill
Essex IG 6R
Tel: (01) 518 4191

West Country Products
51 Lion Road
Twickenham
Middlesex
Tel: (01) 392 1814

Winerite Ltd
Leeds No 4 Bond
Leeds LS12 6HJ
Tel: (0532) 449822

Winter & M. G. Imports Ltd
11 Beaumont Road
Chiswick
London W4 5AG
Tel: (01) 994 4781
          994 7316

HANDS UP FOR RUGBY JOKES

THEY STUCK 'EM UP . . .

Their hands that is, when we asked who wanted yet another collection of the fastest-selling, hilarious, most bawdy load of laughs ever to grace the greasy floor of your rugby club locker room. They demanded, cajoled, bribed and bothered us until we came up with the goods!!

So here it is, pull your pinkies from your pint and let's have a hand for Bill and his Bong, Walker the great talker, the young gasman from Chester who had terrible wind, the Morris Dancer and the Yorkshire minor . . . and many many more!!

And don't forget to intercept:
RUGBY JOKES
SON OF RUGBY JOKES
MORE RUGBY JOKES
WHAT RUGBY JOKES DID NEXT
EVEN MORE RUGBY JOKES
RUGBY JOKES SCORE AGAIN
RUGBY SONGS
MORE RUGBY SONGS
Also available in Sphere Books

0 7221 7256 7   HUMOUR   £2.50

THE MENSA PUZZLE · BOOK

PHILIP CARTER & KEN RUSSELL

This challenging collection of Mensa puzzles is not for the faint-hearted. You'll need all your wits about you to solve the dazzling range of brainteasers – crosswords, word and number games, grid and diagram puzzles – a veritable cornucopia of craftiness.

THE ULTIMATE QUIZ BOOK FOR THE ULTIMATE QUIZ ADDICT

0 7474 0018 7   CROSSWORDS/QUIZZES   £2.99

RUSSELL MILLER
BARE-FACED MESSIAH

THE TRUE STORY
OF L. RON HUBBARD

MESSIAH OR MADMAN?

In 1954, science fiction writer L. Ron Hubbard founded the controversial Church of Scientology. It attracted six million members, made him a millionaire – and could, he claimed, cure all ill, physical or psychological. He alone could save the world. In 1967, pursued by the CIA, the FBI and outraged governments, he set sail with his own private navy and lived at sea for a decade, served by nymphet messengers in hot-pants who dressed and undressed him and were trained like robots to relay orders in his tone of voice. He tried to take over several countries, and at least one continent; described in detail two visits to heaven; plotted to infiltrate the FBI and CIA; and vanished completely in 1980.

In the courts last year, the Church of Scientology failed to suppress this, his extraordinary life story . . .

'An absorbing exploration of one of the muddiest trails ever left by a human being' LISTENER

0 7474 0332 5   BIOGRAPHY   £3.99

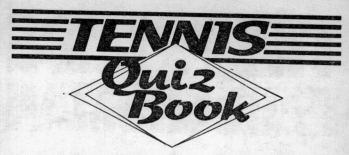

Ian Thomson & Mansel Davies

Anyone for tennis? . . .

At last, the definitive quiz book for the tennis enthusiast who prefers an armchair challenge to an 'on-court' one!

With 1,000 questions ranging from the less taxing:

Who did John McEnroe beat in 1981 to win his first Men's Singles title at the Wimbledon Championships?

Which tournament is traditionally played a fortnight before Wimbledon at London's Queen's Club?

– to those for the hardiest challenger:

Who was the Wimbledon champion who won an Olympic Silver medal in Ice Hockey?

Who, during 1976, became the first European player to pass $1 million in career earnings?

You'll find the TENNIS QUIZ BOOK a formidable opponent with many devious shots to fool and confuse you. But don't be discouraged – in this game, it's guile that gains, not ground play!

And don't miss the other *Quiz Books* in the series:
GOLF QUIZ BOOK
CRICKET QUIZ BOOK
FOOTBALL QUIZ BOOK

0 7474 0110 1   QUIZ   £2.50

THE PALACE
PAUL ERDMAN

The flash of a wheel, the twinkling spin of a ball, the fat slap of a heavy wallet as glazed eyes ignite and bejewelled fingers tremble, urging that faithless harlot, Lady Luck, to stretch out and offer her all. Gambling – compelling, glamorous, sleazy and addictive – is wickedly exposed in Paul Erdman's masterly novel of financial skulduggery on the Big Game circuits. From the vast money-making centres of Las Vegas and Atlantic City to the shadowy, underground gambling dives of London and Beirut, he spins a spellbinding tale of wealth and treachery, intrigue and mob conspiracy. Proud, aristocratic international bankers, sharp-eyed card tricksters, corrupt politicians, professional criminals are all in on the game in this devastatingly suspenseful, cracking-paced thriller that will have you hooked from first page to last . . .

'*Mind-blowing financial scams . . . lively narrative spanning two decades in which fortunes are won and lost . . . very funny and very sharp*'
LITERARY REVIEW

Also by Paul Erdman in Sphere Books:
THE LAST DAYS OF AMERICA
THE CRASH OF '79
THE PANIC OF '89

0 7474 0259 0   **THRILLER**   **£3.50**

BAD MONEY

A.M. KABAL

'Midsummer's Eve, the hard men moved . . .'

01.01 hours GMT: in London, Rome, Panama and Gdansk four men are savagely murdered. No one sees the connection. It's a quiet, efficient start to the international crime of the century . . .

But one victim, reporter Tom Wellbeck, leaves behind his ex-wife, fellow-journalist Caro Kilkenny, who is determined to find the truth about his death. And then there's Tom's friend, John Standing – burned-out, alcoholic, but still the one man with the skill and experience to see the case through . . .

They unravel a thread of intrigue that stretches from Warsaw to Washington, from the silent corridors of the Vatican to the murderous jungles of Central America, a vicious thread of bad blood and bad money. And when Standing detects the hand of his old enemy David Medina, he knows their troubles are just beginning . . .

Financial devilry of a high order . . . knowledgeable and sinister
OBSERVER

Also by A M Kabal in Sphere Books:
THE ADVERSARY

0 7221 5232 9   CRIME/THRILLER   £3.99

PRECINCT: SIBERIA

Tom Philbin

NINE SQUARE MILES OF SAVAGE NEW YORK STREETS

Siberia: the 53rd Precinct. Where the heaviest criminals hang out; where the most hardened cops are sent.

Detective Joe Lawless: tough, street-smart and ruthless, his battles with the brass have landed him in Siberia. Now he's out to nail a sadistic child-murderer before he kills again . . .

Police Officer Barbara Babalino: sent to Siberia for refusing the advances of her boss, she's out to rescue a young hooker. But the girl's pimp knows something that could destroy Barbara's life . . .

Detective Leo Grady: with five months before retirement and a flask of vodka in his pocket, he thinks he can take it easy. He can forget it. Nothing's easy in PRECINCT: SIBERIA

0 7474 0283 3   CRIME   £3.50